Notes on the Minor Prophets

Rex Beck

Copyright © 2019 Greater Purpose Publishers

All rights reserved. No part of this publication may be reproduced, stored in a retrieval system, or transmitted in any form by any means electronic, mechanical, photo-copying, recording or otherwise, without prior written permission from the publisher.

Cover design by Janet Dapo & Julian Taylor
Layout by Joshua Yu

"Scripture quotations are from the ESV® Bible (The Holy Bible, English Standard Version®), copyright © 2001 by Crossway, a publishing ministry of Good News Publishers. Used by permission. All rights reserved."

Published by
Greater Purpose Publishers
2281 Delaware Drive
Cleveland Heights, OH 44106

Email: rex.beck@gmail.com

Printed in the United States of America

First Printing

CONTENTS

	Preface	7
1	Hosea	9
2	Joel	80
3	Amos	98
4	Obadiah	140
5	Jonah	156
6	Micah	169
7	Nahum	231
8	Habakkuk	253
9	Zephaniah	286
10	Haggai	305
11	Zechariah	325
12	Malachi	356
	Bibliography	376

PREFACE

This book has grown out of a study of how God worked in the minor prophets' lives as He developed each prophet's distinct voice. In seeking to know the prophets' experiences, it is crucial to know their work. Originally, I was going to include these notes on the Minor Prophets in their corresponding chapters of *The Voices of the Prophets. A look at the lives of the Minor Prophets.* However, that work seemed better if it was focused on the prophets' lives themselves with only paragraph summaries of their works. This book contains more extensive notes.

Most people overlook the Minor Prophets. They read the books of Moses, the histories, the Psalms and maybe a bit of Isaiah. Then, they hope to get to the New Testament gospels and pass by the Minor Prophets as fast as possible. This is sad because few sections of the Bible present so much color, personality, metaphor, romance and excitement as these books.

The reason for such variety stems from the *many* personalities behind the words. Jonah, Hosea, Habakkuk and the others are surely a motley crew!

The preciousness of these books becomes clear because each prophet portrays messages about Christ and God's great salvation using his unique voice. Together, the Minor Prophets present a grand symphony of God's message. Concerning Christ, the Minor Prophets depict, among many other things, His birth in Bethlehem, His entrance to Jerusalem, His suffering, His death and resurrection and His second coming. The Apostles considered these writings to be a foundation for the New Testament. This is true in regards to their content.

The Minor Prophets also present a foundation for the New Testament in terms of the lives of the prophets themselves. Their patience and interaction with God provide an example for New Testament believers to follow. Paul appreciates the covenant of Abraham, just as Micah sees it. Paul strove to present people as a bride to Christ, just as Hosea travailed for the same thing. The Minor Prophets plant many seeds that grow into the New Testament. This makes them a rich study.

It is the purpose of this book to provide notes that emphasize the general flow of thought for each book, the revelations about Christ and the experiences of the prophets. Hopefully, readers will fall in love with the Minor Prophets and will be helped to have deeper, more colorful experiences of Christ, just like the prophets enjoyed.

CHAPTER ONE

Hosea

Hosea is structured into two broad sections. The first, chapters one through three, centers on Hosea's domestic life. This section includes Hosea's marriage to Gomer and the children they bear, God's message to Hosea explaining how God dreams of a healthy marriage relationship with Israel, and Gomer's restoration to Hosea after she left him. The second section, chapters four through fourteen, contains God's direct speaking to the nation and include Hosea's impassioned appeals for God's people to return to their Lord. Throughout Hosea's writings he remains laser focused on the central message of his ministry, which is to restore Israel to a loving, husband/wife relationship with their God. His central theme is emphasized through Hosea's domestic experience, through his emphasis on spiritual adultery and through his appeals to return to the Lord.

Hosea's marriage to Gomer

Hosea's ministry begins like no other prophet. "When the Lord first spoke through Hosea, the Lord said to Hosea, "Go, take to yourself a wife of whoredom and have children of whoredom, for the land commits great whoredom by forsaking the Lord"" (Hosea 1:2). God asks Hosea to take a "wife of whoredom," in other words, marry a prostitute. In response, Hosea takes Gomer, the daughter of Diblaim, and proceeds to have three children with her.

Much has been written trying to answer the question of whether or not Hosea actually married a woman who formerly had been a harlot, or if the entire "marriage" referred to by Hosea was symbolic. For a relatively complete list of options I refer the reader to Garrett's comments on this section. Many very respectable commentators consider the marriage to be symbolic (see Jerome, Calvin, Keil). Calvin seeking to protect the reputation of the prophet, which he feels would have been marred by his marriage to a former harlot, writes, "Hence almost all the Hebrews agree in this opinion, that the Prophet did not actually marry a wife, but that he was bidden to do this in a vision."

On the other hand, many commentators take Hosea's marriage to be literal. These commentators cite the fact that prostitutes are found in important places in the Divine narrative. For instance, Rahab the harlot is an ancestor of Christ. Furthermore, there is no command stating who prophets can marry, although priests are commanded to marry only virgins or widows of other priests. From this standpoint, then, Hosea's real domestic life helps to strongly convey the central message of his ministry, which is, "Israel has committed great whoredom by forsaking the Lord and should return to their rightful Husband." I agree with Feinberg who considers that if the marriage is taken to be a mere symbol, it ceases to strongly underscore Hosea's central message. "Because this fact has been overlooked, all too often the force of the message of the book has been dissipated by symbolizing the transactions recorded. The message was real because the acts noted were actually lived out in the life of the prophet" (p. 13). For this reason, I will consider Gomer to have been an actual harlot, Hosea's marriage to her to be real, the children born to be fathered by Hosea and Gomer and the return mentioned in Hosea 3:1 to be the return of Gomer back to the marriage relationship with Hosea.

The name Gomer means "perfect, complete" (Jones, p. 132). This may indicate that she "was thoroughly perfected in her whoredom, or that she had gone to the furthest length in prostitution" (Keil, p. 38). Diblaim, the name of her mother, means "two cakes of figs" (Jones, p. 95). Figs are a nourishing product of the land of Canaan, a blessing from God, which were often corrupted to be used in idol worship (like the raisin cakes referenced in Hosea 3:1). Jerome puts this together, saying that Gomer "therefore is a wife taken out of Israel by Hosea, as the type of the Lord and Saviour, viz. one accomplished in fornication, and a perfect daughter of pleasure (filia voluptatis), which seems so sweet and pleasant to those who enjoy it" (Jerome, qtd. by Keil, p. 38).

Gomer, in addition to being a perfect picture of a prostitute, became the wife of Hosea, whose subsequent marriage and family became the perfect message that God wished to send to His adulterous nation. As such, Hosea proceeds to have three children with Gomer. These children are called "children of whoredom" (Hosea 1:2) most likely because Gomer had a history of whoredom. Even though the children are offspring of the marriage between Hosea and Gomer, Gomer's past still taints them in such a way that the children could be considered "of whoredom." The children are given meaningful names, which God uses to send a message to the nation of Israel. Just like Isaiah, whose family was part of his message to the nation, could say "Behold, I and the children whom the Lord has given me are signs" (Isaiah 8:18), Hosea could also point to his household—his wife and children—as being messages God is sending to Israel.

God gives Hosea's first child the name "Jezreel," saying, "for in just a little while I will punish the house of Jehu for the blood of Jezreel, and I will put an end to the kingdom of the house of Israel" (Hosea 1:4). Jezreel historically has been a place of war for Israel (Judges 6:33; 1 Samuel 29:1; 2 Samuel 4:4). It was also a place of bloodshed, where Israelites put other Israelites to death. Ahab killed Naboth in Jezreel (1 Kings 21:1) in order to take his vineyard. Jehu put the house of Ahab to death in Jezreel (2 Kings 9:36; 10:1, 11). Calvin remarks that "The massacre was a crime so far as Jehu was concerned, but with God it was righteous vengeance" (Calvin, qtd. by Keil, p. 41). Here God gives this first child the name Jezreel to indicate that the unrighteous blood that was shed in Jezreel will be avenged. It will result in the termination of the monarchy in Israel, an event which takes place a short number of years after the death of Jeroboam II (2 Kings 17).

God names Gomer's second child "Lo-Ruhamah," (NKJV) which is translated "No Mercy," declaring, "for I will no more have mercy on the house of Israel, to forgive them at all" (Hosea 1:7). Up to this point in the history of the Israelite kings, God had mercy in his dealings with Israel. For example, when Israel under king Jehoahaz was pressed hard by king Hazael of Syria, God eventually relented. After the oppression had reached a certain extent, "the Lord was gracious to them and had compassion [Hebrew "Ruhamah"] on them, and he turned toward them, because of his covenant with Abraham, Isaac, and Jacob" (2 Kings 13:23). God exercised His compassion on the nation in hopes that they might reform and turn back to Him. The birth of this daughter to Hosea was a message that this kind of compassion was now going to end. From this point onward, the "Syrians" would not relent in their discipline of the nation.

God names Gomer's third child "Lo-Ammi" (NKJV), which means "not my people." Here God is laying out the severity of the coming judgment. In Exodus 19:5, when the children of Israel were at Sinai on their way to Canaan from Egypt, God declared, "Now therefore, if you will indeed obey my voice and keep my covenant, you shall be my treasured possession among all peoples, for all the earth is mine." The third child is the final word, symbolizing the breaking of the covenant. Israel as a whole would no longer be the people of God, as He had so lovingly intended from the time that He led them through the wilderness to Canaan.

From these three names we see how fitting Hosea's family is to pronounce God's message to the adulterous nation. Hosea marries Gomer, a wife of whoredom. The fruit of their relationship is three children of whoredom, whose names are "Jezreel," "no mercy," and "not my people." The children show that Israel is now unprotected from God's wrath—the just consequence that God so long delayed in hopes that the relationship would be restored. They will pay for the bloodshed and evil that they committed—Jezreel. They no longer will be able to rely on the God's mercy to avert His severe punishment—Lo-Ruhamah. They no longer will be able to claim a special relationship where they as a nation belong to the Lord and the Lord belongs to them—Lo-Ammi. This is the fruit of their adulterous relationships. These are the children they produced through their wandering, lustful and profligate actions.

God's promised restoration

If God would end His description of Hosea's family here, then He would be giving a bleak, despairing message. Looking at Hosea's family, one could easily think, "All is now lost." However, in verse ten God makes a significant turn. He says, "Yet the number of the children of Israel shall be like the sand of the sea, which cannot be measured or numbered" (Hosea 1:10). In spite of Gomer's children, God reaffirms His promise—that the number of the sons of Israel will be great—like the sands of the sea. God is saying, "There is still hope." These words have even more impact considering their history. Jacob uttered these exact words when he was returning from Haran fearing that Esau would kill him. He used these words to remind God of His promise to him (Genesis 32:12). The message is the same here. Even though Gomer's three sons portend future suffering, God's promise to multiply Israel still stands.

In His following words, God uses the names of Gomer's children to show how He will reverse their effect through His great, promised salvation.

> 10 And in the place where it was said to them, "You are not my people," it shall be said to them, "Children of the living God."
> 11 And the children of Judah and the children of Israel shall be gathered together, and they shall appoint for themselves one head. And they shall go up from the land, for great shall be the day of Jezreel.
> 1 Say to your brothers, "You are my people," and to your sisters, "You have received mercy."
> —Hosea 1:10-2:1

Here, God declares the end: "in the place where it was said to them, 'You are not my people,' it shall be said to them, 'Children of the living God'" (Hosea 1:10). The end is that

God, who in His great love wishes that His people be His family in an organic relationship with Him, declares that they will be "children of the living God." There is family. There is life. There is multiplication. Hosea had "children of whoredom." Israel bore fruits of shame. One day God will have "children of the living God." This is glory. God declares, "You are my people" and, "You have received mercy" (2:1). What a glorious declaration! The Apostle Paul quotes these words in Romans 10:25-26, indicating that in them He sees God's New Covenant promise. They are a declaration that God's salvation will overcome all the failings that occurred under the Old Covenant.

All is not lost. With God there is still hope. The wisdom, the power, the love, the depths, the knowledge, the intricate pathways of God Himself work together for a great reformation among God's people. It is not the place here to explore all the riches of God which pertain to His salvation that would make this reversal possible. It is too much to talk of a virgin birth, incarnation, a sinless life, death, resurrection, ascension, the Holy Spirit, the new birth, sanctification, transformation, and a glorious inheritance. However, what is revealed here is that all will work out to glory. God promised it to Jacob; Jacob reminded God of that same promise. Eventually, there will be children of the living God.

Hosea's commission and education

Hosea 1:1-2:1 is a self-contained message showing the degraded state of Israel and the glorious place to which God will lift it. The remainder of chapter two could be considered God's thoughts about how Hosea would help restore the nation. In this chapter he commissions Hosea, telling him what to do, and also teaches Hosea how He views the nation as His wife and family.

God commissions Hosea with a very simple command—"Plead." God says, "Plead with your mother, plead—for she is not my wife, and I am not her husband—that she put away her whoring from her face, and her adultery from between her breasts" (Hosea 2:2). With these words God commissions Hosea. Hosea is to plead with his mother. Hosea, as an individual member of the nation is to plead with the entire nation, as symbolized by his mother.

God then reminds Hosea what He has lavished upon His wife throughout the history of the nation. God found her (2:3), gave her sustenance—grain, wine, and oil, and multiplied gold and silver for her riches and adornment (2:8). God did so much for the nation of Israel, just as a husband would graciously care for His wife. Years later Ezekiel greatly enlarges on this theme (see Ezekiel 16). Hosea is the first prophet to mention how God views His people Israel in context of a courtship and marriage.

God describes how Israel responded to His gifts and care. She appropriated God's gracious gifts for herself and used them to pursue her adulterous affairs. She attributed God's gifts as wages for her harlotry, saying of the vines and figs, "These are my wages, which my lovers have given me" (Hosea 2:12). Her very face displayed the whoredom she engaged in, while the adultery she was consumed with was between her breasts. God's immediate reaction is, like the names of Hosea's children, to render judgment to her without mercy and to end the relationship where God is their God and they are His people—Lo-Ruhamah and Lo-Ammi. He will expose her before her lovers, lay waste to her vines and fig trees, take away the supply of bread, and remove all her mirth. This judgment will be severe, drastic, and firm.

In this section we see God presenting to Hosea His view about His relationship with His people. It's all about the marriage relationship. Note here that God does not make a case concerning temple rites and offerings, although the Israelites errantly and hypocritically practiced these. God does not lay a charge about how Israelites mistreat the poor among them, although the rich treated the poor with contempt. God does not complain about unfair business practices, although Israeli merchants had diverse weights. God does not complain about the lives of ease and luxury that the upper class was living, although this was true. Here God zeroes in on one thing: "Israel was supposed to be My wife, but she doesn't honor that relationship." In the previous chapter, Hosea's domestic life was a picture of this message. Here, God gives this message to Hosea in clear and certain words.

These words clarify exactly what Hosea's ministry was to become. He was to focus on this relationship. In a certain way one could imagine that Hosea becomes a marriage counselor. God is not interested in mere obedience or sacrifice on the part of His wife. He is interested in restoring a healthy marriage with His people. This involves so much. God, the offended party, is now saying "I will punish her" because "she forgot me" (Hosea 2:13). Hosea, the marriage counselor, has his work cut out for him. He must minister to restore the healthy relationship. Centuries later, the Apostle Paul would pick up a similar goal, ministering so believers would grow a healthy marriage relationship with God. "For I feel a divine jealousy for you, since I betrothed you to one husband, to present you as a pure virgin to Christ" (2 Corinthians 11:2). After hearing God's case, Hosea might have this same "divine jealousy" within him for the people of Israel.

God will woo His wife back to Himself

God tells Hosea just how He intends to woo His wife back. These are some of the most touching words God speaks. The feeling they convey could easily describe the passion of a twenty-year-old man who is absolutely smitten by a certain girl in his calculus class. As if in a whisper, God tenderly voices His plan to Hosea.

> 14 "Therefore, behold, I will allure her, and bring her into the wilderness, and speak tenderly to her.
> 15 And there I will give her her vineyards and make the Valley of Achor a door of hope. And there she shall answer as in the days of her youth, as at the time when she came out of the land of Egypt.
> —Hosea 2:14-15

God declares, "I will allure her" (Hosea 2:14), using the Hebrew word, *pātâ*, translated here as "allure." This is a most interesting word. "The basic verb idea is "be open, spacious, wide," and might relate to the immature or simple one who is open to all kinds of enticement, not having developed a discriminating judgment as to what is right or wrong" (Harris, p. 742). It is translated "seduce" as when a man seduces a virgin (Exodus 22:16) or when Samson's wife entices, or seduces him (Judges 14:15; 16:5). It is used to describe the gentle persuasion of a ruler (Proverbs 25:15). It is also used in instances to denote deception, as when oher gods may deceive the hearts of the Israelites (Deuteronomy 11:16), or when Abner came to deceive David (2 Samuel 3:25). Jeremiah claims that God deceived him, by enticing him into his ministry which seemed so hard and fruitless (Jeremiah 20:17). This word indicates how God will extend Himself to woo, to attract, to entice and finally to win His lovely bride, Israel. He will allure her, attract her, entice her. Every God seeker must see God in this way. God is not hiding. He is not playing "hard to get." Instead, He is like a suiter who has been smitten by a lovely girl who he intends to win so they will marry. God is straining, craning, and stretching out to grab Israel's attention, attract, entice, and seek to win the nation for Him forever.

God wishes to bring his restored wife "into the wilderness" (Hosea 2:14). The best example of a "wilderness" is the desert that Israel wandered through before entering Canaan. That was a place where they learned precious lessons of God's presence and obedience to Him. God remembers Israel's "love as a bride" (Jeremiah 2:2) as they journeyed through the desert. It was a place where God was everything to His people. Where He fed them with manna and watered them from the rock. God seeks to recreate that same wilderness, bridal experience with His restored Israel. It is as if God is saying, "Come away with Me My love. We will only have each other. I will be everything to you. I will supply your every need. We will enjoy one another's company. We will grow together so that you will fully become worthy of being My bride."

In the wilderness God will "speak tenderly" (Hosea 2:14) to His people. The Hebrew word translated "speak tenderly" is literally "I have spoken unto her heart" (Young's Literal Translation). Other versions translate this as "comfortably" (ASV 1901), "speak comfort" (NKJV), and "kindly (NASB). The description paints a picture of God being tender, kind, comforting, and heart-warming toward his bride. In that atmosphere, His words will penetrate all the way to the heart of His wife. What a sweet picture of God's deep love for His people! Commentators consider this boldly anthropomorphic language to be "astonishing." Chisholm writes, "It is in this daring kind of portrayal that the passion of God becomes visible—a passion that does not hesitate at any condescension or hold back from any act for the sake of the beloved elect" (p. 1385).

Not only will God lavish tender words upon His bride, He will also pour out His blessings. He will restore her vineyards. He will make the valley of Achor, which is the valley associated with the shameful, idolatrous sin of Achan (Joshua 7:26), a door of hope. Thus, God will transform Israel's shameful past into a hopeful, eagerly expectant, better future.

"There" Israel "shall answer as in the days of her youth" (Hosea 2:15). In the past, when God blessed Israel, she appropriated His blessings to serve idols. Now, it will be different. Israel will "answer." God recalls the days at Sinai, which He considers to be like a wedding. At Sinai, Moses read the covenant to the people. There they "answered" (the same Hebrew word used here), "All the words that the Lord has spoken we will do" (Exodus 24:3). There God spoke, and Israel responded positively. It was just like a man proposing to a woman on a mountain. To the man's request for marriage, the woman lovingly replies, "I will." In the many years that God spoke to the nation after that time, Israel seldom answered positively. Now, in the restoration of the marriage, God will speak, and Israel will "answer." Many versions translate "answer" in 2:15 as "sing" (Darby, NASB, NKJV, NET). This is very poetic. God allures her, speaks to her heart, brings her to the wilderness, gives her vineyards, and provides her with hope. Her response is to sing, just as Moses sang after leading the people through the Sea.

God wants to be a husband, not a master

After His wife "sings," God describes how He envisions His wife to relate to Him. He will not be her "Baal," but will be her "husband. "And in that day, declares the Lord, you will call me 'My Husband,' and no longer will you call me 'My Baal'" (Hosea 2:16). The term "husband," Hebrew ʾiš, is a very general term, used over two-thousand times in the Hebrew Bible. It is used for "man" and "husband" and "each" referring to individual men. It is the main word used to describe husband and indicates the standard family relationship as such. Dearman sees this as a term of intimacy. Keil describes God's people calling Him *'iš* "when she stands in right relation to Him; when she acknowledges, reveres, and loves Him, as He has revealed Himself, *i.e.* as the only true God" (p. 62).

God makes a contrast between "husband" and "Baal." He declares that His wife, Israel, will no longer call Him, "My Baal." The name Baal could have two distinct meanings, both showing what God does not desire from His relationship with His wife. "Baal" could be understood to mean the name of the gods that Israel was committing adultery with. Israel had the names of the Baals in their mouths (Hosea 2:16) and regularly celebrated feasts to them (Hosea 2:13). Saying they will no longer call God "my Baal" means that they will no longer associate Him with any other god. He will not be one of many, He will be unique. Keil takes this view, saying that Israel, "calls Him Baal, when she places the true God on the level of the Baals, either by worshipping other gods along with Jehovah, or by obliterating the essential distinction between Jehovah and the Baals, confounding together the worship of God and idolatrous worship, the Jehovah-religion and heathenism" (p. 62). Not calling God "my Baal" also has another implication, which comes from other uses of the word "Baal" in the Hebrew Bible. This word is commonly used to denote husband in a very respectable sense. King Ahasuerus was concerned about how the women of his realm would treat their husbands, their "baals," if they found out that queen Vashti dismissed his summons (Esther 1:17, 20). It is used to describe a woman's legitimate and true husband (Exodus 21:22; Proverbs 12:4). "Baal," however, is not only translated as husband. It is also used to refer to leaders as in Judges 20:5, masters as in Isaiah 1:3, and owners as in Exodus 21:28. From a vocabulary standpoint, then, calling a husband "my Baal" includes implications related to master, owner, or ruler. While there is truth to this side of the relationship, God does not want this to be the focus of His relationship with His wife. Dearman notes that no longer calling God "my Baal" "would be a sign of the covenant intimacy…as well as indicating more mutuality between God and people than was found in the hierarchy and role specificity of a Canaanite pantheon" (p. 124). He admits that "As the gracious giver of a covenant to Israel, YHWH is the father, husband, and owner of the people. These are His identities in his relationship to Israel, reflecting modes of His self-revelation. And in his household, he can be known by the simplest relational term, *'iš*'" (Dearman, p. 124).

God's dream marriage

As "husband" God tenderly speaks about how He imagines His future betrothal and marriage to be. "¹⁹ And I will betroth you to me forever. I will betroth you to me in righteousness and in justice, in steadfast love and in mercy. ²⁰ I will betroth you to me in faithfulness. And you shall know the Lord" (Hosea 2:19-20).

Three times God lovingly declares, "I will betroth you." The word He uses for betroth, *'āraś*, evokes great purity in the marriage. It is used in other instances to describe a man's marriage to a virgin. This is striking because of the context. In this renewed marriage, in which God will restore Israel to be His wife, He doesn't see any of her past as a stain upon her. He sees her as a pure virgin, being married for the first time to Him. Calvin remarks, "We now perceive the import of the word, espouse: for God thereby means, that he would not remember the unfaithfulness for which he had before cast away his people, but would blot out all their infamy" (Volume 1, p. 112). Here all is new. Second chances are real. The union is vital. There is a freshness, simplicity, and purity to the whole.

God describes His marriage to be in righteousness, justice, steadfast love and mercy. All these are profound characteristics of God Himself, which He brings into the marriage relationship. Hebrew poetic structure leads us to combine the first two, righteousness and justice, and the second two, steadfast love and mercy.

God's betrothal takes place in an atmosphere of righteousness and justice. Righteousness could be considered as being right oneself. Justice could be considered as the application of righteousness to a situation. A marriage without both parties being right themselves and exercising justice outwardly is far from stable. The problem with the first covenant was that the wife, Israel, could not righteously maintain her responsibility for the covenant. The result was a downward spiral of unfaithfulness. There was no righteousness or justice on her side. God was merciful for a time, hoping that righteousness would be restored. However, eventually the covenant relationship became beyond repair and the relationship was broken, causing God to say, "She is not my wife" (Hosea 2:2).

The coming betrothal will be different. It will be in righteousness and justice. These words are not at all surprising when they are applied to God Himself; they are His attributes, which He exercises in any relationship. The most wonderful aspect of the promise of this future marriage is that the betrothal, involving *both* parties, will be in righteousness and justice. God's wife will be brought up to His standard related to these characteristics. Calvin applies these words to both, "These words must be applied to both the contracting parties: then, by righteousness God means not only his own, but that also which is, as they say, mutual and reciprocal; and by *righteousness* and *judgment* is meant rectitude, in which nothing is wanting. We now then perceive what the Prophet had in view" (Volume 1, p. 112). Some see the righteousness of the bride to indicate God's impartation of His righteousness into His people, which is clearly a New Testament promise. This may be. However, it is more likely that Hosea is concentrating on the result, which is God's wife living out righteousness and justice. His wife will act in a righteous and just way that will cause her not to violate the letter or spirit of her loving covenant with God.

Such righteousness lived out by the wife implies something wonderful. God will work on His wife to make her fitting for who He is. That is the power of His salvation and the wonder of this marriage. "God betroths the church to Himself in righteousness and judgment…by purifying her, through the medium of just judgment, from all the unholiness and ungodliness that adhere to her still (Isa. i. 27), that He may wipe out everything that can injure the covenant on the part of the church" (Keil, p. 64). Calvin sees this in terms of God writing His laws on the hearts and inscribing them on the minds of His people, that they may be truly righteous and true partners in this marriage. Dearman considers that this righteousness should be measured in terms of the relationship, the betrothal, and not in terms of customs, traditions, or even law. "Righteous(ness) (sedeq) means essentially to be rightly related….It represents integrity in communal life as defined by relationships based on solidarity and commitment. One can be in the right in the sense of a commitment to family and community, even if it brushes up against law and custom (so Gen. 38:26)" (p. 127). Such thought brings one close to the danger of defining righteousness based on the feeling of the relationship, without regard for the written word. This is clearly an error. However, this thought places the marriage relationship with God at the center. It can lead the wife into freedom from legalistic practices and requirements which sap the passion, life, and vitality from her loving marriage relationship with God.

God's betrothal is also in steadfast love and mercy. Steadfast love "is an unswerving devotion which fulfills the responsibilities arising from a relationship" (Chisholm, p. 1386). Mercy "is tender feeling which motivates one to gracious action" (Chisholm, p. 1386). These characteristics underscore the feeling in the marriage and, when combined, produce a deep assurance. Both parties possess unswerving devotion to the other. Likewise, both parties are assured that the other is entirely devoted, in a patient enduring way. Mercy implies that there is nothing from the wife's past that will disqualify her from her Husband's steadfast love. Her Husband will be absolutely devoted to her and will never find a reason to desist. This should provide the most wretched feeling soul, solace and balm. "There is then no reason why their own unworthiness should frighten away the people; for God here unfolds his own immense goodness and unparalleled mercies" (Calvin, Volume 1, p. 114). For us, a marriage without steadfast love and mercy is like walking on eggshells all the time. These qualities give deep assurance to the parties of a solid, steadfast relationship. "And yet such is the frailty of man's fallen nature, and so many are the faults and the failings to which he is liable, that loving-kindness (God's condescending love, *chesed*, equivalent to ἀγάπη) and mercies (inmost compassion on man's weakness, *rachamim*, σπλάχνα) on God's part must be added to righteousness and judgment in order to secure the stability of those whom he takes into covenant, and the continuance of the contract" (Spence-Jones, p. 50). In such a confident setting, the relationship can flourish in romantic, exciting ways.

Finally, God intends that His betrothal would be in "faithfulness." This is "the constancy of commitment and compassion. It has the basic meaning of steadiness, constancy, supportiveness (Exod. 17:12)" (Dearman, p. 128). God's faithfulness means constancy in the marriage. One will never hear the words, "Honey, it's complicated, but I have to leave." Rather, the relationship will be in steadiness, supportiveness, dependability, constant loyalty, unwavering steadfastness, and stability. Such assurance is balm to the wounded soul. Faithfulness assures us that this betrothal will persevere. It will indeed be "forever" (Hosea 2:19).

The fitting result to all these characteristics of the betrothal is that the wife will "know the Lord" (Hosea 2:20). Knowing the Lord is no small thing. Because the marriage is so strong and safe, the wife will be free to truly, deeply, profoundly and thoroughly know her Husband. In the end, knowing Him is what deeply satisfies both parties—the wife and even God Himself.

Overflowing blessing due to a healthy marriage

God connects the restoration of His marriage with Israel to the renewal and flourishing of the entire earth. When He betroths His people to Himself, He declares, "And I will make for them a covenant on that day with the beasts of the field, the birds of the heavens, and the creeping things of the ground" (Hosea 2:18). The covenant God will make with the animals will ensure that they will no longer harm mankind (Job 5:23) and will have a peaceable existence towards one another (Isaiah 11). Right now, the living creatures on earth groan, waiting eagerly for the revelation of the sons of God (Romans 8:18-22). When the marriage between God and His people is consummated in righteousness, justice, steadfast love, mercy and faithfulness, the beasts, birds and creeping things will be brought into the freedom of the glory of the children of God. No longer will wild animals need to be at arm's length from mankind.

Not only will animals be free, heaven, earth, and the fruit of the earth will all work together in harmony. "²¹ And in that day I will answer, declares the Lord, I will answer the heavens, and they shall answer the earth, ²² and the earth shall answer the grain, the wine, and the oil, and they shall answer Jezreel" (Hosea 2:21-22). All the elements affecting the produce of earth will acknowledge and answer each other, so that they work together in harmony. God will answer the heavens. The heavens, in turn, will answer the earth, supplying what the fields need to make crops flourish. The earth, then, will answer the vegetation, resulting in rich produce. This vegetation will "answer Jezreel," which means they liberally distribute food, just like the sower scatters seeds. The vegetation will nourish God's people with grain, wine, and oil. Additionally, there will be peace between all men. "And I will abolish the bow, the sword, and war from the land, and I will make you lie down in safety" (Hosea 2:18).

After living in our world where we fear wild animals, witness violence among beasts, struggle to produce enough food, succumb to natural disasters, and wither under wars and conflicts, we may forget that all these phenomena are temporary. They are, in fact, the effects of the degraded relationship between God and Adam, because of which the entire natural world was subject to vanity, corruption, and disharmony. The result was that the earth and its creatures ceased to flourish at their full potential. God's restored marriage with His people precipitates the most radical restoration. The entire earth will change. The restoration of the marriage will once again unlock the potential in God's creation. This will not only affect one small corner of the earth. No, that marriage affects the entire world. Even the entire universe—the heavens and the earth—will resound when the betrothal is restored.

Additionally, God will fully restore His people. All the children of whoredom and all the judgments that resulted from Israel's spiritual adultery will be cleared up. God promises this by referring to each of Gomer's children and demonstrating how He will reverse the meanings of their names. God declares, "and I will sow her for myself in the land. And I will have mercy on No Mercy, and I will say to Not My People, 'You are my people'; and he shall say, 'You are my God'" (Hosea 2:23). When God named Gomer's child "Jezreel" He referred to the place of bloodshed denoted by that name. Here, however, when God declares "I will scatter" (Hosea 2:23), He is referring to the meaning of the name Jezreel, which is "God scatters" (Easton). In the restoration, God declares the meaning of the name "Jezreel" in a positive sense. He will scatter His people as seeds in the restored land and they will produce fruit and bring Him glory. When God named Gomer's child, "No Mercy," He indicated that He will withhold His compassion from His people. Now, God will reverse the judgment by bestowing abundant mercy. Finally, when God named Gomer's child "Not my people," He indicated a breaking of the covenant. Now God will declare, "My People" to the child named "Not My People." In a fitting response God's people will respond to God by saying, "You are my God." All these restorations show that God's overarching desire for a bride who matches Him and who loves Him prevails over the strongest and most severe judgments. He will restore and win His people back as His bride.

Gomer is restored to Hosea's house

Hosea's next action towards Gomer provides a living demonstration in Hosea's domestic life showing that God intends to restore His adulterous wife Israel to Himself. After the birth of their three children, Gomer left Hosea's house and returned to her former occupation as a harlot. God essentially commands Hosea to go and buy his wife *again*. "And the LORD said to me, "Go again, love a woman who is loved by another man and is an adulteress, even as the LORD loves the children of Israel, though they turn to other gods and love cakes of raisins"" (Hosea 3:1). "Go again, love a woman" is God's command for Hosea to go forth again and love Gomer. "Who is loved by another man and is an adulteress" indicates that Gomer is loved by Hosea, the "another man," even while she has forsaken him and is practicing adultery. Gomer's desertion is a picture of Israel's relationship with God. God still loves the children of Israel, even though they have turned to other gods. Furthermore, the children of Israel "love cakes of raisins." This may mean that they are using raisin cakes in their worship of idols (as cakes were in Jeremiah 7:18). It may also mean that they love pleasure, which is symbolized by raisin cakes. Keil speculates that "Loving grape-cakes is equivalent to indulging in sensuality. Because Israel loves this, it turns to other gods" (p. 68). Israel's love of pleasure and worship of other gods combined to turn them away from their true Husband and lead them into a life of adultery.

The amazing thing about God's command to Hosea is that it boldly declares God's own unchanging love for His people, even when they fall away from Him. In fact, this verse uses the word "love" four times. Hosea is to love Gomer, because she is loved by him even while she is committing adultery. God loves the children of Israel. Israel loves raisin cakes. In this small section, God's love for His people is mentioned three times! God loves the children of Israel even though they love raisin cakes and honor other gods. This verse strongly, clearly, firmly, establishes how far and deep God's love extends towards His people. His great love compels Him to work with

His people until they are fully restored to Him. Because of love, he charges Hosea to buy Gomer back and work it out until the love blossoms into a betrothal like God envisioned in Hosea 2:19-20.

Hosea obeys the Lord, seeks out Gomer, and buys her for a little more than half the price of a dead slave (Exodus 21:32). "² So I bought her for fifteen shekels of silver and a homer and a lethech of barley. ³ And I said to her, "You must dwell as mine for many days. You shall not play the whore, or belong to another man; so will I also be to you"" (Hosea 3:2-3). Hosea commands Gomer to stay in his house for many days and to not play the whore. Similarly, he commits to be faithful to her.

Hosea's domestic scene is supposed to convey a message to Israel. They should think about Gomer dwelling in Hosea's house after being purchased again by him. They should also realize that her days in Hosea's house will be purifying—she will have no other men during that time. Similarly, Israel will have a time of purification before returning fully to their God. "⁴ For the children of Israel shall dwell many days without king or prince, without sacrifice or pillar, without ephod or household gods. ⁵ Afterward the children of Israel shall return and seek the LORD their God, and David their king, and they shall come in fear to the LORD and to his goodness in the latter days" (Hosea 3:4-5). Just like Gomer was free from other men in Hosea's house, God prophecies that Israel will experience a time when they will have no king, prince, sacrifice, pillar, ephod or household god. They will be purified. After this time, they will return to Him in a proper way. Verse four is an amazing prophecy that has been fulfilled with Israel for many centuries. From AD 70, when the Roman general Titus destroyed the temple in Jerusalem, the Jews have lived as is described in this verse. They have had no king or prince. Because the temple was gone, they have had no sacrifice. Because the priesthood was destroyed they had no one to wear the Ephod to receive speaking from God. Furthermore, during this entire time they were without idols; they had no idolatrous pillars and no household gods. Israel has been like Gomer in the house of Hosea. She is purchased and purified from all the other things in preparation for a better future. After this period, they will return and seek the Lord and David their king, who is the Lord Jesus Christ. They shall come to the Lord with fear, which is "*reverence* inspired by His goodness realized in the soul (Ps 130:4)" (Jamieson et al, Vol. 1, p. 652). This is the lesson of Hosea's domestic life.

God's speaking directly to Israel

The next section of Hosea, chapters four through fourteen, contain God's direct speaking to Israel. These chapters present a clear contrast to the first three chapters. We've seen how the first three chapters contain details about Hosea's domestic life. There God instructs Hosea on who to marry and how to conduct his household. He also speaks to Hosea concerning the current adulterous state of the nation and of His hopes for the future restoration of His marriage with His people. Hosea does not speak directly to the people in chapters one through three. Rather, the experiences there could be considered Hosea's preparation for speaking to the nation. He learns from Gomer and he learns from God's direct speaking to him. Chapters four through fourteen are different. They contain no more reference to Hosea's family, nor any more of God's speaking to Hosea explaining His views and dreams. Rather, they are Hosea's and God's direct, clear speaking to the nation. They could be considered the application of the message of Hosea's domestic life and of God's initial speaking to the prophet.

Israel's whoredom

Chapter four begins with God presenting His case against Israel. God looks at Israel and declares, "There is no faithfulness or steadfast love, and no knowledge of God in the land" (Hosea 4:1). Faithfulness, steadfast love, and knowledge of God are characteristics of the betrothal God envisions with His people (Hosea 2:19-20). When God examines the nation of Israel He sees no ground for the relationship He desires. Instead, He sees "swearing, lying, murder, stealing, and committing adultery" (Hosea 4:2). Chapters four and five proceed to enlarge upon many aspects of the evil condition of the nation.

One aspect that Hosea particularly emphasizes in this section is the whoredom of the nation. He mentions adultery, whoredom, prostitutes or the like sixteen times in chapters four and five. Some acts of whoredom refer to the physical act while others describe idol worship as a spiritual whoredom. Israel combined the two—idolatry and prostitution—as Hosea describes they, "sacrifice with cult prostitutes" (Hosea 4:14). When Hosea looks at the nation, it is as if this one aspect—whoredom—permeated throughout their culture and character. Daughters, brides and men are all complicit. Israel pursues whoredom in their idol worship and even when there is no more for them to drink at their parties. Children of harlotry fill the land.

The sinister diversion of whoredom has animated the nation, insulting God as their Husband and driving them to go farther astray. Hosea points out the evil force that is driving them. They do not deviate into whoredom simply by the exercise of their own whims and fancies. Rather, they are animated by a spirit of whoredom, driving them away from God. Hosea says, "For a spirit of whoredom has led them astray, and they have left their God to play the whore" (Hosea 4:12).

Again, "Their deeds do not permit them to return to their God. For the spirit of whoredom is within them, and they know not the LORD" (Hosea 5:4).

Outwardly, whoredom characterized the nation. Inwardly a spirit of whoredom drove and animated individuals. The spirit of whoredom is some demonic power that occupied the hearts of the people. When that spirit was in them, there was no room in their hearts for the knowledge of the Lord. They were taken over on the inside with this demonic power. It caused them to be led astray and leave their God. Calvin speculates that this spirit of whoredom would put the people into a kind of shameless frenzy. They would openly pursue their whoredom with no thought of distinction between right and wrong, propriety, or shame. Israel, "inflamed with lust, ran headlong into evil" (Calvin, Volume 1, p. 163). Such a spirit is not a thing of the past, today, there is a "spirit that is now at work in the sons of disobedience" (Ephesians 2:2), driving people to do evil and separate from God. This shows that Israel's problem was not merely a behavioral one. The root of their problem was spiritual. It was a spirit of whoredom. This means that the solution could not merely be an adjustment to behavior. It was deeper than that. The demonic spirit knew the most crucial spot to wage its attack. It attacked the relationship full force. It wasn't the spirit of stealing, murder or lying, although all those were present. Instead the spiritual attack was accomplished by the spirit of whoredom. This was sure to take the place of the knowledge of God in people's heart, lead them astray and cause them to abandon their God to play the whore.

Priests were not able to help the people out of their errant condition. Instead the priests themselves rejected the knowledge of God and forgot His law (Hosea 4:6). The priests themselves fed on the sin of the people (Hosea 4:8), wanting them to sin so that the people would offer a sin offering from which the priests could take a portion. There was no help from the priesthood and even no help from the prophets

Because the people of Israel were ferociously determined to pursue whoredom, it was very difficult for anyone to sway them. Even God could not reason with them or touch them by displays of His grace. His only recourse was to exercise His harsh judgment, explaining that, "Ephraim is oppressed, crushed in judgment, because he determined to go after filth" (Hosea 5:11). God then decided to be against His people, likening Himself to a ferocious lion, preparing to tear its prey. "For I will be like a lion to Ephraim…I, even I, will tear and go away" (Hosea 5:14). After tearing, He planned to withdraw, until Israel emerged from their stupor, admitted their wrongdoings, and began to seek Him. He says,

> 15 I will return again to my place, until they acknowledge their guilt and seek my face, and in their distress earnestly seek me.
> —Hosea 5:15

Hosea's first plea to return

The prophecy of Hosea takes a drastic turn in chapter six. Here Hosea pleads for the nation to return to the Lord. Possibly Hosea was taken aback as he considered the harsh judgment God just pronounced upon the people. When Hosea considered God's intention to become like a lion and eventually leave His people until they change, a deep reflexive outburst erupted from him. A terrifying thought of the plight of the people who would no longer have God's presence rushed through the prophet's mind. Standing at this "precipice" the prophet burst out.

> 1 "Come, let us return to the Lord; for he has torn us, that he may heal us; he has struck us down, and he will bind us up.
> 2 After two days he will revive us; on the third day he will raise us up, that we may live before him.
> 3 Let us know; let us press on to know the Lord; his going out is sure as the dawn; he will come to us as the showers, as the spring rains that water the earth."
> —Hosea 6:1-3

I consider these words to be a direct appeal on behalf of Hosea to the people, asking them to return to the Lord. Commentators differ on this view. I agree with Keil, who says, "It would be…in harmony with the general style of Hosea….to take the words as a call addressed by the prophet in the name of the Lord to the people, whom the Lord had smitten or sent into exile" (p. 94). This is the prophet's impassioned plea to the people who may have been woken out of their stupor by his previous message. The people heard that God will be a lion to them, tear them, and withdraw until they change. Hosea begs them to be different. He implores them to join him as he returns to the Lord, pursues God, and seeks to know God. Hosea is seeking to restore the vital aspect of the relationship; they must return to their Husband.

Hosea's impassioned plea contains his profound understanding of who God is, what He will do, and what a proper attitude of a returned Israelite should be. First, Hosea displays that he knows God. God said He would be like a lion to the nation, yet Hosea sees God as much more that simply a lion who would tear them. Hosea says, "he has torn us, that he may heal us" (Hosea 6:1). Hosea recognizes that yes, God has torn them. However, he sees a purpose in the tearing—that He may heal us. The people may see God as simply a lion, tearing and leaving. Hosea sees God as more like a surgeon, removing the tumor so healing can take place. Job uses this Hebrew word for torn "He has torn me in his wrath and hated me" (Job 16:9), only to later testify how much he has grown from the Lord's severe discipline. In Hosea's sight, God's tearing is for good, so that real health and wellness may come from God. Similarly, Hosea says, "he has struck us down, and he will bind us up" (Hosea 6:1). The Hebrew word for struck, *nākâ*, is used for severe hitting that sometimes ends in death. However, here, God's *nākâ* is not for death. It will leave a wound, which God Himself will bind up. To bind up simply means to wrap a bandage around the wound. Hosea sees God's purpose here. Yes, God caused pain for Israel. However, His tearing and wounding were intended for good—to break Israel out of their determined whoredom and free them from the spirit of whoredom that was preventing them from returning. Upon their return, God would heal them and bind up their wounds. Anyone who has known God's discipline, knows that the tears and wounds that He administers, once healed and bandaged by Him, become the source of grace, strength and life in the relationship with Him. This is Hosea's realization.

Second, Hosea sees what God will do, "he will revive us… he will raise us up, that we may live before him" (Hosea 6:2). Hosea sees God as the life-giver and declares the benefits of the power of that life. Hosea uses the common verb, *ḥāyâ*, "to live," in the piel stem, which indicates that God will make His people live or give them life. The eternal life that God has and that God imparts makes all the difference. It was the weakness of the human life and the frailty of the isolated human heart that allowed the people to be filled with the spirit of whoredom and fall so far away from God. The problem was that they didn't have the divine life, which would have the stamina, purity, vigor, power, and virtue to stay true to God, love God, and be the wife of the eternal God. God, after healing the tear and binding the wound, would impart the life required for His people to begin to match Him. Ezekiel expands the picture of how God will give life in his vision of a valley of dry bones representing Israel who is without hope and dead. God declares to those bones, "I will cause breath to enter you, and you shall live" (Ezekiel 37:5).

Not only will God impart His eternal life, he will also "raise" them up (Hosea 6:2). The word for raise up means to establish. It is used by Moses to describe how God will set Christ up as a prophet before His people. "The Lord your God will raise up for you a prophet like me from among you, from your brothers—it is to him you shall listen" (Deuteronomy 18:15). Because Jesus had life and even was life, God could establish Him in power. Here Hosea is promising the same to God's people. God will establish His people after He has given them His sure, eternal, incorruptible life. Before they received life, how could God establish them or raise them up? He could not establish a people who have the spirit of harlotry in them! However, when they receive His life, then they are substantial. They become true, solid, real. Then God can raise them up, establishing them as something solid. The result is "we may live before him" (Hosea 6:2). People with the life of God may live before the face of God. This is a factor of life. With eternal life it is not necessary for people to do things to make God happy in order to live before Him. Rather, the life itself qualifies them to live before God. A fly with a fly's life can be around a person with a human life. However, that fly cannot stay there and may even be expelled from a person's presence. However, if a fly is given a human life and human body, then that person can be in the presence of human beings simply by virtue of the life. They have human life, therefore contact with a human being fits. Here it is the same. God's people have God's life, they are established by God and they can live before God. This is the virtue of eternal life, not the result of any actions or other qualifications.

Third, Hosea sees what a person who has returned to God should be like. Hosea encourages the people to have an active life of getting to know the Lord, "Let us know; let us press on to know the Lord" (Hosea 6:3). Hosea declares that getting to know the Lord is the most exciting, most glorious life. Gaining such precious knowledge is worth "pressing on." The Hebrew word for press on, *rādap*, occurs over one-hundred-fifty times in the Old Testament and usually describes an army following after its enemy. Abram pursued the armies of the four kings to rescue lot (Genesis 14:14). Only here and in Isaiah 51:1 (you who pursue righteousness), does this word indicate how we should be with God and the things of God. Hosea is inviting God's people to pursue the knowledge of God. He is encouraging God's people to think about how an army goes after an enemy. Think about the intensity of a military struggle—all your powers are focused, all your strength is applied, and all your thoughts are channeled. That same intensity should be channeled for the purpose of gaining the knowledge of the Lord. The word "press on" is also translated "persecuted." Hosea is calling out those who might respond to his words to change their focus, adjust their direction, and find God with all their strength. The Apostle Paul presents a similar New Testament example. He says, "I press on to make it my own, because Christ Jesus has made me his own" (Philippians 3:12). It is as if Paul heard Hosea's plea and forgot everything else to pursue the knowledge of God in Christ Jesus. Hosea is calling the people to a life of pursuing experiential knowledge of God. "The knowledge of Jehovah, which they would hunt after, i.e. strive zealously to obtain, is a practical knowledge, consisting in the fulfillment of the divine commandments, and in growth in the love of God with all the heart. This knowledge produces fruit. The Lord will rise upon Israel like the morning dawn, and come down upon it like fertilizing rain" (Keil, p. 96).

Hosea gives the people ample reason to press on to know the Lord—the reason is that God is so good. He is like the rain and like the spring rains that water the earth (Hosea 6:3). "The latter rains occur during March and April, while the former rains (q.v.) begin the season of rain, usually including severe thunderstorms, in the second half of October to November (or even as late as January in a bad year). The latter rains of March and April are desperately needed for the coming harvest, hence Job's description of his miserable comforters in a marvelous simile (Job 29:23)" (Harris, p. 483). When God rains, fruit grows. "he will give the rain for your land in its season, the early rain and the later rain, that you may gather in your grain and your wine and your oil" (Deuteronomy 11:14). This is a marvelous picture of the goodness of God and of the blessing that a revived person who is pressing on to know Him will experience.

The people's response to Hosea's appeal

A very reasonable question after Hosea's passionate, learned and hopeful appeal, is "How did that go?" In this case, the answer is not that simple. The very next verse after the prophet's appeal contains a question from God, who is wondering what He should do with His fickle people. "What shall I do with you, O Ephraim? What shall I do with you, O Judah? Your love is like a morning cloud, like the dew that goes away early" (Hosea 6:4). The answer to the question of how the people responded to Hosea's appeal depends on the flow of thought between Hosea's plea in verses one through three and God's question in verse four. Commentators vary greatly in their opinions. Keil sees them as not related at all, considering the transition as just another abrupt jump which is characteristic of Hosea's writings. Calvin speculates that 6:1-3 records what Hosea says to the *remnant* of responsive Israelites and that 6:4 is God's speaking to the *whole* nation, which is largely apostate from God. Others say 6:1-3 is addressed to a *future* remnant, while 6:4 is spoken to the *present* nation. Dearman speculates that Hosea appealed to the people to return, but they never actually returned to the Lord. "If they [Hosea 6:1-3] represent what Judge YHWH wishes to hear, then it is obvious from what follows [Hosea 6:4-6] that he did not hear it from his people" (Dearman, p. 193). He considers 6:4-6 to be "God's response to the people's continuing unfaithfulness" (p. 195). I think Dearman is right, especially considering the people's hypocrisy described in chapters six and seven. Some Israelites might have pretended to "return" to God, speaking the words of Hosea 6:1-3. However, their cry was not from their heart (Hosea 7:14) and their "return" was not truly upward, to God Himself (Hosea 7:16).

God's complaint concerning Israel is that their love, *chesed*, is transient and fleeting. This love should be steadfast, the way God describes the love in His betrothal (Hosea 2:19). However, it is "like a morning cloud" and "like dew that goes early away" (Hosea 6:4). Their best intentions are fleeting, momentary and wisp away like a morning cloud. They are like dew that dries up under the sun before its life-giving water can make the plants grow. Ephraim and Judah are completely unreliable, even when they display "steadfast love."

God then emphasizes exactly what He wants from the nation. "For I desire steadfast love and not sacrifice, the knowledge of God rather than burnt offerings" (Hosea 6:6). God would rather have people who love Him than those who offer sacrifices to Him. He would rather have people know Him than offer burnt offerings. Steadfast love and knowing Him make God happy. The word "desire" in this verse is the Hebrew word, ḥāpēṣ. "In the case of ḥāpēṣ, the object solicits favor by its own intrinsic qualities. The subject is easily attracted to it because it is desirable....[ḥāpēṣ] means "to experience emotional delight." (Harris, p. 310). God is simply delighted in steadfast love and in His people knowing Him. Sacrifices and burnt offerings could be given to Him in a rote, dutiful, mechanical way. He has no delight in that. Rather, He dreams about steadfast love and true knowledge in His betrothal to His lovely bride.

Israel falls short of God's delight

The remaining verses in chapter six and show that Israel is still beset with problems. Far from possessing a steadfast love, they still deal faithlessly and are consumed by all kinds of lusts. Clearly there was a problem with their "return" to the Lord. Possibly their corruption worsened because they didn't follow God's requests thoroughly. God expected them to return *and* to admit their guilt, declaring that He would withdraw "until they acknowledge their guilt and seek my face" (Hosea 5:15). In their return in 6:1-3, they acknowledged God according to Hosea's profound knowledge of Him. However, in that "return" they never acknowledged their own errant condition. Thus, they are still full of corruption, as the following verses portray. The priests murder (Hosea 6:9) and Ephraim's whoredom is still haunting the house of Israel (Hosea 6:10). They never addressed the root of their problem.

God reveals that Israel's genuine return to Him will be different, saying, "When I restore the fortunes (literally turn) of my people, when I would heal Israel, the iniquity of Ephraim is revealed" (Hosea 6:11-7:1). When God restores the people to Himself, He will truly heal them *and* reveal Ephraim's guilt. A return according to God doesn't only involve promises of healing as in Hosea 6:1. It also involves the iniquity of Ephraim being revealed, so that it can be brought to the light and eradicated. It's as if 6:1-3 only took care of one side—seeking God—but not the other. Thus, in chapter seven God continues to expose the root of Israel's persistent problems, which ultimately impede His vibrant relationship with Israel His wife.

Chapter seven uses four colorful metaphors that powerfully depict the plight of the fallen nation. Ephraim is like a burning oven, an unturned cake, a silly dove, and a treacherous bow. These metaphors greatly help visualize Israel's iniquity. First, they are like a "heated oven," because their adulterous lusts burn within them (Hosea 7:4-7). While the fire burns inside them, the baker (maybe the spirit of whoredom who animates them) ceases to stoke the burning coals for a short time until the bread is leavened. When the bread leavened, signifying the wickedness has ripened, then the fire is stirred to a ranging flame and the bread is baked. The Israelite's anger smolders all night, just like that oven smoldering as the bread is leavened. In the morning their whoredom blazes and they commit all kinds of apostasy.

Second, Israel has mixed herself with the surrounding nations and has become "a cake not turned" (Hosea 7:8-10). Since the time of Judges, God used the nations surrounding His people to test Israel (Judges 3:1-2). If a neighboring country would attack Israel, the nation would learn war, trust in God, and seek to return to God. The war would "bake" God's people, so that they would return to God. However, in this case, as the surrounding nations "baked" Israel, they never turned to God. Instead, they simply mixed with the nations, taking on their way and even worshipping their gods. The result is that Israel has become like a cake that is put on the fire and is burnt to charcoal on one side and still liquid, raw and doughy on the other. They never turned. God testifies about this unturned cake, "yet they do not return to the LORD their God, nor seek him, for all this" (Hosea 7:10).

Instead, they have become like a "dove, silly and without sense" (Hosea 7:11-13). A dove will flit about to any place that it may perceive that there is food and have no understanding that a trap is set right at that place. Ephraim is like that dove, "silly and without sense, calling to Egypt, going to Assyria" (Hosea 7:11). As Ephraim sought protection from these two countries, they were so silly that they didn't realize that God, the one who they should have sought for protection, had turned against them, saying, "As they go, I will spread over them my net" (Hosea 7:11).

Finally, Ephraim is like a "treacherous bow," which is a bow that malfunctions when the arrow is placed in it and the string is pulled back (Hosea 7:14-17). Instead of shooting the arrow to where the archer aims, the string breaks, or the bow twists and sends the arrow in another direction. For Ephraim, this meant that when they were aiming at returning to the Lord, it wasn't with their whole heart or sincerely. Thus, they ended up at another place, far from God. "They do not cry to me from their heart, but they wail upon their beds" (Hosea 7:14). If they cry to the Lord at all, it is not purely. God says, "They return, but not upward; they are like a treacherous bow" (Hosea 7:16). They might have intended to return, but never did it. They were like a person who was trying to lose weight, aiming to eat less, yet finding themselves at the donut shop with a half-dozen in front of them.

A heated oven, an unturned cake, a silly dove, and a treacherous bow are four metaphors that might describe anyone who is not doing well with the Lord. Within them there is a lust which is only tempered until their situation is right for fulfilling it. Their oven of lust is banked for the night until the bread is leavened, then their lusts come out in full. They are like unturned cakes. The difficulties in their life are allowed by the sovereign God in order to turn them to God and to teach them to trust and know God. Instead, the difficulties simply make these people calloused and bitter. They don't turn to God. Rather they get burned by the world, and just stay there and take it. They are like silly doves, playing with dangerous things in the world, thinking that those things will not hurt them, but will help them. Little do they know that there is a trap waiting. They are like treacherous bows. They intend to return to God, but never succeed. Instead they shoot their arrow somewhere else and become distracted. At different times we all exhibit some aspects of the heated oven, unturned cake, silly dove, and treacherous bow. These pictures may help us genuinely know who we are apart from Christ and how serious is our fallen condition.

The coming, deserved judgment

The next section, Hosea 8:1-9:9, highlights the coming judgement on Israel who has acted as a hypocritical, idolatrous and adulterous nation. It begins by God announcing to the nation, "Set the trumpet to your lips! One like a vulture is over the house of the Lord" (Hosea 8:1). Sounding the trumpet is a sign that the enemy is approaching. A vulture is a bird of prey that God uses to represent invading armies (Deuteronomy 28:49). These words indicate that the enemy army is approaching and that it will devastate the nation. The trumpet call is needed, because Israel seems to be completely clueless about impending disaster. They've transgressed God's covenant, rebelled against His law, and at the same time cry out to God, "My God, we—Israel—know you" (Hosea 8:2). This section seems to be designed to make Israel abundantly clear, that the vulture is coming, judgment is near, and that the veneer of their lip service and so called "sacrifice" to the true God will not stem the coming destruction.

God is like a loving parent in chapter eight, laying out how His child has transgressed, determining the coming punishment, and addressing all the creative ideas that the child may have for avoiding the coming discipline. God first lays out the transgression, "They made kings but not by me" (Hosea 8:4), referring to the establishment of many kings of the northern kingdom of Israel through the people's choice (many times by violent coups) and not by God. Additionally, "with their silver and gold they make idols" (Hosea 8:4). God declares there will be a consequence for these transgressions, saying, "For they sow the wind, and they shall reap the whirlwind" (Hosea 8:7). For Israel to sow the wind means that they played with these transgressions through their own strength and means. They set up kings apart from God and they made idols out of their own resources. When they did this, they "sowed the wind," and will thus bear the consequences of what they put in the ground to grow. They will "reap the whirlwind," a common symbol of God's judgment (Isaiah 66:15). They tapped into the universal law of consequences—they will reap what they have sowed (see Galatians 6:7). They sowed something that was odious to God, they will reap judgment from God.

The remainder of the chapter eight contains a list of creative ways that Israel employed to get out of the judgment. The first was to run to other nations, Egypt or Assyria, for protection. To this God says, "Though they hire allies among the nations,

I will soon gather them up" (Hosea 8:10). These nations do not have the metal to protect Israel from impending doom. Israel also sought to sacrifice more, in a seeming vain attempt to stem the coming disaster. They "multiplied altars for sinning" (Hosea 8:11) seeking to sacrifice in order to gain favor. They even sacrificed to God Himself, "As for my sacrificial offerings, they sacrifice meat and eat it, but the Lord does not accept them" (Hosea 8:13). Just like the nations will not help them, the sacrifices they offer, even to God Himself, will not make their future better. The real problem is that, "Israel has forgotten his Maker" (Hosea 8:14). Only addressing this real problem will help them.

In the next section, Hosea 9:1-9, Hosea speaks directly to the nation, telling them not to be happy. It is amazing that they were so aloof from their dire condition that they seemed to be rejoicing, exalting, and partying. Hosea then says, "Rejoice not, O Isreal!" (Hosea 9:1), as if to say, "Israel you should be crying and mourning, not partying! The reason you should be sad is the same reason that Hosea has been speaking about from the beginning of his prophecy, "You have played the whore, forsaking your God"" (Hosea 9:1). The judgment is that "They shall not remain in the land of the Lord" (Hosea 9:3) and that the festivals of celebration to God will cease. Thus, Hosea asks, "What will you do on the day of the appointed festival, and on the feast day of the Lord?" (Hosea 9:5). Hosea is questioning these dense, aloof, unsuspecting, clueless people. They are rejoicing now. However, they don't know that soon they will be evicted from the land and there will be no more festival days in which they will rejoice. The party is truly going to be over. The nation is not just a silly dove, but a stupid, clueless, completely-on-another-planet dove. God reiterates, "The days of punishment have come; the days of recompense have come" (Hosea 9:7). "They have deeply corrupted themselves as in the days of Gibeah: he will remember their iniquity; he will publish their sins" (Hosea 9:9). Hosea brings to remembrance the evil sins associated with Gibeah (Judges 19:16-22) and applies that state of corruption to the current condition of Israel. The day is near for God to bring to light their sins and execute a fitting judgment.

God's lessons from Israel's history

Chapter nine verse ten starts an entirely new idea in the prophesies of Hosea. From this point to the end of chapter thirteen, Hosea uses many examples from Israel's history to teach lessons about God's faithfulness, to show how the nation was given so much by God and now deserves God's judgment, and to enlighten the people about how they might return to God. These chapters demonstrate how God is remembering many instances in Israel's history and, based on them, planning how to go forward. God remembers the good old days, "Like grapes in the wilderness, I found Israel" (Hosea 9:10), the riches of the nation, "Israel is a luxuriant vine that yields its fruits" (Hosea 10:1), her past glories, "Israel was a trained calf that loved to thresh" (Hosea 10:11). He remembers His past care for the nation, "When Israel was a child, I loved him" (Hosea 11:1). He fondly recalls the past struggles that brought the nation this far, including those with Jacob, "He strove with the angel and prevailed...He met God at Bethel" (Hosea 12:4) and the broader nation, "I spoke to the prophets; it was I who multiplied visions" (Hosea 12:10). He remembers the past glories "When Ephraim spoke, there was trembling; he was exalted in Israel (Hosea 13:1) and how He brought the nation out of Egypt to those glorious places, "It was I who knew you in the wilderness in the land of drought"

(Hosea 13:5). From Hosea 9:10 to the end of chapter thirteen we find no less than eight different references to events in the past that provide glimpses, though fleeting, of what God envisions His glorious relationship with His people will be.

I am so glad that Hosea makes a turn like this here. Even though I understand what God is getting at in Hosea 4:1-9:9, that section is very much focused on the current state of Israel, God's frustration with it, and the coming judgment. That section is necessary, but it lacks historical context, which is exactly what Hosea 9:10-13:16 bring to the table. We no longer see that we are just concerned with Israel as it is right now. Rather, we begin to see God's persistent hope for His people and God's joy for His people. The people may be errant now, but at one time, God found them like grapes in the wilderness. History gives context. Through historical context, the nation can begin a period of self-examination.

This section could be likened to the experience of an aged alcoholic. Imagine a person in his fifties who lived a normal life until he was overcome by alcoholism in his thirties. As he thinks back upon his life, he examines the positive seeds planted in him before alcohol took over. Those seeds did not bear fruit in his decades of alcoholism. However, now he's looking to the future and considering that his roots have potential. There is hope! Those seeds still have time to grow in the last decades of his life. This thought helps us appreciate the second half of Hosea. Hosea will still highlight some of the nation's current unfaithfulness. However, their problems do not dominate this story. There are some very good seeds that God sowed in the nation throughout its history. In this section those seeds begin to speak.

Like grapes in the wilderness

Hosea begins the first historical section, Hosea 9:10-17, with a beautiful description of the overwhelming joy God experienced when He first witnessed the nation emerge from Egyptian bondage to come to Him at Sinai. "Like grapes in the wilderness, I found Israel. Like the first fruit on the fig tree in its first season, I saw your fathers" (Hosea 9:10). God likens His joy to the experience of a person traveling through a dry wilderness, who may pass by a hidden crevice where a vine and fig tree are growing. The ripe grapes quench his parched mouth and the figs are a surprising sweet nourishment. Even more, the figs are the very first figs that the young tree has ever grown. They are, "the first-fruit, which the fig-tree bears in its first time, at the first shooting" (Keil, p. 125). God's joy at finding Israel, finally alone and set apart for Him in the wilderness was just like this. God was bubbling over with satisfaction, delight, and love.

The lesson here is that even though Israel was so satisfying to God at the beginning, they didn't stay that way. These bridal days were tragically short lived. "But they came to Baal-peor and consecrated themselves to the thing of shame, and became detestable like the thing they loved" (Hosea 9:10). At Baal-peor Israel committed fornication with the Midianite women and were drawn away to worship Baal (Numbers 25:1-3). When God first found them, they were like an unexpected fruit in a dry place. Afterwards, they became detestable, just like the idols and foreign women that they loved. God thus turned and spoke of the judgment to come—"Ephraim must lead his children out to slaughter" (Hosea 9:13).

At this point, Hosea cries out. His prayer is from a person who understands how far Israel had fallen and could not bear it any longer. "Give them, O Lord—what will you give? Give them a miscarrying womb and dry breasts" (Hosea 9:14). The prophet prays according to a holy indignation that he feels due to the corruption he sees in the nation. Here, the prophet feels the same as God. He hears about the joy God felt when He found Israel and tastes the pain that Gad feels when He considers their corruption. He prays for justice to be applied to the profligate nation.

God answers the prophet's prayer, indicating how He hates the nation, will love them no more, and will prevent their increase, saying, "Even though they give birth, I will put their beloved children to death" (Hosea 9:15-16). The section concludes with the prophet declaring how God will reject the nation because they have not listened to Him (Hosea 9:17).

A luxuriant vine

Hosea 10:1-10 forms another historical section. Here, Hosea describes Israel as a luxuriant vine that gives much fruit. "Israel is a luxuriant vine that yields its fruit" (Hosea 10:1). The nation of Israel did, in fact, bear much fruit in many different ways. It enjoyed rich produce from the land. It experienced a great expansion of territory under Jeroboam II. Throughout the years, it also produced many able, spiritual individuals. It produced Elijah, Elisha, Jonah, and the seven thousand that did not bow their knee to Baal.

The lesson of this historical example is that the fruit Israel produced did not result in the nation honoring God. In fact, the more fruit, "the more altars he built" (Hosea 10:1). The more the land developed and improved, the more "he improved his pillars" (Hosea 10:1). Now, the nation's false heart must bear its own guilt (Hosea 10:2). The Lord will bring judgment upon them. God's judgment will be so severe, that the people will simply wish to hide, or even be killed by some natural catastrophe. In words echoed by that New Testament to describe the terrors of the end times, the Israelites "shall say to the mountains, "Cover us," and to the hills, "Fall on us"" (Hosea 10:8). Their cry "expresses the desire to be buried under the falling mountains and hills, that they may no longer have to bear the pains and terrors of the judgment" (Keil, p. 86). Such will be their despair as God moves to "discipline them" (Hosea 10:10).

A trained calf that loves to thresh

The next historical example is that Ephraim was a nation that God took pains to care for. He expresses His care by saying, "Ephraim was a trained calf that loved to thresh" (Hosea 10:11). This is good. A calf that is threshing wheat is useful; he walks the threshing floor to process grain. Plus, he gets to eat as much grain as he desires (Deuteronomy 25:4). Compared with fieldwork, threshing is one of the easier duties of the ox. Ephraim is like that. In His tender care for the nation, God gave Ephraim this wonderful job. God remarks that He "spared her fair neck" (Hosea 10:11), indicating that he enabled her to live this kind of easy life. Ephraim loves this kind of life, doing the easiest work and eating the most. However, the problem is that, now, the easy work is not good enough.

The lesson that God is teaching with this example, is that from this point forward, He is going to change His treatment of the nation. Now, He will give Ephraim harder work to do, saying, "I will put Ephraim to the yoke" (Hosea 10:11). In His great wisdom, God will place a more severe yoke on the bull. His intention in this is not simply judgment. He desires that Ephraim would produce something better and more worthwhile.

God's intention is that Ephraim's harder would result in flourishing, productive fields. He commands them, "Sow for yourselves righteousness; reap steadfast love; break up your fallow ground, for it is the time to seek the Lord, that he may come and rain righteousness upon you" (Hosea 10:12). The three commands here are telling—sow, reap and break up. God commanded them to sow righteousness. Previously, they sowed the wind (Hosea 8:10). Here they are to work hard to plant righteousness and witness the harvest that comes from that. They are to have a righteous living, enjoy the righteousness of the Lord, and seek out His righteousness. That is the new seed that they are to sow. From sowing righteousness comes reaping of steadfast love. The Hebrew word for steadfast love, *ḥesed*, is the same word in which God seeks to betroth his people—"I will betroth you to me in righteousness… in steadfast love" (Hosea 2:19). It is the same steadfast love that God delights in (Hosea 6:10) and it is the same steadfast love that God couldn't find among the nation (Hosea 4:1). One may wonder, if God is seeking this steadfast love from them, then how could the people actually have it? The answer is here. They are to grow it. God commands that if they sow righteousness, they will reap steadfast love.

This planting and reaping require that the fallow, empty ground that was in their lives and hearts be broken up. This means that there were fields right there before them. However, they were lying fallow. There were places that surely had the capacity to bring forth fruit. However, there was no produce, no fruit, no steadfast love, because this ground was not broken up or tilled. God commands them to get to the ground, till it, and plant righteousness in it. Then they will reap steadfast love, which is the delight of God and the base for His betrothal to His people. While the field is growing, they may seek the Lord. He, in turn, will cooperate by raining righteousness upon them.

God uses Ephraim's past—as a trained, threshing calf—as a basis to outline a realistic pathway for His people to get out of their predicament. What they need to do is stop threshing, a light activity where they eat their fill with almost no work. They need to look at the fallow field that could be productive, break it up, and sow righteousness. Then God will come in and cooperate with their work. God will rain righteousness upon them. They will reap steadfast love. Together, man and God, God and man will work together to see blessing and loyalty fill the land. This is fertile soil for the betrothal God is seeking.

It is hard to say if God's appeal for them to take up this yoke had any effect on the people of that time. It seems like they did not heed the word and did not followed the pathway for restoration that God laid out. Instead of sowing righteousness and reaping steadfast love God remarks, "You have plowed iniquity; you have reaped injustice; you have eaten the fruit of lies" (Hosea 10:13). God's appeal to the people might have educated *Hosea* about what God requires for them; but it didn't help the *nation*. In this sense it might have helped Hosea understand, consider, and further refine his appeal to the people. However, apart from educating the prophet, we see no immediate fruit in the people. Instead they still are sowing things that will grow into shameful fruit that will eventually be destroyed.

Israel was a lovely child

Chapter eleven contains a description of some of the tenderest care that God gave to Israel in the early days. It is a beautiful, intimate testimony given by God Himself about how He felt, what He did, and what His intentions were. It is like an interview of a person who passed through a momentous event, allowing them space to fill in the feelings and emotions of the time. Reading Exodus may give us the facts and stories. That would make a great movie. Hosea gives us the feelings and internal states. This would make a great novel. Consider the beauty of God's internal state when He utters the following statements. "When Israel was a child, I loved him." "Out of Egypt I called my son." "It was I who taught Ephraim how to walk." "I took them up by their arms." "I healed them." "I led them with cords of kindness, with the bands of love." "I became to them as one who eases the yoke on their jaws." "I bent down to them and fed them." (Hosea 11:1, 3-4). Each of these statements is simply beautiful and unveils the beautiful feelings of the Lord!

When Israel was a child, I loved him

When Israel was in Egypt, under the bondage of Pharaoh, God considered him to be a child. As a child, Israel did not have the law, offered no sacrifices, held no feasts, did not have an army that could fight for God, had no temple, and had no freedom to carry out their own will. They could not inherit His land, could not occupy Jerusalem, and could not establish a kingdom on earth for God. Here God declares that He loved Israel, even though the nation could do almost nothing for Him. This verse points to a beautiful blossoming that was in God's heart. His central motivation was love—pure, simple love.

A careful reader of the Old Testament will realize that there are, in fact, very few verses in the Hebrew Bible that describe God's love to His people. The entire list can be enumerated in this small paragraph. The first mention of love, which provides the base in type for God's true love, occurs in Genesis 22:2, where God tells Abraham, "Take your son, your only son Isaac, whom you love, and go to the land of Moriah." Moses writes about God's unconditional love for the nation only two times, speaking of a first love, "he loved your fathers" (Deuteronomy 4:37) and an enduring love, "the Lord your God turned the curse into a blessing for you, because the Lord your God loved you" (Deuteronomy 23:5). The sons of Korah mention God's love to Jacob (Psalm 47:4). Three other prophets describe God's love for His people (Isaiah 43:4; Jeremiah 31:1; Malachi 1:2). Hosea is the first of the prophets to emphasize God's love and to describe it as His motivation for a persistent pursuit of His wife (Hosea 3:1; 11:1). To ears accustomed to the New Testament message, hearing that God loves His people may seem very common. However, Hosea was a trailblazer in terms of this revelation, basing His word of God's love on only about three written references that existed at the time of His speaking. Now we see that Hosea's message of God's love has fully blossomed in the New Testament age. The central message of the New Testament, "But God, being rich in mercy, because of the great love with which he loved us…" (Ephesians 2:4) is the same as it was here in Hosea's time—"When Israel was a child, I loved him." God was motivated to show His rich mercy upon Israel, not because He wanted to get something done, or make some effect in the universe. He was motivated because of His simple, single, profound, pure, and unadulterated love.

Out of Egypt I called my son

Not only did God love His child, He also called His son. God called Israel out of Egypt, so that He could enrich His relationship with them as they travelled through the desert toward Sinai. When God calls, it means that He desires to be in fellowship with the one He calls. He desires to share who they are, have them in His presence, be with them, and continually deepen the relationship. God's calling of His son means that He wishes that His people would be in the family, working with Him, serving Him, and enjoying His love. God desired that His calling would increase, declaring in 11:2, "The more they were called." Dearman remarks on this, "YHWH's calling of Israel in vv. 1-2 was not simply a one-time event, even though it is founded on the historical redemption from Egypt. The term also characterizes an ongoing relationship between Deity and people, not simply the moment of choosing or acquisition" (p. 280).

Yet it was I who taught Ephraim to walk; I took them up by their arms

God cared for Israel just like a parent would take care of their baby. Spence-Jones describes the feeling this image portrays, "This picture of God's guiding and guarding care of Ephraim is very touching and tender. It is that of an affectionate parent, or tender nurse teaching a child to walk by leading-strings; taking it up in the arms when stumbling or making a false step; and in case it fell curing the wound. Thus, nurse-like, God taught Ephraim, his wayward perverse child, to use his feet (so the original word imports), all the while lending considerate help and seasonable aid" (p. 330). Garrett describes the way God took them by the arms, "The picture is of a father teaching his child to walk; one does this by bending over and holding the child's arms, not by picking up the child. The metaphor of teaching to walk appears to relate to Israel's walking out of Egypt" (p. 223).

Hosea does not use the common Hebrew word "walk" in this description. Instead, he uses the Hebrew word *rāgal*, translated here "taught to walk." *Rāgal* is based on the root meaning "foot" and is mainly used to denote spies or scouts. Moses sent spies into the land of Canaan to view it in preparation for their possession (Deuteronomy 1:24). Joshua sent spies to Jericho before they circled the city (Joshua 2:1). God tenderly taught Israel to walk with a definite purpose in view—He was preparing them to inherit the land. We know from the book of Joshua how God offered the land to the people and how they fought to possess it. Here we see the groundwork training God lovingly administered that would make the later possession possible. As a loving parent, God took them by the arms as they placed one foot in front of the other. The purpose of that tender action was that eventually they would gloriously possess the land God would give them.

I healed them

In His tender, parental, loving care, God healed His children. Israel may not have known all that God healed, because He actually *prevented* many diseases from afflicting them. This was symbolized when God healed the bitter waters at Marah, so that the nation could drink. There He declared, "If you will diligently listen to the voice of the LORD your God, and do that which is right in his eyes, and give ear to his commandments and keep all his statutes, I will put none of the diseases on you that I put on the Egyptians, for I am the LORD, your healer" (Exodus 15:26).

I led them with cords of kindness, with the bands of love

God led His nation just like a kindly master would lead his livestock—with cords of kindness and with bands of love. God did not train them harshly, with bit and bridle, as the Psalmist describes the usual training of animals, "Be not like a horse or a mule, without understanding, which must be curbed with bit and bridle" (Psalm 32:9). Instead, God's firm, steady leading was gentle and kind. "Cords of kindness" are literally, "ropes of adam." Darby, ASV, and NASB all translate this as "cords of a man." God led His people with human cords. Some reasonably understand this to describe God leading His people using men who could exercise compassion on the nation. For instance, Moses led the people and prayed for God to show mercy to them. Similarly, other prophets provided a very human, kind, gentle leadership to the nation to train it. It is not a stretch to say that the incarnate Christ is the ultimate picture of "cords of a man," leading God's people as a man who was like us in all respects, yet without sin (Hebrews 2:17; 4:15).

The phrase "bands of love" uses the Hebrew word, *ăbōt*, for bands. This is the same word that Moses uses to describe the gold twisted cords that connect the breastplate of the high priest to the Ephod. Just as the breastplate containing the names of the twelve tribes is held against the loving breast of the high priest, God holds His people close to Him through His love. These bands that hold His people to His breast are the means that He uses to lead them. These two phrases answer to each other. The cords of a man are the bands of love. This means that God keeps His people close to Him in love through the men that he sends to mercifully and compassionately lead them onwards. Moses and the prophets did this. Christ Himself is *the* perfect fulfillment.

I became to them as one who eases the yoke on their jaws

Far from using a harsh bit and bridle to train the nation, God worked to make their yoke easier. "This figure leads on to the kindred figure of the yoke laid upon beasts, to harness them for work. As merciful masters lift up the yoke upon the cheeks of their oxen, i.e., push it so far back that the animals can eat their food in comfort, so has the Lord made the yoke of the law, which has been laid upon His people, both soft and light" (Keil, p. 90). God gave the yoke of the law to His people. However, He also gave the tabernacle to them. Through the sacrifices at this altar, His people could receive atonement for transgressions and enter into a rich enjoyment of fellowship with Him. The peace offering is the best example of pure, deep fellowship with God. God also gave the people feasts, at which they would enjoy and rejoice in His rich, gracious provisions. All these are ways God "eases the yoke" on the nation, bringing them into enjoyment and not merely servitude.

I bent down to them and fed them

Lastly, God describes how He lowered Himself to feed the nation. God bending down implies that God inclined his ear, reached down to their level, extended Himself so that He might help them. God went out of His way, extended Himself from His high place, and came all the way down to the level of His people. In this low place, God fed them. Moses testifies this, "And he humbled you and let you hunger and fed you with manna, which you did not know, nor did your fathers know, that he might make you know that man does not live by bread alone, but man lives by every word that comes from the mouth of the LORD" (Deuteronomy 8:3).

Israel's sad response

Sadly, Israel's response to all of God's care described here was disappointingly lacking. Their response was "The more they were called the more they went away," (Hosea 11:2) and "they did not know that I healed them," (Hosea 11:3), and "they have refused to return to me" (Hosea 11:5). The result now is that God declares, "My people are bent on turning away from me" (Hosea 11:7). The Hebrew word *mĕšûbâ* translated, "turning away" signifies apostasy or backsliding. After all God's tender care in extending Himself to uphold His people, they have become characterized by turning away, backsliding, and apostasy from Him. The result is harsh judgment. God declares, "Assyria shall be their king" (Hosea 11:5) and "The sword shall rage against their cities" (Hosea 11:6).

God's heart recoils within Him

If the lesson from this historical event would stop here, then it would teach a similar lesson as the last two events have taught; Israel did not return the love that God's care deserved, therefore they will be judged. However, the wonderful thing about this lesson is that it goes farther. Here we see how much God's care for Israel was an expression of His unwavering love for His people. Furthermore, God uses the historical backdrop of that care to show how much He is, in fact, committed to the marriage and its recovery. In what might be one of the most amazing change of heart recorded in the Bible, God describes how His own heart recoils from the judgment He intended and warms again to His people.

> 8 How can I give you up, O Ephraim? How can I hand you over, O Israel? How can I make you like Admah? How can I treat you like Zeboiim?
> My heart recoils within me; my compassion grows warm and tender.
> 9 I will not execute my burning anger; I will not again destroy Ephraim; for I am God and not a man, the Holy One in your midst, and I will not come in wrath.
>
> —Hosea 11:8-9

These words give us a window into God's divine deliberation. First, He considers that He really had in His power the ability to eradicate the nation for its flagrant apostasy. "'How thoroughly could I give thee up!' If I were to punish thy rebellion as it deserves" (Keil, p. 141). To illustrate this, He refers to Admah and Zeboiim, two cities that were overthrown along with the destruction of Sodom and Gomorrah (Deuteronomy 29:23). God had it in His power to destroy the nation like these cities were destroyed. He even had the right to do this based on the nation's response. However, God's heart changed. He says, "My heart recoils within me." The word *hāpak* translated "recoil" is the same word used to describe how God "overthrew" Admah and Zeboiim. "Significantly, Hos. 11:8 also uses the verb *hāpak* to describe YHWH's change of heart from anger to compassion for wayward Israel, not to describe the fate of Admah and Zeboiim. Almost certainly the verb is chosen in v. 8 because it is part of the judgment tradition associated with Admah and Zeboiim" (Dearman, p. 288-289). The placement of the word here paints a striking picture of what went on within God's heart. Just like Admah and Zeboiim drastically changed from existence to eradication, God's heart went through a drastic upheaval. He changed from wrath bent on destruction to compassion where He sought a way through for His people to receive salvation and restoration.

Accompanying this change, God's compassion grew "warm and tender" (Hosea 11:8). The word for "grew warm" is used when Joseph saw Benjamin after years of separation and when the woman whose baby was alive heard Solomon's suggestion (Genesis 43:30; 1 Kings 3:26). In the same way, God's compassions grew warm and tender. His rekindled compassions and changed heart caused Him to decide and act, declaring "I will not execute my burning anger." He gives reason for this, "For I am God and not man," showing that, unlike man who can change his overall purpose, God will not change His. His initial purpose was calling His son because He loved Him. In spite of the current apostasy, which deserves just recompense, His heart changed. He will not eradicate the nation. Rather, He will work to bring in salvation. His compassion is warmed; His heart is changed. He will continue along the lines of His persistent purpose until it is accomplished.

As a fitting end to this section, Hosea prophesies that the nation will one day go after the Lord, be gathered together, and return to their homes.

> 10 They shall go after the Lord; he will roar like a lion;
> when he roars, his children shall come trembling
> from the west;
> 11 they shall come trembling like birds from Egypt,
> and like doves from the land of Assyria, and I will
> return them to their homes, declares the Lord.
> —Hosea 11:10-11

This prophesy looks forward to a day when Israel is scattered, being dispersed in Assyria, Egypt, and even in the west. In the day of restoration Israel will go after the Lord from all these places. God will roar like a lion and call all His people together from these different places, just like a lion would roar so that the pride will gather. In other places in Hosea's prophesies God likens Himself to a lion which is intent on tearing the nation (Hosea 5:14) or ripping open their breasts and devouring them (Hosea 13:8). Here the lion will roar to gather His people and return them to their homes and to Himself.

Jacob is their ancestor

Hosea's next historical lesson reviews the experience of their ancestor Jacob to highlight a way that they might return to the Lord. Hosea particularly emphasizes Jacob's life-long struggles that eventually led him to meet the Lord at Bethel.

> 3 In the womb he took his brother by the heel, and in his manhood he strove with God.
> 4 He strove with the angel and prevailed; he wept and sought his favor. He met God at Bethel, and there God spoke with us—
> 5 the Lord, the God of hosts, the Lord is his memorial name:
> —Hosea 12:3-5

From birth to manhood, Jacob showed one overarching quality—he struggled to lay hold of the best God could give. In the womb Jacob struggled, holding onto the heel of his brother Esau, wrestling with him, trying to come out first and claim the birthright (Genesis 25:26). The Hebrew word *'āqab,* meaning supplant or deceive and translated literally "took by the heel," is where Jacob got his name. Throughout his life, Jacob demonstrated the meaning of his name, deceiving his father and supplanting his brother in order to gain God's blessing. In his manhood, when he was strong, his struggle continued. While Jacob rested by the brook Jabbok, a man who was God, came and wrestled with Jacob for the entire night. Jacob eventually prevailed in this wrestling match, causing God to touch his thigh and make him lame. When Jacob prevailed, he told God, "I will not let you go unless you bless me" (Genesis 32:26). Hosea may very well have interpreted this act for us in describing Jacob as "he wept and sought his favor" (Hosea 12:4). Jacob asked God for His name, yet God would not reveal His name until Jacob came to Bethel. There God appeared to Jacob and revealed His name (Genesis 35:11).

Why did God review the struggles of Jacob's life? He wanted to teach Israel the lesson of Jacob. God wanted to show the people the supreme value and preciousness of struggling with God. Jacob is a picture of a deeply flawed person who exhibited one cardinal virtue—he persistently sought God's blessing. God wanted Israel to seek Him, struggle through all their flaws and go after God. Jacob's story means that God did not want them to become perfect like Joseph or Joshua or Samuel. Rather, in spite of all the flaws, God wanted them to seek, struggle, grab a heel, and wrestle. God wonders about the nation, "Can you show some pulse, some interest, some struggle, some fortitude to go after Me with all your might?" If they would, then God would surely bless them, just as He did with the highly flawed Jacob. "Jacob is a flawed figure whom God nevertheless sustained, and is thus an appropriate figure with whom to compare and contrast his descendants. The emphasis of Hosea's retelling of the story is that in his life's struggles, Jacob is also the recipient of divine care and blessing and not simply the recipient of negative consequences for his transgressions" (Dearman, p. 307).

Immediately after presenting Jacob's example, Hosea charges them to strive for God's blessing and presence. "So you by the help of your God, return, hold fast to love and justice, and wait continually for your God" (Hosea 12:6). The words "by the help of your God" indicate that God would greatly help them, if only they direct themselves rightly—to return to God. God is saying, "Don't worry about generating strength for yourself. Just return. Just seek out God. Hold fast to loyalty, in the way Jacob did. Throughout his whole life, in spite of his flaws, he kept seeking God. This is the loyalty and justice I'm talking about. He sought God when he was in the womb and when he became strong—all the time. This is a great example of loyalty. Also, wait for your God just as

Jacob did. When he came to Bethel the first time, he heard God's speaking. Then, twenty years later, he wrestled with God. When he came to Bethel the second time, he learned God's name and heard words that still speak to us today. Jacob did not understand God right away. However, his loyalty kept him seeking and eventually rewarded his seeking. Israel, this is your ancestor. Can you seek just like Jacob? Yes, his life was messy. However, his priorities were right, so he eventually met Me."

Sadly, this plea also falls on deaf ears. Even though they have an ancestor such as Jacob whose seeking of God fits the deceptive nation's situation so well, they lack that drive in them that propelled Jacob to God. Instead, they are complacent. "Ephraim has said, "Ah, I am rich; I have found wealth for myself; in all my labors they cannot find in me iniquity or sin"" (Hosea 12:8). Jacob had flaws but still sought God. Israel has flaws but doesn't recognize them and sees no reason to seek after God. They have Jacob's DNA, yet they do not live it in their lives.

God delivered Jacob and Israel from many hardships

In the next section, Hosea 12:9-14, God reminds Israel of instances of His care that enabled Jacob and the nation to overcome many hardships. He declares, "I am the LORD your God from the land of Egypt" (Hosea 12:9), reminding them that He has been their Lord since they were in hardship in Egypt. God promises them restoration, "I will again make you dwell in tents" (Hosea 12:9), assuring them that He will eventually cause them to celebrate the Feast of Tabernacles, fully delivering them out of their past trials.

Throughout their history God delivered His people out of many trials by working through prophets who He sent to them. "I spoke to the prophets; it was I who multiplied visions, and through the prophets gave parables" (Hosea 12:10). God spoke to the prophets so that the nation would be nourished through His words. God gave prophets visions so that the nation would have direction. He supplied parables to the prophets so that the nation could understand Him. These provisions were God's grace to His people, so that the fields of their hearts would be plowed and they could grow fruit to glorify God.

God gives the example of how Jacob their ancestor overcame hardship, which eventually worked out for his good. "Jacob fled to the land of Aram; there Israel served for a wife" (Hosea 12:12). In spite of Jacob's flawed character and deceitful actions that caused him to need to flee to Aram, he got a wife there. He worked hard for her, watching sheep for fourteen years. In this trial, he was able to advance in his relationship with God and even further the purpose for which he was called—he bore many sons in that foreign land who would become the tribes of Israel. There was hardship due to Jacob's flaws, yet through God's arrangement and Jacob's seeking God, he advanced even in exile in the land of Aram.

The nation's sojourn in Egypt followed a similar pattern. Jacob's descendants found themselves in slavery in Egypt. However, their trial was not a dead end. God brought them out of Egypt by a prophet, guarding them by Moses. This was another instance when Israel was "out of the land," in some kind of predicament, but was brought to blessing through God's provision. Moses guarded them and gave them great blessing.

Hosea applies these lessons from Israel's past to their current setting. Now, Israel is in a terrible predicament, largely of their own doing. However, God is saying, "Right now you are simply like Jacob who was in Aram because he was a deceiver. Or, you are like Israel who was in slavery in Egypt. However, in both these situations I was able to bring them to blessing. Now, Israel is in a poor place, yet that is not too much for Me. Hosea is the prophet. He can give visions, parables and My words to lead you out. My provision is here. The history shows it can work."

Sadly, in spite of God's offers and provisions, there is *still* no seeking on the side of Israel. They are complacent, self-satisfied, and hardened. Therefore, they cannot repeat the historical victories of Aram and Egypt. Instead, "Ephraim has given bitter provocation; so his Lord will leave his bloodguilt on him" (Hosea 12:14).

Exalted Ephraim whose words produced trembling

The last two historical examples show the depths of Israel's fall and the lengths God will stretch to redeem him. God first reminds His people of their former exultation: "When Ephraim spoke there was trembling, He was exulted in Israel" (Hosea 13:1). He recalls how Ephraim once held an ascendant place, possibly referring to the time that Jeroboam was king of the northern kingdom.

The lesson from this is simple. They fell terribly from the height they once occupied. They never learned the lessons from Jacob and Moses that God spoke to them in the last chapter. Instead, "now they sin more and more," even to the point of committing despicable acts, "Those who offer human sacrifices kiss calves" (Hosea 13:2). Here, God describes Ephraim at his worst—offering human sacrifices. It was the offering of such sacrifices by the nations inhabiting the land of Canaan that provoked God to eradicate them. When God touched this among the nations, His judgement came down strongly. Now, Israel, the nation which was supposed to conquer the Canaanites, committed the heinous act themselves. God's response is to make the nation disappear.

> 3 Therefore they shall be like the morning mist or like the dew that goes early away, like the chaff that swirls from the threshing floor or like smoke from a window
> —Hosea 13:3

God uses transitory images to describe His severe punishment. The nation will be like morning mist, dew, chaff and smoke. These disappear in the sun or are scattered by wind. Ephraim will be transitory. They fell to the depths, so God will cause them to evaporate.

God knew them in the wilderness

However, God's memory of Israel's "bridal days" is still with Him. The final historical lesson will show just how far God will go to redeem His fallen people. We've already seen in chapter twelve, how Jacob's faults were no barrier to God's salvation and how Egyptian bondage could be overcome. Here we will see that even death cannot stop God's great salvation.

God begins by reviewing the facts of who He is in relation to His history with the nation.

> 4 But I am the Lord your God from the land of Egypt; you know no God but me, and besides me there is no savior.
> 5 It was I who knew you in the wilderness, in the land of drought;
> —Hosea 13:4-5

Here, God lays special emphasis on immutable facts, unchanging characteristics of who He is: "I am the Lord your God" and "besides me there is no savior." He also sees the good in Israel, "you know no God but me," declaring this, in spite of how far they have fallen. Here, God is looking at the eternal part of Israel's experience. The eternal part is their experience with Him—the only God and Savior; the temporary part is their worship of idols. Here God is uplifting them to show them His divinity and the power that He alone has to save. It was He, as God and Savior, who knew them in the wilderness. It was He, as God and Savior, who gave them water even when they passed through the land of drought.

Even though God presents a new historical angle compared with his other references to Israel's history in Hosea, Israel does not respond in a different way. Just as in so many other historical lessons, here Israel falls away and justly deserves God's judgment. God declares that after all His care, Israel "forgot me" (Hosea 13:6). Thus, He will become to them like a lion, leopard and bear (Hosea 13:7-8) to destroy them completely, so that no one will be able to save (Hosea 13:9-11).

The pangs of childbirth

In Hosea 13:13, God describes His coming judgment with an entirely new angle. No longer is His judgment simply for destruction. Here he presents it as a birth, declaring, "The pangs of childbirth come for him" (Hosea 13:13). Keil sees the glorious hope contained in this image, "The pains of childbirth are not merely a figurative representation of violent agony, but of the sufferings and calamities connected with the refining judgments of God, by which new life was to be born, and a complete transformation of all things effected" (p. 159). God emphasizes that His judgment is a birth, a pathway to newness for the nation. Thus, God presents them with hope.

Sadly however, even in light of this hope, Israel will fail to present themselves in a way in which God's arrangement will work out to their purification and restoration. Hosea describes this missed opportunity, saying of Ephraim, "at the right time he does not present himself at the opening of the womb" (Hosea 13:13) As the birth was happening, Ephraim, as the child being born, did not present himself at the opening of the womb. "Ephraim is an unwise son, inasmuch as even under the chastening judgment he still delays his conversion, and will not let himself be new-born, like a child, that at the time of the labour-pains will not enter the opening of the womb and so come to the birth. (Keil, p. 159).

This picture of a breech birth presents God an opportunity to reveal something marvelous about Himself. In most cases, a situation where the child is not positioned correctly for birth leads to danger. Many times, it results in the death of both mother and child. The birth, then, leads to death. Here, God interjects with His most marvelous promise.

> 14 I shall ransom them from the power of Sheol; I shall redeem them from Death. O Death, where are your plagues? O Sheol, where is your sting? Compassion is hidden from my eyes.
> —Hosea 13:14

God declares that He will ransom them from the power of Sheol and redeem them from death. He boldly taunts death, "where are your plagues" and defiantly taunts Sheol "where is your sting?" Previously, in the breech birth, it seemed like death will win. It seemed like the power of Sheol will swallow up the people. The whole nation might disintegrate. However, God, who is the only Savior, will reverse it. He declares, "I shall ransom them" and "I shall redeem them." These are truly words of grace. "God here promises them deliverance from utter ruin; the grave shall be thus deprived of his victim, and the victim rescued out of the tyrant grasp of death" (Spence-Jones, p. 402). "Hosea has been speaking about a situation which could easily, and often does, issue in death (see v. 13).

Now the Lord promises the death of death itself. Grace shines through in the midst of words of judgment" (Feinberg, p. 65). Garrett writes, "The metaphor of death follows from the previous passage, in which Ephraim is like a woman giving birth to a breech baby, but it also describes in general terms the condition of national demise and exile. Ezekiel develops the idea of national resurrection further in his dry bones text (Ezek 37:1–14). As in Ezekiel, the message of resurrection applies first of all to the restoration of Israel, but it also looks ahead to a personal, bodily resurrection. Here, as elsewhere, the prophet develops a type. Both national and personal resurrection legitimately arise from the idea that God can restore that which has died" (p. 265).

God concludes this verse with "Compassion is hidden from my eyes." This is not to be understood as a statement that God will no longer have compassion on the nation. The word for "compassion," *nōḥam* is from the Hebrew root, *nāḥam,* meaning "**be sorry, repent, regret, be comforted, comfort**" (Harris, p. 570). Darby, ASV, NASB translate this, "repentance." Jamieson et al. describe this as "**repentance shall be hid from mine eyes**—that is, I will not change My purpose of fulfilling My promise by delivering Israel, on the condition of their return to Me" (Vol. 1, p. 662). God is saying, "Even if this breech birth will result in death, I have risen up with all My power and will defang death. I will ransom and redeem my people from the power of Sheol and from death. That is because I have a purpose from the very beginning. I will not repent from that purpose. I will gain My bride in a glorious state. I will accomplish this. Repentance, a change of purpose, is hidden from My eyes." This shows the persistent purpose of God.

Hosea 13:15-16 conclude this section by addressing the upcoming judgment on the nation. This judgment will bring the birth pangs, which are intended to purify and transform the nation. "Though he may flourish among his brothers, the east wind, the wind of the Lord, shall come….his fountain shall dry up….they shall fall by the sword; their little ones shall be dashed in pieces, and their pregnant women ripped open" (Hosea 13:15-16). Even though Israel may not present themselves correctly, God, in His unique ability as Savior, will ransom His people, bring them out of death, and win them back to Himself as His lovely bride. This is salvation!

A true return and a genuine confession

Now that the lessons from history have been taught, Israel is ready to hear another plea to return to the Lord, as recorded in chapter fourteen. This is the second call to return, after the first call in chapter six fell upon hypocritical, proud ears. The people should be different by this time, because the examples from history have taught them many lessons. They should now realize their good beginnings with God, God's constant care, how their fathers have overcome hardships, their fall from God's grace, the coming judgment, the unfitness of the nation to allow that judgment to do its intended work, and the fact that God will redeem them from Death. With this added confidence that God will save, their return to God this time has the possibility to be full. Their return in chapter six was a faulty return, with no thought of repentance. It was partial. Here, they will return to God *and* acknowledge their sin. Hosea thus pleads for the people's full return.

> 1 Return, O Israel, to the Lord your God, for you have stumbled because of your iniquity.
> 2 Take with you words and return to the Lord;
> say to him, "Take away all iniquity;
> accept what is good, and we will pay with bulls the

> vows of our lips.
> 3 Assyria shall not save us; we will not ride on horses; and we will say no more, 'Our God,' to the work of our hands. In you the orphan finds mercy."
> —Hosea 14:1-3

There are many admirable aspects to Hosea's appeal here as compared with his appeal in chapter six. First, Hosea uses a stronger word in his appeal here as compared with his plea in 6:1. There, when Hosea asked Israel to "return to" the Lord, he used the Hebrew word el for "to." Here, Hosea uses a different word for "to." It's not el it is ad. Ad indicates a stronger, more thorough return. God uses this stronger word in Joel 2:12, saying, "return to me with all your heart." Thus, here Hosea is appealing that God's people would not simply return, but return in a complete, full, whole-hearted way. As Keil writes, Hosea is aiming for a "complete conversion" (p. 163).

Such a complete conversion must be associated with repentance. There are three other appeals to return to God in Hosea (6:1; 10:12; 12:6). None of them include any repentance. This one is different and much more thorough. "If the conversion is to be of the right kind, it must begin with a prayer for the forgiveness of sin, and attest itself by the renunciation of earthly help and simple trust in the mercy of God" (Keil, p. 164). Here, Israel acknowledges their iniquity, renounces any reliance on Assyria and horses (signifying their own strength), and resolves to never again say to an idol, "you are my god." This confession is like a breath of fresh air. Finally, in this full return, God's people acknowledge the real problems. Sins are brought into the light and fully confessed before God.

In this return they rely on God for their cleansing and offer back to Him what has been cleansed. They offer what is good in them—"accept what is good"—but realize the "good" they have is only present because God has taken away what is evil—"take away all iniquity" (Hosea 14:2). "For unless Thou hadst borne away our evil things, we could not possibly have the good thing which we offer Thee" (Jerome, qtd. By Keil, p. 164). In this return, they also realize the mercy of God—"In you the orphan finds mercy" (Hosea 14:3). God's people, who are supposed to be His sons, realize that they are in fact like orphans, they've been living as if they had no father. They come back to Him, realizing that He is a merciful recipient of those who have no father. In this genuine return they have contrition, repentance, truth, acknowledgment, purity, simplicity, and a deep understanding of God.

God's loving response

God's words in Hosea 14:4-8 show that God fully accepts their return. God's heart is ravished by their whole-hearted return. Unlike the other appeals to return in Hosea, here God does not utter one word of condemnation or grief. He doesn't point out that their lusts are like an oven, or that they are like silly doves or treacherous bows. He doesn't say they have sowed the wrong thing or have denied their Jacobian makeup and have become corrupt businessmen. Rather, with open arms He accepts their contrite repentance. "In response to such a penitential prayer, the Lord will heal all His people's wounds, and bestow upon them once more the fulness of the blessings of His grace" (Keil, p. 165).

God responds to them, promising them that He will heal their apostasy (Hosea 14:4). They did not get rid of their apostasy by their own strength. They simply returned with their whole heart, confessed their wrong, and sought God's mercy. God stepped in and healed all the vile effects and festering sores from their apostasy. He is the healer. He just needed to hear true repentant words and be invited back.

Furthermore, God promises them that He will love them freely (Hosea 14:4). God was like a great big river wanting to flow blessings to His people. However, because they were unrepentant, the flow was dammed. Now, the floodgates are opened and God's great love, His essence, what has driven him to desire this marriage, is now in a place where that bounty can be freely poured out. He will love them freely. The Hebrew word translated "freely" is used to describe freewill offerings at the temple. The Lord did not require these offerings. Rather, freewill offerings were fruits of any Israelite who had an overflowing heart who desired to offer something to God. This word is also used to describe how God caused it to rain on His people in the desert, "Rain in abundance, O God, you shed abroad" (Psalm 68:9). When God says He will love them freely, He is describing a love that is given not because of any obligation or requirement. It is given because there is joy in showering it upon them.

Furthermore, God will be like the dew to His people (Hosea 14:5). He will water them and refresh them with gentle dew that falls in the morning. Previously Hosea used the image of dew to denote the fickleness and transitory nature of Israel's loyalty to God (Hosea 6:4). Here, all things are positive and restored. Dew is a picture of God's refreshing, thirst-quenching gentleness. It harkens back to Isaac giving all the dew of heaven to Jacob, "May God give you the dew of heaven" (Genesis 27:28) and to the picture of dew being the blessing of life from God (Psalm 133). Dew shows that God is a supplier of life to His repentant and restored people.

Because of all these good things given by God, Israel will flourish. He will be healed of apostasy because God healed him. He will thrive under God's freely given love. He will be watered, refreshed, and kept by the abundance of dew.

The flourishing of Israel under God's care

> 5 he shall blossom like the lily; he shall take root like the trees of Lebanon;
> 6 his shoots shall spread out; his beauty shall be like the olive, and his fragrance like Lebanon.
> —Hosea 14:5-6

What a beautiful picture of flourishing life! Compared with deceitful bows, silly doves, heated ovens and unturned cakes, this portrayal catapults Israel into another realm. All the plants here are meaningful. Lilies are pictures of purity and vibrant life (Song of Songs 2:1). "It is said that one root can produce as many as fifty bulbs" (Feinberg, p. 67). The cedars of Lebanon are lofty (Isaiah 2:13) and very good for building (1 Kings 5:6). They are "proverbial for firmness and durability (Feinberg, p. 67). The shoots of these trees depict new growth and young life in vitality (Job 14:7; Ezekiel 17:22). The olive tree is beautiful and green (Psalm 52:8), a picture of "abundance, by which gods and men are honored" (Judges 9:9). Olive trees are the source of oil which is a picture of the Holy Spirit (Leviticus 24:2; Zechariah 4). The result is that Israel will have a pleasant fragrance, a "fragrance like Lebanon." "The smell is like Lebanon, which is rendered fragrant by its Cedars and spices (Song of Sol. iv. 11). The result of God being like dew to Israel is this picture of a flourishing nation. One plant is not enough to express the graces of God's elect people. The *lily* depicts its lovely growth; but as it wants duration and firmness, the deeply rooted cedars of Lebanon are added; these, however, are fruitless, therefore the fruitful, peace-bearing, fragrant, ever green olive is added" (Jamieson et al, Vol. 1, p. 663). "The rooting indicates stability; the spreading of the branches, propagation and the multitude of inhabitants; the splendour of the olive, beauty and glory, and that constant and lasting; the fragrance, hilarity and loveliness." (Rosenmuller, qtd by Keil, p. 166).

When Israel is healthy, vibrant, and flourishing, other nations and peoples may find refuge under his shade.

> 7 They shall return and dwell beneath my shadow;
> they shall flourish like the grain; they shall blossom
> like the vine; their fame shall be like the wine of
> Lebanon.
> —Hosea 14:7

Most versions (e.g. Darby, ASV, NKJV, NASB, NET) do not write "my" shadow in the first line of the verse. My shadow indicates that it is God speaking about people dwelling beneath His shadow. Rather, these versions write "his" shadow, meaning Israel's shadow. The Hebrew agrees with "his," as opposed to "my." Some translations use "my" because they may feel there is a corruption in the text. Darby translates this verse, "They shall return and sit under his shadow; they shall revive *as* corn, and blossom as the vine: the renown thereof shall be as the wine of Lebanon."

This verse is a picture of the flourishing effects of the growth of Israel. The nations and peoples of the earth will return and dwell beneath the shadow of God's people, Israel, who are flourishing under God's rich care. Those nations, then, shall flourish like grain, blossom like the vine, and become famous like Lebanon's wine, "which has been celebrated from time immemorial" (Keil, p. 166). This indicates that not only Israel will be restored by God's presence, healing, and blessing. The nations will all benefit by being associated with God's people.

The last words God speaks to Israel are like words that a loving, caring husband would speak to his faithful, loving wife.

> 8 O Ephraim, what have I to do with idols? It is I who answer and look after you. I am like an evergreen cypress; from me comes your fruit.
>
> —Hosea 14:8

The loving God tells His loving wife, "What have I to do with idols?" In saying that He has nothing more to do with idols it also implies that His wife "Ephraim is to have nothing more to do with them" (Keil, p. 166). In other words, idols are no longer an issue. The couple is happily in love and joyfully faithful to each other. As God speaks this, He is reinforcing that happy fact. Furthermore, God declares that He will "look after" His wife. For this, He uses the Hebrew word, *šûr*, which means to be anxious about or care for, as in Job 24:15. The Lord's attention is always on His dear wife. Lastly, God is like an evergreen cypress, giving fruit to His people. "God compares Himself to a cypress becoming green, not only to denote the shelter which He will afford to the people, but as the true tree of life, on which the nation finds its fruits—a fruit which nourishes and invigorates the spiritual life of the nation" (Keil, p. 167). In this wonderful, restored marriage, there is no more competition from other men. There is no more need for the husband to withhold any of his blessings because His wife is squandering them on other lovers. There is simply a pure mutuality, a tender care, an evergreen freshness, and a fruit that is constant and increasing.

We see how precious this chapter has become. It describes a restored, renewed relationship where God's people are returning to God in a humble, repentant way. God, in turn, heals their apostasy and removes all the evil things from them. He waters them as the dew. They flourish under His care and, in turn, make the world grow and enlivened. The couple are in a pure, beautiful relationship. There are no more idols that entwine Ephraim or need to be spoken about by God. Instead,

God watches over His people, caring for them at all times. God is even a tree of life to them, where they can eat of His fruit. This is God's dream. This is the betrothal He has longed for. This is the fulfillment of the divine romance.

Hosea concludes by speaking about the wisdom of God in His divine plan.

> 9 Whoever is wise, let him understand these things; whoever is discerning, let him know them; for the ways of the Lord are right, and the upright walk in them, but transgressors stumble in them.
>
> —Hosea 14:9

CHAPTER TWO

JOEL

The book of Joel can easily be divided into two sections. The first, Joel 1:1-2:17, describes a plague of locusts and a gathering of the people to cry out to God for deliverance. It includes a description of the locust plague and drought (1:2-19), transitions to a description of the coming day of the Lord (2:1-11) and ends in a plea for a great gathering in Jerusalem where the priests lead the cry "Spare Your people" (2:12-17). The second section, Joel 2:18-3:21, describes God's restoration in response to the peoples' prayer. It includes a description of the physical restoration of the land (2:18-27), the spiritual restoration that results when God's Spirit is poured out on all flesh (2:27-32), God's judgment of all nations and the refuge He gives His people (3:1-16), and the restoration of the entire earth (3:17-21). The book follows a clear progression, presents a definite response of the people, and is straightforward in its message showing God's work.

The locust plague

Joel opens his book by relating God's direct speaking to the nation concerning a coming, devastating plague of locusts. In the opening verses God speaks in the first person, declaring how the locusts will swarm against "my land" (Joel 1:6), laying waste "my people" and splintering "my fig tree" (Joel 1:7). He begins, "Hear this, you elders; give ear, all inhabitants of the land! Has such a thing happened in your days, or in the days of your fathers? ³Tell your children of it, and let your children tell their children, and their children to another generation. ⁴What the cutting locust left, the swarming locust has eaten. What the swarming locust left, the hopping locust has eaten, and what the hopping locust left, the destroying locust has eaten" (Joel 1:2-4). God asks the elders and inhabitants of the land to be in awe of what is coming. He then describes how four locust types—the cutting, swarming, hopping, and destroying—will consume all that is in the land. Differentiating the meaning of each of these four types of locusts has been attempted by many commentators. After finding no solid significance in their difference, Keil concludes "The only thing that has any real significance is the number four, as the four kinds of punishment in Jer. 15:3, and the four destructive judgments in Ezek. 14:21, clearly show. The number four, "the stamp of oecumenicity" (Kliefoth), indicates here the spread of the judgment over the whole of Judah in all directions" (p. 182). The locusts will devastate all vegetation. God asks that even the drunkards wail, because the wine has been cut off from their mouth. God's vine is laid waste. His fig tree is splintered, having its branch made white because it is stripped of its bark (Joel 1:5-7).

This opening section of Joel's prophecy contains God's direct speaking to the nation. In the next set of verses, Joel 1:8-18, the person speaking changes. Here we find Joel speaking directly to the people. In this section, God never says "I" or "My." Instead, the prophet speaks to the people as a fellow Israelite, using phrases like "my God" and telling the people how they should behave towards "your God" (Joel 1:12-13).

Just as God asked the drunkards to wail in Joel 1:5, Joel asks the people to "lament like a virgin wearing sackcloth for the bridegroom of her youth" (Joel 1:8). The reason he commands them to lament is because the locusts' devastation will end the temple offerings. "The grain offering and the drink offering are cut off from the house of the Lord" (Joel 1:9). Essentially, Joel is saying that the result of this locust plague will be that the nation's fellowship with God, as symbolized by the offerings at the temple, will be cut off. "Any further offering is rendered impossible by the failure of meal, wine, and oil. Now Israel could not suffer any greater calamity than the suspension of the daily sacrifice; for this was a practical suspension of the covenant relation—a sign that God had rejected His people" (Keil, p. 184). This is the real tragedy of the coming swarm, affecting all levels of society. For this reason, "the priests mourn" (Joel 1:9), the ground mourns (Joel 1:10), and the tillers of the soil will be ashamed (Joel 1:11). The calamity will not only be due to the swarm of locusts. A severe drought will also ravage the land. "The vine dries up, the fig tree languishes, pomegranate, palm, and apple, all the trees of the field are dried up" (Joel 1:12). Joy will be sapped from the nation and "gladness dries up from the children of man" (Joel 1:12).

Joel pleas for the nation to gather together because of the day of the Lord

Joel's response to the coming calamity is to implore the priests to lament and to charge them to gather the elders and people at the temple so that they all might cry out to the Lord (Joel 1:13-14). The reason Joel states for the gathering is not only the locust plague and drought. He goes beyond this immediate catastrophe and points the people to the spiritual significance of the locusts and drought—the coming day of the Lord, "Alas for the day! For the day of the Lord is near, and as destruction from the Almighty it comes" (Joel 1:15). In using the phrase, "the day of the Lord" Joel is employing a well-known idea that there will come a day when all things are reckoned to the Lord. Keil well describes "the day of the Lord" as a day "through which everything that has been brought to eternity by the stream of time unjudged and unadjusted, will be judged and adjusted once for all, to bring to an end the whole development of the world in accordance with its divine appointment, and perfect the kingdom of God by the annihilation of all its foes (p. 186).

Joel sees the present locusts as a harbinger of the coming day. Thus, he asks those who will gather in the solemn assembly to look at the details of the present calamity as they cry out to the Lord. Joel tells them, "Is not food cut off before our eyes, joy and gladness from the house of God? The seed shrivels under the clods; the store houses are desolate; the granaries are torn down because the grain has dried up. How the beasts groan! The herds and cattle are perplexed because there is no pasture for them; even the flocks of sheep suffer" (Joel 1:16-18). Joel places these images before the people's eyes as if he is trying to make them viscerally aware of the impact of the coming day of the Lord. Joel is trying to stir them up to lament and cry from their heart in their solemn assembly.

Joel's first prayer

Joel 1:19-20 records Joel's prayer. Here, we see that the prophet himself is actually the first one to cry out to God, thus setting the example of what should go on in that solemn assembly. It is as if his attempts to waken the people have actually awakened his own desperation to call out to the Lord. This is Joel's prayer. "To you, O Lord, I call. For fire has devoured the pastures of the wilderness, and flame has burned all the trees of the field. ²⁰Even the beasts of the field pant for you because the water brooks are dried up, and fire has devoured the pastures of the wilderness" (Joel 1:19-20). Joel is joining with creation, groaning for God's deliverance along with all the beasts who are also crying out to God. Calvin understands that Joel's prayer, while being an example of calling out to God, is also a sign that the people have thus far failed to respond. "When the Prophet saw that he succeeded less than he expected, leaving the people, he speaks of what he would do himself, *I will cry to thee, Jehovah*. He had before bidden others to cry, and why does he not now press the same thing? Because he saw that the Jews were so deaf and listless as to make no account of all his exhortations: he therefore says, "*I will cry to thee, Jehovah;* for they are touched neither by shame nor by fear. Since they throw aside every regard for their own safety, since they account as nothing my exhortations I will leave them, and will cry to thee;" which means this, — "I see, Lord, that all these calamities proceed from thy hand; I will not howl as profane men do, but I will ascribe them to thee; for I perceive thee to be acting as a judge in all the evils which we suffer." Having then before declared that the Jews were more tardy than brute animals and having reproached them for feeling less acutely than oxen and sheep, the Prophet now says, that though they all remained obstinate, he would yet do what a pious man and a worshipper of God ought to do, *I will cry to thee — Why? Because the fire has consumed the pastures, or the dwellings, of the wilderness"* (Volume 2, p. 40).

God's response to the prayer and description of the "day"

Joel 2:1-9 could be considered as God's response to Joel's prayer in 1:19-20. Joel calls out to God. In response, God proclaims "Blow the trumpet on Zion," which points to a solution—the solemn assembly spoken by Joel in 1:13-14. A trumpet was used to gather the people throughout Israel's history (Numbers 10:3-4). God commands the gathering trumpet to be blown and, at the same time, that a warning would be given—"sound an alarm on my holy mountain" (Joel 2:1). Trumpets were not only used to call an assembly, but were also employed to indicate an alarm, as when the nation was to go to war (Numbers 10:7-9). God's response here is twofold. The first is to assemble the people; the second is that war, as described in what will take place in the coming day, is imminent.

In Joel 2:2-9 God describes the coming day. This description is intended to stir up the people who are assembled on Zion to cry out to the Lord from their hearts. God vividly paints the picture of the coming "day" as a day of darkness under the fear of a coming invading army. It will be "a day of darkness and gloom, a day of clouds and thick darkness! Like blackness there is spread upon the mountains a great and powerful people; their like has never been before, nor will be again after them through the years of all generations" (Joel 2:2). This army executes complete destruction on the land—"The land is like the garden of Eden before them; but behind them as desolate wilderness" (Joe. 2:3)

The appearance of the army is supernatural and shows great similarities to the description of the army of locusts, who also look like horses, that emerge from the open pit in Revelation 9:7-11. Here the locust's "appearance is like the appearance of horses, and like war horses they run. ⁵As with the rumbling of chariots, they leap on the tops of the mountains, like the crackling of a flame of fire devouring the stubble, like a powerful army drawn up for battle" (Joel 2:4-5). This army is focused, un-distractible, and efficient. "They do not jostle one another; each marches in his path; they burst through the weapons and are not halted. ⁹They leap upon the city, they run upon the walls, they climb up into the houses, they enter through the windows like a thief" (Joel 2:8-9).

Joel picks up the dialog at 2:10 and describes that while this army marches, the earth quakes, the heavens tremble, the sun and moon darken and the stars withdraw their shining (Joel 2:10). Joel describes God Himself as being the head of this army, "The LORD utters his voice before his army, for his camp is exceedingly great; he who executes his word is powerful. For the day of the LORD is great and very awesome; who can endure it?" (Joel 2:11). This indicates that the army of devastation described here is actually carrying out God's command. The day of the Lord is where unrighteousness and evil are brought to judgment according to the will and the powerful word of the Lord.

God and Joel plea for the people to return

In light of this coming, great judgment and catastrophe, God pleads with the people, "return to me, with all you heart, with fasting, with weeping, and with mourning; and rend your hearts and not your garments" (Joel 2:12-13). Here we see God's true purpose for speaking about the great and mighty day of the Lord. It was not to judge His people. Rather, it was to stir His people so that they might return to Him. Oh,

God yearns for His people to return to Him! This is His heart, His dream, His wish, His desire. Such a return is what the plague of locusts and the vivid description of the day of the Lord are supposed to effect. To rend their hearts and not their garments indicates God seeks truth in the inward parts, and not merely an outward display of contrition. He wants their hearts. He wants them to be broken inside. He wants their inward being to be open and contrite toward Him.

Joel echoes God's plea and directs the priests and people how to carry out that return. Previously God had said, "Return to me" (Joel 2:12). Now Joel sends the exact same message, pleading with his people for them to "Return to the LORD your God" (Joel 2:13). Joel explains to them just how good God is. "For he is gracious and merciful, slow to anger, and abounding in steadfast love; and he relents over disaster" (Joel 2:12). Here Joel presents the most compassionate description of God, which is even more striking considering the context. God had just warned the people about the locusts devouring the land and making the temple offerings cease. He had just let the people know about the severe drought. He had just vividly described the terrifying army, executing the word of God Himself, that would wreak disaster on the land in the day of the Lord. All this did not change Joel's appreciation for the true character of God. Judgment, Joel knew, was the strange work of God. Compassion, Joel was convinced, is the true nature and blissful delight of the Lord. He pleads to the people here based on the compassion and mercy of God, not based on his anger or threat of judgment.

One phrase stands out on Joel's list, "abounding in steadfast love." This word describes God in His steadfast relationship with His people. It is like the solid, healthy relationship between husband and wife. In fact, Hosea uses this same Hebrew word, *chesed*, to describe the kind of love God has toward His bride, the nation of Israel, "And I will betroth you to me forever. I will betroth you to me in righteousness and in justice, in steadfast love and in mercy" (Hosea 2:19). "The prophet thus points the people to the covenant-making and covenant-keeping God; your God specifically emphasizes the personal relationship between the LORD and his people" (Prior, p. 54). Joel's hope is that with such a return, God may turn from His judgment, restore the land and thus restore the temple offerings to Him (Joel 2:16).

The great assembly

Joel once again and finally encourages the people to gather together. He wants everyone to be there—old men, priests, Levites and even the nursing children. He wants the all the people to stand before the Lord and, as an entire nation, cry out to God. "[15]Blow the trumpet in Zion; consecrate a fast; call a solemn assembly; [16]gather the people. Consecrate the congregation; assemble the elders; gather the children, even nursing infants. Let the bridegroom leave his room, and the bride her chamber. [17]Between the vestibule and the altar let the priests, the ministers of the LORD, weep and say, "Spare your people, O LORD, and make not your heritage a reproach, a byword among the nations. Why should they say among the peoples,'Where is their God?' " (Joel 2:15-17). "In order that none may think themselves exempt, the people are more precisely defined as old men, children, and sucklings. Even the bride and bridegroom are to give up the delight of their hearts, and take part in the penitential and mournful worship. No age, no rank, is to stay away, because no one, not even the suckling, is free from sin; but all, without exception, are exposed to the judgment. "A stronger proof of the deep and universal guilt of the whole nation could not be found, than that on the great day of penitence and prayer, even new-born infants were to be carried in their arms" (Umbreit)" (Keil, p. 197-198).

God responds to the cry of the assembly

The remainder of Joel's book could be considered as God's response to this collective, corporate cry. "Then the LORD became jealous for his land, and had pity on his people" (Joel 2:18). Both words in this verse are used by God to denote his energies for restoring His people. The word "jealous" is used by Zechariah to describe how God will restore Jerusalem and Zion after they had been devastated by the Babylonians (Zechariah 1:14; 8:2). There God's jealousy meant that God would move to rebuild. The word "pity" is used by Malachi to describe how God will spare his people from judgement, just like a father would spare his own son (Malachi 3:17). For the Lord to have pity on His people means that He will spare them from judgment. For Him to be jealous for His land means that He will restore the land that was ravaged by the locusts.

Physical restoration

Restoration is exactly what God does. He first sends them produce, which they were sorely lacking, "Behold, I am sending to you grain, wine, and oil, and you will be satisfied; and I will no more make you a reproach among the nations" (Joel 2:19). He will take the locust swarm away, "I will remove the northerner far from you, and drive him into a parched and desolate land" (Joel 2:20). He will remember the beasts of the field, who cried out to Him, "Fear not, you beasts of the field, for the pastures of the wilderness are green; the tree bears its fruit; the fig tree and vine give their full yield" (Joel 2:22). He will open the heavens and pour out abundant rain, "for he has given the early rain for your vindication; he has poured down for you abundant rain, the early and the latter rain, as before" (Joel 2:23). He will restore all that they lost through the judgment of every kind of locust, "I will restore to you the years that the swarming locust has eaten, the hopper, the destroyer, and the cutter, my great army, which I sent among you" (Joel 2:25). Finally, He will dwell in the midst of His people who will eat plenty and praise His name, "You shall know that I am in the midst of Israel, and that I am the Lord your God and there is none else" (Joel 2:27).

The spiritual restoration

Then, there is a transition. Just as Joel transitioned from describing locusts to speaking about the coming day of the Lord in Joel 1:15, God transitions from describing the material restoration of the produce of the land to speaking about the future spiritual restoration—the outpouring of the Spirit. "I will pour out my Spirit on all flesh; your sons and your daughters shall prophesy, your old men shall dream dreams, and your young men shall see visions. [29] Even on the male and female servants in those days I will pour out my Spirit" (Joel 2:28-29). Just as God promised to pour out rain upon the fields in His physical restoration, here He promises that He will pour out His Spirit upon all flesh. Pouring out symbolizes abundance, "to pour out, signifies communication in rich abundance, like a rain-fall or water-fall. For the communication of the Spirit of God was not entirely wanting to the covenant nation from the very first. In fact, the Spirit of God was the only inward bond between the Lord and His people; but it was confined to the few whom God endowed as prophets with the gift of His Spirit. This limitation was to cease in the future. What Moses expressed as a wish—namely, that the people were all prophets, and the Lord would put His Spirit upon them (Num. 11:29)—was to be fulfilled in the future" (Keil, p. 139).

In this marvelous promise the abundant Spirit is poured out upon "all flesh." Just like Joel gathered the entire nation from every walk of life to come to Jerusalem to cry to the Lord, here the Spirit is poured out upon all. It includes old men, young men, women and even slaves. Keil remarks concerning slaves, "Not a single case occurs in the whole of the Old Testament of a slave receiving the gift of prophecy.…The gospel has therefore also broken the fetters of slavery" (p. 140). The coming Spirit described here, is truly the fulfillment of John's description that before Jesus was glorified the Spirit was not yet (John 7:39). However, after His glorification, on the day of Pentecost, Peter could utter these words of Joel, as He witnessed the abundant pouring out of the Spirit. When the Spirit was poured out, salvation was poured out onto all mankind.

The coming judgment and salvation

The outpouring of the Spirit was a prelude to the coming day of the Lord, which will include judgment for all evildoers and salvation for all God's people. "For Joel the day of the Lord was not exclusively judgment or salvation; it was simply the coming of God to deal with people. For some this means life; for others it means death (2 Cor 2:16)" (Garrett, p. 370). "[30] And I will show wonders in the heavens and on the earth, blood and fire and columns of smoke. [31] The sun shall be turned to darkness, and the moon to blood, before the great and awesome day of the Lord comes. [32] And it shall come to pass that everyone who calls on the name of the Lord shall be saved. For in Mount Zion and in Jerusalem there shall be those who escape, as the Lord has said, and among the survivors shall be those whom the Lord calls" (Joel 2:30-32).

These verses show that both God's judgment and His salvation have wide effects. Blood, fire, smoke, the darkened sun and moon all speak of the coming severe judgment that God will unleash on the ungodly of the earth. His judgment will encompass the land, the people and even the heavenly bodies. Just like His judgment will be broad, His salvation will grow in its extent—it will be offered to all. Joel describes that salvation will be available to "everyone"—to all who *will*—even to Gentiles. He boldly claims, "everyone who calls on the name of the Lord shall be saved." This is marvelous! Calling on the name of the Lord is the way to participate in the salvation that is available to any who seek it. ""Calling upon the name of Jehovah" signifies not only the public worship of God, but inward worship also, in which the confession of the mouth is also an expression of the heart" (Keil, p. 214). Not only do people call on God; these verses show that God calls those who call on Him, "among the survivors shall be those whom the Lord calls" (Joel 2:32). There are two sides of salvation: on the one hand the believers call on the name of the Lord, become saved and survive. On the other hand, God calls from among the survivors. This is a picture of full salvation: the believers call on the name of the Lord, they escape, God calls from among the survivors. We see man and God working together so that God may enact His salvation and man may enjoy God's salvation to the full extent.

The judgment of the nations in the day of the Lord

In chapter three God describes the future judgment of all the nations, which will take place after the restoration of Israel. "When I restore the fortunes of Judah and Jerusalem, I will gather all the nations...And I will enter into judgment with them" (Joel 3:1-2). God's judgment will be based on how those nations have treated His people, "because they have scattered them among the nations and have divided up my land" (Joel 3:2), as well as many other atrocities. God gives specific examples of how some nations—Tyre, Sidon and Philistia—engaged in these atrocities and will reap punishment for them (Joel 3:4-8).

Just as Joel transitioned from the present locust swarm to the future day of the Lord in 1:15, and as God transitioned from the present blessings concerning the fruitfulness of the land to the future outpoured Spirit in 2:28, Joel transitions from the judgment of Tyre, Sidon, and Philistia to the future world-wide gathering for judgment of all nations in 3:9. Here Joel taunts all the nations who are rising up against God, saying, "Consecrate for war; stir up the mighty men...Beat your plowshares into swords and your pruning hooks into spears...Hasten and come, all you surrounding nations, and gather yourselves there" (Joel 3:9-11).

Joel's second prayer

At this point, Joel utters his final prayer of the book. With the nations bent on war surrounding the city of God, Joel looks to God, and utters this marvelous plea, "Bring down your warriors, O LORD" (Joel 3:11). This is essentially a plea for God to return and for Him to bring His warriors with Him. When Joel cries "bring down," he utters this word in the Hebrew Hiphil stem, which indicates that the Lord should send the warriors down and come down with them as well. Joel's first prayer, uttered as he described the beasts of the field calling to God, was as if he joined the creation in calling on God for deliverance from the drought (Joel 1:19-20). This prayer is as if the prophet is putting himself in the city he is describing as it is surrounded by nations. "This prayer almost seems like a sudden response to the prophet's realization that the battle lines are being drawn in very unequal numbers—all the multitudes of the nations against the LORD and his people" (Prior, p. 93). Ironside defines the warriors as the Lord's saints, indicating that the Lord will return with the matured and ready saints, just as the picture in Revelation 19 conveys. "The whole land will be overrun with them; and all human help for the remnant of Israel, who cleave to the Lord, will be gone. Therefore they cry in the hour of their deepest distress, "Thither cause Thy mighty ones to come down, O Lord." Knowing that the hour has struck when the saints shall take the kingdom, they turn heavenward in their affliction, calling for the descent of their once-rejected Messiah and His glorious train. The answer to their prayer is given in the riding forth of the warrior on the white horse, with all the armies of heaven, as recorded in Rev. 19. He executes summary judgment upon the armed hosts of the nations" (p. 94).

This prayer is nothing short of marvelous. It is the prophet's voicing of what God has wanted to do for so long—return. In uttering this prayer, Joel is voicing a cry that has resounded from within God's people throughout history. Since ancient times, even during the time of Enoch, God's people have been yearning for Him to return with His saints (Jude 14). The final prayer recorded in Revelation is the same—"Come Lord Jesus" (Revelation 22:20). It is a recognition that God is yearning to return. The wonderful thing about Joel's prayers, is that God does not return alone. He returns with His warriors, His saints.

The warriors being the saints, as they are in Revelation 19:14, means that they are believers who will return with the Lord as part of His glorious train. This is not the first time

Joel refers to believers or saints in his prophesy. Previously we have learned how the Spirit is poured out upon them, how they will call on the Lord to be saved, and how the Lord will call them (Joel 2:28-32). Those steps could be considered the beginning stage of the process of their full salvation. In Joel's prayer, we see the same people at a much more mature stage of their relationship with God. Here they are warriors, clothed in white garments, and returning with the Lord to fight with Him and establish His kingdom on earth. When God would hear Joel utter such a prayer, one could think that God's heart would be stirred up with joy. Joel is not praying this prayer in order to request help for his own selfish needs. Rather, he is asking God to do what He has wanted to do for so long. God desires that the believers that have called upon Him would mature into warriors who could return with Him. Furthermore, God yearns that He would be able to return. Here Joel, like the one who utters the final prayer in Revelation, is pounding on a door that God Himself has wanted opened for so long—He wants to return with His mature saints to set up His kingdom. On earth the battle lines are drawn. In heaven the saints who called on the name of the Lord have grown and have been prepared as warriors. Now, the only thing left to do is for the Lord to bring down His warriors and to come down with them.

The harvest of the righteous and wicked

God's joyous response to Joel's prayer is in Joel 3:12-15. He declares the coming judgment of all the nations, "Let the nations stir themselves up and come to the Valley of Jehoshaphat; for there I will sit to judge all the surrounding nations" (Joel 3:12). Then, He commands that a great harvest would begin, "Put in the sickle for the harvest is ripe. Go in, tread, for the winepress is full. The vats overflow for their evil is great" (Joel 3:13). God alludes to the harvest of two different crops—wheat and grapes. The Hebrew words for "sickle" and for "harvest" are used only in regards to wheat (Jeremiah 50:16 and Deuteronomy 24:19). Treading the winepress clearly indicates a harvest of grapes. The thought of this verse is repeated by John in Revelation 14:14-20. There, the reaping of the ripe grains is a sign of the reaping of mature believers before the final battle. There, the grapes in the winepress are a sign that the evildoers of the earth have been harvested and are facing God's wrath. Here the thought may be the same. God's response to Joel's prayer is His command that the earth be reaped, which includes both the good and the bad. The good will be rewarded and the wicked judged in God's great winepress. God declares that this will be accomplished in the midst of great, supernatural effects that darken the sun, moon, and stars (Joel 3:15).

Joel's final direct speaking comes in Joel 3:16. He declares how awesome God will be in the day of the Lord. To God's enemies, he will be like a roaring lion, shaking the heavens and the earth, "The LORD roars from Zion, and utters his voice from Jerusalem, and the heavens and the earth quake" (Joel 3:16). However, to the Lord's people, those who receive Him, fear Him, and even serve Him, He will be a refuge and a stronghold, "But the LORD is a refuge to his people, a stronghold to the people of Israel" (Joel 3:16).

The glorious end

The remainder of the book is written in the first person, involving God speaking directly to His people through Joel, describing the glorious future of Judah and of all the earth. God describes how He is their God "who dwells in Zion, my holy mountain" (Joel 3:17) and that all Jerusalem will be holy. All the mountains will drip sweet wine. The hills will overflow with milk. The streambeds will flow with water. Furthermore, the Lord's house will become the source of living waters blessing the earth—"a fountain shall come forth from the house of the Lord and water the Valley of Shittim" (Joel 3:18). Like Ezekiel 47:1-12, Zechariah 14:8, and Revelation 22:1, Joel prophesies how the house of God will become the source of salvation for the earth. Living waters will flow and restore all the dry places of the earth. This is a picture of God's spiritual salvation reaching all the barren, dry people of the earth.

God concludes by declaring how Egypt and Edom will be judged and how Judah will dwell in Jerusalem forever (Joel 3:19-21). Egypt and Edom are types signifying all the nations. Judah is a type signifying all God's people. Thus, God is declaring that all the nations will be judged and cleared of any authority that is not from God. Likewise, all God's people will be brought to dwell securely with Him in the holy city of Jerusalem.

The closing picture is a marvelous display of what will happen after God descends with His warrior saints. God will gain a glorious earth that is fully cleansed, holy and restored. It produces wine, milk and food in abundance. Its waters flow. The center of the restored earth is the house of the Lord, from which living streams of salvation proceed. All the wicked nations are corrected and judged. God dwells in Zion where His people dwell securely for eternity. Marvelous!

CHAPTER THREE

Amos

The book of Amos can be divided into three parts. The first section begins and ends with a lion's roar (Amos 1:2-3:8), which is God's way of sounding out His voice in the book. This section unveils how the prophet's intimate fellowship with God results in his yearning for righteousness among the nations and within God's people. The second section begins with foreign nations learning about the judgments coming upon Israel and ends with a foreign nation gathering round Israel to execute that judgment (Amos 3:9-6:14). This section mainly contains God's speaking to Israel as it was at Amos' time. He warns of coming judgments, reviews past calamities allowed by God in an attempt to turn Israel back to Him and urges people to seek good and the living God Himself. The last section contains five visions (Amos 7-9). This section reveals God's judgment on Israel, shows how God will save a faithful remnant, and portrays how that remnant will become a seed to bring God's salvation to His people and the Gentiles. This last section also reveals Amos' commitment in his ministry to the faithful remnant God desires.

God is roaring like a lion

Amos begins his prophecy with God roaring like a lion from Zion. "The LORD roars from Zion and utters his voice from Jerusalem" (Amos 1:2). The Hebrew word translated "roar" is used mainly in reference to lions roaring (see Amos 3:8). In Amos' understanding there is always a purpose for a lion's roar—a lion doesn't roar unless there is some prey (Amos 3:4). Likewise, God is roaring because there is a definite reason—a problem with the nations and with Israel. The place God roars from is also significant here. Even though Amos is prophesying to the northern nation of Israel from the city of Bethel, Amos indicates God's roar comes from the southern nation, from Zion and Jerusalem. In saying this, Amos is pointing back to the temple in Jerusalem, the place where God has put His name, in contrast to Bethel where the Israelites are currently engaged in a false worship of God. Thus, at the beginning of his book, Amos firmly declares that he respects God's revealed place, Jerusalem, considers that to be the source of God's speaking, and humbly puts himself in obedience to God's revelation from there.

Roaring at the nations

One might think God's roar from Zion would first be aimed at a problem He sees with Israel or with Judah. However, His roar is not concerned with either of these at first. Rather, the roar from Zion and the voice from Jerusalem first concern themselves with the nations, the Gentiles surrounding Israel.

It is almost as if Amos is saying that the God who roars from Zion is Lord of the whole earth. If He sees a problem in His sphere of influence, He will say something about it.

God first addresses His roaring words to six surrounding nations, repeating the phrase, "For three transgressions and for four" for each nation. This phrase should not send the Bible student on a quest through the history of these nations to find three transgressions and then a fourth. Rather, this phrase is an idiom denoting that the transgressions have been filled up to such an extent that their behavior now deserves to be addressed. It is like a parent saying to a child, "This is the last time I want to see you doing that." In each case, God addresses a specific act committed by the nation and usually highlights an evil characteristic. In response, God will administer just punishment to that nation.

God first speaks to Damascus, Gaza, and Tyre, which are cities from the nations of Syria, Philistia, and Phoenicia, respectively. These countries, while having no historical blood relation with Israel, are located near Israel and had business dealings with them. Each of these nations has committed violent acts. God points out that Damascus "threshed Gilead with threshing sledges of Iron" (Amos 1:3), which is a reference to the king of Syria savagely attacking the Israelites in Gilead. Elisha foresaw this heinous crime when he saw the Syrian king ripping open pregnant women and hamstringing oxen. (2 Kings 8:12). There was no need for this kind of savagery in his attack of the weaker nation. God describes how Gaza "carried into exile a whole people to deliver them up to Edom" (Amos 1:6). Tyre did a similar, unfeeling, cruel act: "they delivered up a whole people to Edom" (Amos 1:9). When Tyre sold these people, they "did not remember the covenant of brotherhood" that they had with Israel, even though they had a history of good relations with the kingdom. They supplied materials for the building of the temple at Jerusalem, received payments of wheat and oil from Israel, and even went on joint shipping ventures with the nation. In violation of this history of cooperation, they turned on their brothers by selling a whole group of Israelites to Edom.

The next group of nations—Edom, Ammon, and Moab—are historically related to Israel by blood. Edom is descended from Jacob's brother Esau. Ammon and Moab are descended from Lot, Abraham's nephew. Each of these committed violent acts. Edom "pursued his brother with the sword and cast off all pity" (Amos 1:11). When Israel was being persecuted by other nations, Edom had no mercy on the Israelites fleeing the violence, preying upon the helpless in spite of Jacob being Esau's brother. Furthermore, Edom nursed a continual, burning hatred for Israel, "his anger tore perpetually, and he kept his wrath forever" (Amos 1:11). The Ammonites mercilessly "ripped open pregnant women in Gilead that they might enlarge their border" (Amos 1:13). Moab showed blatant disrespect for the dead—"he burned to lime the bones of the king of Edom" (Amos 2:1). For each of these transgressions, God promises to bring the deserved punishment on the cities of these nations through fire. Six times the Lord declares, "I will send fire" (Amos 1:4, 7, 10, 12, 14; 2:2). Thus, the Lion roars from Jerusalem.

God's prophecies to these nations reveal Amos' worldview. They show that he is broadly concerned for the whole earth. Other prophets, like Hosea, don't address heinous acts of any other nation, but only show concerned for Israel. Amos is much broader. He involves himself in foreign affairs and concerns himself with the unrighteous actions of foreign powers. The actions Amos chooses to highlight are also instructive. He doesn't focus on the other gods that these nations worship, although they surely worship many other gods. He doesn't focus on the rampant idolatry that they practice and use to corrupt God's people. Instead, Amos focusses exclusively on their behavior, specifically, their relationships with other nations. Amos holds the behavior of these foreign nations to a definite standard, asking them, "How are you treating your fellow men?" Even though these nations have no special revelation of God in their history, they are God's creatures. As such, Amos understands that they have responsibilities as human beings who are members of the human race. In his New Testament writings, the Apostle Paul understood that God's law has its imprint in Gentiles who have not had any special revelation from God, saying, "They show the work of the Law written in their hearts" (Romans 2:15). Amos is wondering concerning these nations, "How is the Law that has been written on your hearts being lived out in the actions of your nation?"

Such concerns show that Amos is a person hungering and thirsting for righteousness. His hunger extends worldwide and applies to all people. It crosses cultural boundaries, is not limited to the people of special revelation, and is expected for every person who is a member of the human race. When Amos sees any country on earth, he will wonder, "How is righteousness being lived out with you?" Here, Amos declares that God will send fire upon these nations for their shortfalls. Later, we will see that Amos' grand dream of righteousness spreading to all mankind will eventually be fulfilled. When God's kingdom is established on earth, Amos' hunger and thirst for righteousness will be satisfied, even among the Gentiles.

Roaring to Judah and Israel

The lion's roar now turns to the people who have had a history of special revelations from God—Judah and Israel. The people of Judah "have rejected the law" and "have not kept his statutes" (Amos 2:4). The result is that "their lies have led them astray" (Amos 2:4). The people of Israel fail greatly in how they treat the poor among them. "They sell the righteous for silver…trample the head of the poor into the dust of the earth" (Amos 2:6-7). In their religious worship they oppress the poor, laying "themselves down beside every altar on garments taken as a pledge," drinking wine taken from "those who have been fined" (Amos 2:8). Moses commanded the people not to take a garment as a pledge (Exodus 22:26) and to worship with the abundance of produce from the land that the Lord has blessed. Instead the Israelites are twisting their false worship and finding ways to oppress the poor even in so-called "worship" to God.

The Israelites acted like this in spite of the fact that God had revealed Himself to them in so many gracious ways. He fought for them, reminding them that He, "destroyed the Amorite before them" (Amos 2:9). He shepherded them, testifying "it was I who brought you up out of the land of Egypt" (Amos 2:10). He cared for them, raising "up some of your sons for prophets" (Amos 2:11) and led them through the wilderness. Despite God's gracious, persistent care, His people did not honor Him, receive His provisions, and especially did not produce a righteous life in which they would treat the poor with dignity and justice.

From this we can see Amos' view for God's people, those who have had a special revelation of God. We have already seen how Amos expects Gentiles to act as responsible members of the human race. Here, we see how Amos expects God's people to act in a way that is according to how God treated them. Amos measures God's people based on what they have received from God, which in this instance is the Law of God (Amos 2:4) and the care of God (Amos 2:9-11). God's Law is not simply the ten commandments and additional requirements laid out by Moses. God's Law was the full provision that He gave His people, which includes the tabernacle, with its altar and sacrifices. The standard of conduct given by the law is high. However, for those who miss that, God's full Law also gave a provision for sin and sins, which enabled God's people to continue in fellowship with Him. Additionally, God gave His special care to the nation, leading them out of Egypt, provisioning them with food and drink, and even fighting for them. The full gamut of care that God's people have received should enable them to act justly and especially mercifully toward their weaker brethren. Motyer notices these things, writing, "First, the object of divine saving outreach is a company of helpless slaves, guilty sinners, frail mortals….. Secondly…what the Lord did for his people was to furnish them with a full salvation, thus depriving them (and us) of every excuse for failing to be like their God" (p. 62). Amos' yardstick for measuring God's people is how they have taken all these God given provisions and put them to use in their relationships with others.

The result of Amos' measurement of Israel is a failing grade. Israel will receive its just punishment; God will judge the nation. Amos points out their special place and the special judgment that comes from that unique place they hold with God. God declares, "You only have I known of all the families of the earth; therefore I will punish you for all your iniquities" (Amos 3:2). This shows that special revelation and special gifts from God bring with them special responsibilities. If the responsibilities are not met, then God's people will also taste His unique punishment. As Peter says, "It is time for judgment to begin at the household of God" (1 Peter 4:17).

Amos concludes this section with a basic message, "I am a prophet and I am speaking. This means something is wrong that you, Israel, have to adjust." Amos however, presents this message in a much more interesting way. He lists seven different scenarios which only happen if a purpose is present (Amos 3:3-6). These scenarios bring out Amos' shepherding background in a most colorful way. He gives examples of two men meeting in a lonely sheep pasture, lions roaring, birds being trapped and snares springing from the ground. Amos' bucolic background shines through, conveying that traps, lions, and a meeting in the wilderness all happen for some purpose. His conclusion brings all these scenarios back to God, and particularly to the message God is giving right now through Amos. "The lion has roared; who will not fear? The Lord GOD has spoken; who can but prophesy?" (Amos 3:8).

Amos' secret fellowship with God

Immediately before describing the Lion's roar, Amos gives a window into why he can prophesy the way he does. Amos' prophesy comes from his intimate fellowship with and knowing of God Himself. He testifies, "For the Lord GOD does nothing without revealing his secret to his servants the prophets" (Amos 3:7). This verse shows how Amos knew God. In turn, God "revealed His secret" to Amos the prophet. The Hebrew word *sôd* translated "secret" is an extremely intimate word. "The primary meaning of the word is "confidential speech" (cf. Arabic *sā'wada* "speak secretly"), hence, "counsel." The emphasis on confidentiality marks a distinction between this word and the more general *'ēṣâ* (q.v.) "advice," "counsel"" (Harris, p. 619). It is sometimes translated friendship, "The friendship of the LORD is for those who fear him" (Psalm 25:14). It conveys the thought of a secret that is only shared with the closest associates, as seen in Proverbs, "argue your case with your neighbor himself, and do not reveal another's secret" (Proverbs 25:9). Amos heard these secrets from God, just as if an intimate friend reveals something deep on his heart.

The Hebrew word for "reveal" used in this verse is employed in the Hebrew Bible to describe uncovering. It is used to portray Noah laying "uncovered" in his tent (Genesis 9:21). Furthermore, it is used to describe God revealing Himself to His people, as He did to Isaiah (Isaiah 22:14), to Samuel (1 Samuel 9:15), and to Jacob when he was at Bethel, "he built an altar and called the place El-bethel, because there God had revealed himself to him" (Genesis 35:7). It is also used for companions speaking to one another. Saul revealed what he was doing to his son Jonathan (1 Samuel 20:2) and Boaz told his situation to his relative (Ruth 4:4). For God to "reveal his secrets" to Amos gives a picture of a man sitting in front of his friend uninhibited, not trying to put on any airs, but simply opening up his heart as he would to his closest friend. This intimate fellowship with God is the fountain of Amos' prophesy.

This shows that Amos did not simply get words from God and become a kind of mindless repeater of the syllables that he heard. Rather, Amos was brought into a friendship with God, where he could hear God's intimate counsel. One could think of this as Amos spending time with a leader, finding out what the leader thought, valued, and treasured. He would find out what really bothered the leader, what "red lines" he would not cross and what things he could let slide for now. Afterwards, Amos could go away from the leader and reflect what the leader felt, said and thought. Amos relationship with God was like this. We could imagine an open conversation between them. God would reveal to Amos what His assessment of the situation was, what His thoughts were and what His plans were. From that intimate knowing, Amos could speak and reflect the secrets he heard from God. It wasn't that God gave him exact words and he mindlessly repeated them. Rather, God showed Amos His secret counsel. Amos internalized that and spoke about it in the way he was accustomed to speak. This is why Amos' words contain so many shepherd and pasture references. He was not a mindless predictor. He was a friend of God who spoke what he heard in his own words.

The picture of Amos in fellowship with God informs us a great deal about the nature of Amos' prophecy and of true prophecy in general. Motyer describes how this process allows Amos to write both "the words of Amos" and "the words of the Lord." "That they were *the words of Amos* forbids us to think in any quasi-mechanical terms, as that Amos became God's typewriter on animated tape-recorder: he was there in the fulness of his individual personality, temperament and humanity; that they were *the words of the Lord* forbids us to allow that as originally given they partook of or were in the least infected by human sin or error" (p. 74).

One might ask how is such a needle to be threaded in this way, where a believer can maintain his personality and individuality, yet still speak the pure words of the Lord? The answer is that the root of all prophecy is not in channeling words, but in knowing God. Ministry is the product of a man spending time in God's presence, being adjusted and changed by God, and speaking as a changed person, who, at the same time, is still himself. Ministry and prophecy come from knowing Him, hours and days and weeks and months and years and decades of being in fellowship with Him. In the intimate fellowship, something marvelous happens: God can speak through His prophet.

Words to the Nation

In the second section of his prophecy, from Amos 3:9 to the end of chapter six, Amos turns his attention to the nation as it was at his time. If the book of Amos is a roaring lion, and Israel is a rabbit, this is the section where the lion has the rabbit directly in his sights and is giving full chase. Here, Amos tries to change his current generation and really make a difference. He roars about the coming calamity, the profligate culture, the attempts God has made to wake up the nation, God's call for some to seek Him, and the futility of their false religion. We will see that the sad result of lion's roar is….nothing—no change, and no repentance. It was as if Amos were talking to cows.

God's coming judgment

Like Amos began the last section with reference to the Gentiles, Amos begins this section with an invitation to Gentile nations (the Philistines and the Egyptians) to come to the hills of Samaria and see the tumult that will soon happen to the nation of Israel (Amos 3:9), for the nation does not "know how to do right" (Amos 3:10). Thus, God's punishment will fall on Israel; their opulent houses of ivory and the altars of the false religion at Bethel will be destroyed (Amos 3:14-15).

Amos describes the destruction with a colorful image, which fits a shepherd who spent many years with the sheep. "Thus says the Lord: "As the shepherd rescues from the mouth of the lion two legs, or a piece of an ear, so shall the people of Israel who dwell in Samaria be rescued, with the corner of a couch and part of a bed" (Amos 3:12). When a shepherd watched over sheep he was required to give evidence if a sheep were eaten by a wild beast, or else he could be accused and held accountable for stealing it (see Exodus 22:13-13). So, the shepherd would produce a leg or a piece of an ear to show that the sheep was taken. Israel was about to be that sheep devoured by the wild beast. However, instead of leaving an ear or a leg, the only thing that would be left of Israel is a small part of couch or bed. This is very symbolic. Couches and beds characterize the lavish extravagance and selfish opulence that characterize the nation (Amos 6:4). After judgment the only evidence of their extinction will be a few broken tokens of their profligate, lavish lifestyle, a memento of how they used to lie on their couches.

God's attempts at turning the self-satisfied nation

In the next section Amos shows his ironic side, by sarcastically addressing the wealthy women and by mocking the futility of their false religion. Amos mocks, "Hear this word, you cows of Bashan…who oppress the poor, who crush the needy, who say to your husbands, 'Bring, that we may drink'" (Amos 4:1). "The expression *cows of Bashan* is used by the prophet to address the wealthy women of Samaria, who demand that their husbands satisfy their cravings. The derogatory language perhaps suggests that they, like the livestock of Bashan, were well fed, ironically in preparation for the coming slaughter" (NET, Notes). In using this bovine analogy with the women, Amos genuinely showed himself as "talking to the cows." He warns that these cows will soon be carried away on a hook, which NASB translates as "meat hooks" (Amos 4:2, NASB). Then Amos mockingly invites them to try to stem the coming judgment through the practice of their false religion. "Come to Bethel," he invites, "and transgress…bring your sacrifices every morning, your tithes every three days….for so you love to do" (Amos 4:4-5).

While they were active in bringing their offerings and tithes to Bethel, God was active in doing something quite different. He was active in allowing calamities to fall upon the nation, so that perhaps possibly they might turn to Him. Amos describes how God sent famine in some places, withheld rain from some cities, struck their vineyards with blight, allowed their fig and olive trees to be devoured by locusts, sent pestilence among them, carried away their horses, and even overthrew some of them just like God overthrew Sodom and Gomorrah (Amos 4:6-11). God allowed all these things for one purpose: that Israel might wake up and return to Him. However, God testifies five times "yet you did not return to me" (Amos 4: 6, 8, 9, 10, 11).

The Israelites did not see that each of these troubles had a purpose behind it. Some of the troubles were relatively minor, a garden struck with blight or rain not coming on one city but falling on another. Such troubles, while bothersome, did not present existential threats to the nation. Other events were more severe, a famine in the land or pestilence. Still others made it seem for some that their entire lives were crashing around upon them, they were overthrown as when God overthrew Sodom and Gomorrah. Those who survived such upheaval were just like a brand of charred wood plucked out of a fire. It was as if God arranged a wide range and intensity of troubles to see if anything would provoke a turn. The bothersome calamities didn't wake up these "cows." Even the most severe, biting calamities resulted in no turn to God. Israel was satisfied in their false, compartmentalized religion of Bethel to such a great extent that they were not willing to see troubles in their environment as being from the hand of God.

Prepare to meet your God

God's conclusion is to warn them that judgment indeed will come, that they are to be prepared to meet Him, and that He is, after all, the Lord of all.

> 12 "Therefore thus I will do to you, O Israel; because I will do this to you, prepare to meet your God, O Israel!"
> 13 For behold, he who forms the mountains and creates the wind, and declares to man what is his thought, who makes the morning darkness, and treads on the heights of the earth— the Lord, the God of hosts, is his name!
>
> —Amos 4:12-13

God declares that He will enact judgment upon the nation and that they will indeed meet their God. Meeting God who reveals Himself in Amos should not be merely thought of as meeting a fiery judge. Meeting God is meeting God, the whole God, with his Judgments, standards, and wrath, but also with His grace, compassion and care. It is all there. God's point was not that they would meet one side of Himself only. His desire was that they would meet Him. "Wherever the idea of meeting God is found in the Bible it has a connotation of grace. The nearest parallel to this verse in Amos is Exodus 19:17 where Moses leads out the people from the camp 'to meet God'" (Motyer, p. 100).

The God they were falsely worshipping at Bethel was a far cry from the Almighty God, the Lord of hosts, who Amos reveals in 4:13. Here God displays Himself as the One who is above all, treading on the heights of the earth. He is the God who is Creator, forming mountains and creating wind. These attributes of God show His power, His effectiveness, and His impact. As the people carried out their rote "worship" in Bethel, they were far from a God like this, who could change nature, affect the world, and even change them. Not only could the living God bring judgment; He could also bring grace and mercy. It is a shame that the nation was so far from this vibrant, effective and exciting God.

Amos sees the potential of a remnant

I consider chapter five to be a turning point for the book of Amos and for Amos' ministry. In this chapter, Amos turns from aiming at the reform and return of the *entire* nation. Instead, he begins aiming at a remnant, a smaller part, who would finally fulfill Amos' deep hunger and thirst for righteousness (Amos 5:15). The events that transpire in the chapters following this one make sense if one considers that Amos changed his focus in chapter five. Amos' motivation has turned to the calling out and establishing of that remnant who would know God's grace and live out God's righteousness.

This chapter begins with a dirge, a lamentation for the house of Israel. Amos laments, "Fallen, no more to rise, is the virgin Israel; forsaken on her land, with none to raise her up" (Amos 5:2). It is as if Amos is lamenting that all the calamities sent by God described in chapter four did not result in Israel returning to the Lord. Instead there is apathy and, as a result, death in Israel. God describes the coming devastation, "The city that went out a thousand shall have a hundred left, and that which went out a hundred shall have ten left" (Amos 5:3). God shows that out of the entire nation, only a small part, here ten percent, will emerge from the coming judgment. We will see later on in this chapter, that there is hope in even a small number. If this remnant that survives is faithful, they will receive God's grace and glorify Him.

It was evident from chapter four, that sending troubles to the nation did not work to tuirn the people to God Himself. So, here, God begins a different tactic—He begins calling out all who will. Like an army recruiter looking for volunteers, God sounds out a call for all who are willing. God voices the precious words, "Seek me and live" (Amos 5:4). He also begins differentiating Himself from other things, contrasting His positive invitation for volunteers with a prohibition, "but do not seek Bethel" (Amos 5:5). In choosing the word for "seek" here Amos had two choices from the Hebrew language, *bāqaš* and *dāraš*. *Bāqaš*, which is a more common word, means to seek so as to discover something that is not found. For instance, Amos uses *bāqaš* to describe how people who don't have the word of God will look so that they might find it (Amos 8:12). Amos does not use this term here. Instead he uses *dāraš*, which includes the meaning of carefulness. "Our word is distinguished from its frequent parallel and equivalent *bāqaš* (q.v.) ... inasmuch as it 1. means "to seek with care" (I Sam 28:7)" (Harris, p. 198). When Moses wanted to know what happened to the sin offering, he carefully investigated and sought diligently, *dāraš* (Leviticus 10:16). Here God is asking His people to seek Him carefully.

The result of such seeking is God's wonderful promise—life. "Seek me and live" (Amos 5:4). Living is the ever-present result of being in the presence of the living God, who is the source of all life, spiritual, eternal, physical and otherwise. This is the clarion call that God sends forth to Israel for whoever might hear. God no longer is looking to send troubles in order to return the nation to Himself. Now it is a call for volunteers to seek with care, to diligently inquire, to carefully investigate God Himself. The rich reward for finding God is life, which can be gained in no other place and in no other way than from God—the living source Himself. Only such a life will be able to withstand the coming fiery judgment. In consideration of this, it may not be too much to say that this life is resurrection life. Only in that life is there power to withstand the fire. Bethel has no comparison to this. God declares "Seek the Lord and live, lest he break out like fire in the house of Joseph, and it devour, with none to quench it for Bethel" (Amos 5:6).

Amos contrasts the life that comes only from the living God Himself with the common religious practice of the Israelites, which was worshipping at Bethel, entering Gigal and even making pilgrimage to Beersheba (Amos 5:5). Life cannot compare with this rote practice of the false religion. Life, as God has it, changes a person and false religious worship does not. The Israelites surely needed a change, because they have "cast down righteousness to the earth" (Amos 5:7). The change that would bring righteousness back into their living can only come from the living God imparting His divine life. Amos colorfully describes how God changes His true worshippers by listing many things that God affects in nature. God's work in nature demonstrates that the living God makes a difference. In Amos 5:8-9 God describes Himself as the agent of change as regards to stars, days, and waters. "He makes seasonal changes. This (8a) appears to be the force of the reference to *the Pleiades and Orion*, constellations which were used in the ancient world to mark the turn of the seasons (*cf.* NBCR, p. 734). He also makes the daily changes, when *deep darkness* becomes *morning* and subsequently *day* yields to *night*. He makes occasional changes (8b), as when the sea wall is breached and land is inundated, and the historical changes, when *the strong* and *the fortress* fall before the destroyer (9). But this fine hymn is bracketed about with reference to a people who resist change. They come to Bethel (7) and they go from Bethel (10-12) totally unaltered…Amos' exposure of religion that leaves life untouched could not have been more brilliantly accomplished" (Motyer, p. 111-112). When we touch God as the agent of change, we change. This is the vibrancy of the life that God has and gives. However, a worship at Bethel, Gilgal, and Beersheba, is devoid of the living God and thus devoid of the changes that come from Him. The sad thing is that the Israelites practicing this false religion not only avoid change, they also hate everyone who reproves them and tries to wake them out of their stupor. While they resist change, the continue in their unrighteousness; they "trample the poor" and "exact taxes of grain from him" (Amos 5:10-13).

What a God-seeker looks like

When God sounds out a call to seek Him, He is calling for people who would be wholly devoted to Him. In the following verses He expands and explains the meaning of His call. When God sends out His call, He includes a call to seek good, hate evil, love good, and establish justice in the context of "seeking Him." This expansion shows that God is looking for those seekers who will devote their whole being to Him so that they may please Him in every department of life. God's thought is that some, even if it is just a few, will respond, will seek righteousness with Him and will enjoy His grace. It is interesting that while God is calling, He does not lower His standard until He finds enough people who will be for Him. Instead of lowering His standard, He raises it, and will be happy to give grace to any who may respond, even though they might be a small number. God calls,

> 14 Seek good, and not evil, that you may live; and so the Lord, the God of hosts, will be with you, as you have said.
> 15 Hate evil, and love good, and establish justice in the gate; it may be that the Lord, the God of hosts will be gracious to the remnant of Joseph.
> —Amos 5:14-15

Previously Amos described the way for people to live, saying, "Seek the Lord and live" (Amos 5:6). Here Amos presents the same reward—"that you may live," this time by seeking good and not evil. In Amos' mind, these two objects of seeking are the essentially the same. "The command to seek and love good is practically the same as that to seek the Lord in vers. 4, 6; and therefore the promise is the same, "that ye may live." But it is only in fellowship with God that man has life" (Keil, p. 284) In Amos' understanding a person cannot seek God and not seek good. One cannot seek God and seek evil. These things are incompatible. For those who seek God, there must be a living out of that seeking that looks like seeking good. Seeking evil while seeking God is a contradiction that cannot be. Furthermore, Amos promises that seeking good will result in God's presence. He adds "and so the Lord, the God of hosts, will be with you, as you have said" (Amos 5:14). Here, Amos promises that the result of seeking good will be an enjoyment of the presence of the Lord. No wonder the result is life! When a person seeks good, he enjoys the presence of the Lord, who is life.

Amos then adds a bit of irony to his saying. He adds, "as you have said" (Amos 5:14). Here he is addressing a false claim voiced by the Israelites because of their assiduous practice of the Bethel religions. They claim that the Lord is with them and have confidence in their claim because of the false religion they are practicing. However, Amos corrects them here.

He says that God will truly be with them, as they falsely claim He is now, once they seek good and not evil.

Amos continues to increase the standard for which God is calling by directing the emotions and actions of the people. Not only are His people supposed to seek good and not evil, but they are to "hate evil" and "love good" (Amos 5:15). This shows that God wants His called people's feelings to correspond to His. God wants His people to go beyond simply avoiding evil; they are to also hate evil. He wants His people to go beyond simply seeking good out of duty; they are to love good and delight in it. Furthermore, they are to "establish justice in the gate." This indicates that they are not only to appreciate righteousness, but they are to shape their environments according to the righteousness that they possess.

God is painting a picture of what He wants. God, like Amos, is hungering and thirsting for righteousness. God desires that His people would seek good, not seek evil, hate evil, love good, and establish justice in the gates. God desires that their whole being would be directed towards righteousness. This includes what they carefully seek, what they feel and what they do in their community. It involves their emotions, actions and even their courts of law.

A remnant according to grace

The surprising thing about this call from God, which seems so much based on righteousness and justice, is that it will result in grace—" it may be that the LORD, the God of hosts will be gracious to the remnant of Joseph" (Amos 5:15). Seeking good etc. results in a remnant knowing God by His wonderful grace. The order of God's thought is first righteousness is lived out, then grace comes from God. This is a beautiful picture of

God and a wonderful portrait of the remnant He is seeking.

God's promise here—"it may be that the Lord, the God of hosts will be gracious to the remnant of Joseph" (Amos 5:15) is very significant. This phrase could be considered as the turning point in the book. Interestingly, it probably means different things to different groups of people. To the vast majority of Israel who read these words of Amos, the emphasis may be on "it may be." The Hebrew word translated "it may be" emphasizes potentiality and insecurity. The problem with Israel was that they were lulled into complacency by their false worship at Bethel. This false sense of spiritual security allowed them to live devoid of righteousness, where they could trample the poor while they lived in ivory houses. These people needed to hear a big "perhaps" from God, to show them that they were not secure. They needed to wake up to see that their emotions needed to hate evil and love good, that their careful seeking needed to be directed towards good and God, and that they needed to fill their society with justice. In short, they needed to seek God, because they didn't have God as they claimed. The "perhaps" of this call would be very useful to them. They might see that they are far from grace and that grace is not a surety by any means.

To another group the word "remnant" might speak loudly. The verb root of this word "remnant" "seems to be used almost exclusively to indicate the static action of surviving after an elimination process" (Harris, p. 894). Joseph considered himself and his family to be a remnant and associated himself with the preservation of the life of the nation, "And God sent me before you to preserve for you a remnant on earth, and to keep alive for you many survivors" (Genesis 45:7). This small group of seekers in Israel might feel very tiny or insignificant. Maybe there is only one or two in a household. Maybe there are only ten who live on a street. Maybe there is only a group of thirty in an entire city. The word "remnant" would indicate that God does not actually need the entire nation to reform in order to achieve His purpose, although He would be pleased with that. He can accomplish His purpose with a small portion, a remnant. Thus, this group would not be discouraged if their numbers were small. This verse would make them see that God is working with "small." For those in the midst of their corrupt society to seek good and not evil, love good, hate evil, and try to establish justice in the gates, may lead them to walk a lonely path. The masses may never seek God. However, that does not mean that the seeking remnant is insignificant.

Others may be encouraged by the word "gracious." It is significant that this promise involves grace. "The teaching is that when the people of God set themselves in the way of holiness, the way which accords with the will and heart of God, they come into possession of life (14a), of the reality of the presence of the omnipotent Yahweh with them (14b) and, hopefully, of a fresh experience of His grace (15b)" (Motyer, p. 125). The fact that the remnant is a product of grace shows what the remnant is not and what it is. Because they are a product of grace, we realize that this group is in need of supply from God. They are not strong in themselves. Nor are they "superhuman" God seekers as they powerfully seek out good and hate evil. Instead, they are a remnant who receives grace. This means they are not perfect, nor are they complete in themselves. Perhaps, this group is inclined to seek God, in spite of many problems they have. They are directed towards what God desires. However, they are not perfect to the point of not needing grace. They are still in great need of the supply God gives in order to live out that kind of life. As they seek God, grace works in them so that they seek good and hate evil. Grace works in them so that their emotions are trained to align with God's—they love good and hate evil. Grace works in them so that they seek to establish justice around them. They are not super human. Rather, they are recipients of grace. As such, God's virtues are exhibited in more and more aspects of their lives. They have the presence of God and enjoy the grace of God. God's grace enables them to continue their seeking God, loving good, and establishing justice even though their surroundings may be strongly contrary.

Judgment for the majority of the nation

After the glimpse of the remnant which receives grace, Amos returns in his writings to address the vast majority of the nation. At this point, Amos has little hope that this majority will return to God. Instead, they will face judgment, "In all the squares there shall be wailing….In all the vineyards there shall be wailing" (Amos 5:16-17). Amos continues to undermine their false sense of security, which is based on the so-called "power" of their false religious practice. They are so secure that they "desire the day of the Lord" (Amos 5:18), thinking that they will be rewarded on that day. Amos, however, corrects them, saying of the day "It is darkness, and not light" (Amos 5:18). No feast in Bethel, assembly, or burnt offering will "brighten" the day of the Lord, altering it from the gloom that Amos is predicting. In fact, God tells the nation, "I hate, I despise your feasts, and I take no delight in your solemn assemblies….Take away from me the noise of your songs" (Amos 5:21-22). Instead, God announces His yearning for righteousness, which is in stark contrast to His hate for their religious rites, "But let justice roll down like waters, and righteousness like an ever-flowing stream" (Amos 5:24).

Chapter six is a colorful picture of the complacency of the nation and the coming, severe judgments. Unlike chapter four, which described partial calamities that were sent to turn the nation, the calamities in this chapter are full and final. Unlike chapter five, which contained a call for people to seek, this chapter contains no offer of redemption. It says nothing about the remnant or the grace that might be received. Instead, it announces that the self-secure nation is about to be overrun by Assyria.

It begins, "Woe to those who are at ease in Zion, and to those who feel secure on the mountains of Samaria" (Amos 6:1). It continues, "Woe to those who lie on beds of Ivory…who sing idol songs to the sound of harp and like David invent for themselves instruments of music, who drink wine in bowls…but are not grieved over the ruin of Joseph" (Amos 6:4-7). Judgment will come first to these people. "They shall be the first of those who go into exile" (Amos 6:7). God simply cannot work with such a complacent, hard-hearted nation. Working with this nation would be like trying to get a horse to run on rocks or like plowing with oxen on a rock field and trying to make it fertile. The nation is far removed from justice, "you have turned justice into poison and the fruit of righteousness into wormwood" (Amos 6:12). Therefore God "will raise up against you a nation" (Amos 6:14). The majority will be destroyed.

Visions of complete destruction

Up to this point, we have mainly seen Amos speaking about righteousness, proclaiming God's judgments and making a call for a remnant to seek God. Now Amos begins to see visions. The first three visions Amos receives show us something more about him, because the visions give Amos an opportunity to speak to God. These interactions give us a window into Amos' thoughts about the coming judgment,

God's work, and highlight the concern that has developed in Amos' heart for the gracious remnant called out by God.

Chapter seven begins with Amos seeing a vision of a locust swarm devouring the grass of the land. "This is what the Lord God showed me: behold, he was forming locusts when the latter growth was just beginning to sprout, and behold, it was the latter growth after the king's mowings" (Amos 7:1). Amos is alarmed at this vision. When he sees the locust swarm, he understands them to be an existential threat to the entire nation. It was a vision of total destruction. Amos, who is normally a very calm person, responds to God with alarm and passion. "When they had finished eating the grass of the land, I said, "O Lord God, please forgive! How can Jacob stand? He is so small!" (Amos 7:2). When Amos cries out to the God to "forgive" he uses the same word as Moses did (pardon) when he prayed that God would be with the people in their journey through the wilderness "pardon our iniquity and our sin" (Exodus 34:9). It was like Amos saw the locusts and realized that this judgment was too much, too far, and too final. He cried out "forgive" and God relented in His course, "The Lord relented concerning this: "It shall not be," said the Lord" (Amos 7:3).

The next vision presents a similar interaction. This time, the vision is of fiery judgment. "This is what the Lord God showed me: behold, the Lord God was calling for a judgment by fire, and it devoured the great deep and was eating up the land" (Amos 7:4). Amos, had a similar, strong response to this vision, crying out that the Lord would refrain from wiping out the very existence of the nation, "O Lord God, please cease! How can Jacob stand? He is so small!" (Amos 7:5). This time, Amos asks God to "cease" a word never uttered by Moses in his prayers to God. It is a word used to denote a situation that is poised to happen yet does not. The king of Israel asked the prophets about a coming battle, saying, "Shall I go to battle against Ramoth-gilead, or shall I refrain [cease]?" (1 Kings 22:6). Amos, passionately pleas to God to refrain and not let fire devour the great deep and eat up the land. Again, as in the vision before, God hears Amos' prayer and relents, "The LORD relented concerning this: "This also shall not be," said the Lord GOD" (Amos 7:6).

Before we consider the amazing power of prayer that Amos demonstrates in these two scenes, it is helpful to consider exactly what the visions may mean. On this, commentators are divided. In the first vision, some do not see any symbolism in the vision and consider the vision to be literal; it predicts a swarm of insects swooping down on the land and devouring the grass. For them, the latter growth, which is "after the king's mowings" means the following. The king would collect the first mowing of the grass as a kind of tax on the land. The second mowing, which is the latter growth, would be fodder for the animals of the people. If the locusts devour that, then the people are left with nothing and, in Amos' eyes, the nation will not stand. Others view this as a highly symbolic vision. For them, the kings mowing represents the first cut of the grass made by the king, who is God. This first cut could be considered the troubles sent by God to the nation described in Amos chapter four. The latter growth is the rebounding of the nation from those calamities and the locusts are symbolic for armies of attacking nations. Here, Amos sees the advancing armies as completely destroying what is left, the latter growth, of the nation and thus eradicating it totally.

Most commentators see the second vision as more symbolic and supernatural. The "great deep" is a picture of the nations, as in Habakkuk 3:10, Ezekiel 26:19 and the land is a picture of Israel as in Isaiah 8:8. Fire devouring the great deep indicates God's judgment will come severely on the nations. Fire eating the land is a symbol that Israel will be utterly burnt up. Thus, the vision indicates that God's judgment will come to the nations, destroy them, and even reach to Israel, consuming it completely.

These first two visions, therefore, represent universal, complete judgments; the first upon Israel, the second encompassing Israel and the entire world. In response to both Amos pleads and prays that the Lord would remember His people and avoid a complete destruction. God turns because of the prophet's prayer, an amazing example of the power and efficacy of a man praying to God according to God's will.

One might ask, "How can God repent?" It is clear in this example that God has two powerful urges within Him. The first is a righteous anger causing Him to pour out His wrath upon sin. The second is a strong desire to give grace and save. When God sees sin, His wrath rightly is stirred to judge. However, the prayer of a man who knows God's deep intentions is enough to cause Him to act upon His mercy instead of His wrath. The power of Amos' prayers allowed God to withhold from a complete destruction of the nation and instead look for another way. Whenever we might think prayer is vain, we should remember these prayers of Amos.

After Amos portrayed such a thorough picture of the nation's sins in chapter six, one might think that Amos would realize the inevitability of the total destruction described by these visions. On the surface, Amos might have thought that these were pictures of the sad result of years of falling away from God and no one responding to God's call. However, Amos doesn't simply agree with the total destruction he sees. It is entirely possible that when Amos was praying for God to cease judgment, he was thinking about the remnant that might receive grace from God. If the whole nation were destroyed, then there is no nursery for the remnant. Maybe

Amos knew by this time that the vast majority of the nation should perish. However, there is still the remnant. As long as there is some possibility that the remnant may receive grace, Amos prays, labors, and ministers in hope. Thus, he pleads for God to cease from complete destruction. The remnant very well might have been the root reason for his boldness in prayer to God. The remnant may have also been the reason God listened to Amos' prayer and withheld His complete judgment.

Vision of a plumb line

Amos' next vision is different in nature from the first two. No longer does it present an indiscriminate locust swarm or fire. Instead God's judgment takes the form of a plumb line, which can measure, discriminate, and decide what should be judged and what should stay. In this vision Amos first sees the Lord, "behold, the Lord was standing beside a wall built with a plumb line, with a plumb line in his hand" (Amos 7:7). Here the Lord Himself is wielding the measuring tool—a plumb line—and he declares to Amos, "Behold, I am setting a plumb line in the midst of my people Israel; I will never again pass by them" (Amos 7:9).

A plumb line in the Old Testament is a measuring tool that is used for both building and destruction. It is used in the Old Testament to indicate building, as when God makes "righteousness the plumb line" (Isaiah 28:17) in His restoration. The plumb line is also used for destruction, as when God "determined to lay in ruins the wall of the daughter of Zion" (Lamentations 2:8) by stretching out His line, and when God shall "stretch the line of confusion over it; and the plumb line of emptiness" (Isaiah 34:11) over a desolate kingdom.

The plumb line and the Lord with a plumb line in His hand make us think of the standard which God will use in His judgment and edification of the nation. God's plumb line is nothing short of God's full characteristics. He will measure the nation based on His Person, which He has been revealing to His people throughout their history with Him. Many commentators (Calvin, Motyer, and others) see the plumb line in the hand of God as representing the past ways that God has dealt with the nation, which God will now use as a measuring tool for them. One may think that the plumb line is only God's righteous legal requirements and the harsh consequences of falling short of them. However, if we consider the line to be the complete God, we will see that the line has law *and* grace in it. Motyer sees this a containing both God's legal, righteous requirements and His caring, gracious ways, "The plumb-line given to them to build the fabric of life consisted in the law of God for their obedience and the grace of God available in blood-sacrifice to cover their disobedience" (p. 182). Thus, he understands this picture to mean that God will evaluate each individual in the nation in terms of His law and in terms of His gracious care. At first the plumb line being the law *and* grace may seem to be a lower standard than simply if the line were simply the law. However, it actually is a far higher standard. The plumb line of law *and* grace not only judges a person for not following the law, but also judges a person for not taking the grace in instances where they fell short of the law. The plumb line being God Himself in His law *and* in His grace takes away all excuse for those who fall short. It is the most righteous standard, one which is according to God Himself.

The take-away from this vision is that God's judgment will no longer be indiscriminate. He will measure each situation against His law, His grace and His person. He will evaluate according to the line. God will destroy the high places and sanctuaries, as well as the errant Israel leadership—all who do not measure up. However, He will no longer destroy the whole. "The Lord had turned from any thought of the total elimination of the people, but what had He turned to? The answer is now provided: a discriminating test, separating one from the other, this from that" (Motyer, p. 160). With the plumb line it is possible to imagine a situation where a remnant according to grace could be preserved.

After the vision of the Lord with the plumb line, Amos offers no desperate prayer for the Lord to cease His judgment. This indicates that Amos approved and felt no urge within him to seek to mitigate God's wrath. The Lord with the plumb line showed discernment and gave Amos assurance that some, even though it may be a small number, will prevail in the judgment and stand before the Lord as a seed. Amos' concern for the remnant is satisfied.

Amos' trial from man

Immediately after these visions, where Amos boldly prayed on behalf of the people, Amos encounters another challenge. This time it comes from man, specifically from Amaziah, who is a priest of the false religion set up at Bethel. Amaziah firstly warns King Jeroboam about Amos, saying, "Amos has conspired against you in the midst of the house of Israel. The land is not able to bear all his words" (Amos 7:10). He then twists Amos words in his report to the king, saying that Amos said that Jeroboam shall die by the sword (Amos 7:11). Amos, in fact, never said this. He only said that the house of Jeroboam will fall. Furthermore, Amaziah speaks directly to Amos, telling him to get out and do his work elsewhere, "O seer, go, flee away to the land of Judah, and eat bread there, and prophesy there, ¹³ but never again prophesy at Bethel" (Amos 7:12-13).

Amaziah employs falsehood, intrigue, threats and even pictures of attractive opportunities in his attempt to move Amos from his town. He doesn't want to kill Amos, just make him prophesy elsewhere. His falsehood and intrigue consist in his political maneuvering to make it difficult for Amos to be welcomed by the government in the land. Amaziah's threat consists in portraying Amos' future in the land of Israel as harsh and unwelcoming. Amos is confronted by the fact that now the king is against him. He may face political and legal opposition in the future. He may also face scarcity—not knowing where his bread will come from, nor having any confidence in its continued supply. Amaziah doesn't stop at simply describing the trials Amos will face if he stays. He also paints a picture of how good Amos' life might be if he leaves. He doesn't tell Amos to stop speaking or to cease "fulfilling his ministry." He simply tells him to do his ministry somewhere that would be more comfortable. He can go back to Judah where he will be welcomed and will have no worries for his sustenance; he can surely "eat bread there." Furthermore, he still can fulfill his ministry by prophesying there.

If Amos would really consider what Amaziah presented, he might come away with a list of pros and cons. The cons of staying in the north were political opposition, acrimony, insult and food scarcity. The pros of going south were plenty of bread, friendly neighbors, being welcomed from his people, and the freedom to write and carry out his ministry. Amos might have thought that he could still write exactly what he was writing at Bethel, but it would simply be a much easier pathway. This whole temptation might be likened to a church board telling a pastor, whose annoying adherence to the gospel exasperated them, to go to a richer, larger church, where he can do his work, get more pay and be out of their hair.

Amos was faced with the same kinds of warnings and temptations here.

Amos replies in a most excellent way. He essentially says, "I'm nobody. I'm just following the Lord." If Amos had a yearning for comfort or appreciation or "spiritual position," he might not have been able to say this. However, we see that Amos was pure, seeking God, and seeking what God was after. He tells Amaziah, "I was no prophet, nor a prophet's son, but I was a herdsman and a dresser of sycamore figs. ¹⁵ But the LORD took me from following the flock, and the LORD said to me, 'Go, prophesy to my people Israel'" (Amos 7:14-15). Here Amos the prophet claimed that he was no prophet—in other words he didn't stand on his title, nor seek appreciation from the men around him. He also revealed how God told him to prophesy to Israel—in other words, he rejected the idea of fulfilling his ministry in a way that could give him an easier life. God put him here and he honored that and stood by that. "This little piece of personal narrative about Amos reveals him at his courageous best, but, more than that, provides us with deep instruction about the nature and function of the man of God, the experiences he may expect to encounter, the resources on which he can draw and the persevering fortitude which is to mark his career" (Motyer, p. 169).

He proceeds to tell Amaziah, the priest of Bethel, about the future judgment that will come on him specifically. His wife will become a prostitute, his children will be killed, his land will be divided up and he will die in exile (Amos 7:17). Here we see God's discriminating judgment, laying hold of a family who has stood against Him. "The encounter between Amos and Amaziah provides a clear example of the plumb-line" (Motyer, p. 170).

Amos' motivation for withstanding the threats and the temptations associated with Amaziah's threats may have been deeper than simply saying, "God told me to be here." By this time in his ministry, he may have truly imbibed God's thought for gaining the remnant. Even though most of the nation was to taste the fullness of God's wrath, some might still receive His grace. It might have been this realization that caused Amos to pray so desperately when he saw God's harsh judgment in the first two visions. This same realization might have also motivated Amos to stay in Bethel in the face of Amaziah's machinations. He was not there for the whole, but for that small group—the remnant—who might receive grace. That group was better to him than the assurance of food in Judah. It was better to him than being able to write a book of prophesies far away from them. That group focused him, became the reason he was willing to suffer, and became the base for his understanding of why God called him from caring for sheep and trees to prophesy in this harsh land.

The fourth and fifth visions—the final judgment on the nation

In his fourth vision Amos sees a basket of summer fruit that symbolizes the end of the nation. "This is what the Lord GOD showed me: behold, a basket of summer fruit. ² And he said, "Amos, what do you see?" And I said, "A basket of summer fruit." Then the LORD said to me, "The end has come upon my people Israel; I will never again pass by them"" (Amos 8:1-3). The connection between summer fruit and the end of the nation depends on a play on words evident in the Hebrew language. "The vision in verses 1-3 depends for its meaning on a pun in the Hebrew. In reply to the Lord's question (2), Amos *replies qayis, then the Lord said....qes*. In sound these two words are virtually identical and the transition from one to the other would come with natural ease to the subtle and perceptive mind of Amos" (Motyer, p. 177).

Amos proceeds to review how the Lord notices all the evil deeds of the nation. They "deal deceitfully with false balances" (Amos 8:5) and "buy the poor for silver" (Amos 8:6). The Lord will "never forget any of their deeds" (Amos 8:7). In return, God will withdraw many blessings that He had been giving to the nation. He will "turn your feasts into mourning" and "your songs into lamentation" (Amos 8:10). Furthermore, He will withdraw His words from the land. "I will send a famine on the land—not a famine of bread, nor a thirst for water, but of hearing the words of the Lord" (Amos 8:11). At the time of Amos' speaking, the nation is flooded with the words of God from prophets, like Elijah, Elisha, Jonah, and even Amos. Because they have not responded to these words, God will one day withdraw them, and cause there to be a famine of the word. This famine shows that when it comes to God's words, silence is worse than words of condemnation. At least when God's words condemn, there is a possibility of turning and grace. However, silence means there is little hope for response. People will "run to and fro, to seek the word of the LORD, but they shall not find it" (Amos 8:12).

Amos final vision is of the Lord standing beside the altar at Bethel. "I saw the Lord standing beside the altar" (Amos 9:1). From this standpoint, He proclaims thorough judgment upon the nation. "Strike the capitals until the thresholds shake, and shatter them on the heads of all the people; and those who are left of them I will kill with the sword" (Amos 9:1). There will be no place to hide, "If they dig into Sheol, from there shall my hand take them; if they climb up to heaven, from there I will bring them down" (Amos 9:2). When this judgment arrives, no historical experience that Israel had with God will serve to save them. God will not consider their exodus from Egypt, the manna, the law, the prophets, the sacrifices they made as reason to lessen His wrath. God reminds them "Did I not bring up Israel from Egypt, and the Philistines from Caphtor and the Syrians from Kir" (Amos 9:7). "The Exodus as a historical fact enshrines no more of God than does the coming of the Philistines from Caphtor or the Syrians from Kir and no more brings automatic benefit than do those other divinely engineered events. One divine government rules all, and (8a) one moral providence observes all, and judges all. The Lord does not look on people in light of their historical past but in the light of their moral present" (Motyer, p. 197)"

At this point, the visions seem quite clear that there will be total destruction for the nation. One might think, "Where is the remnant?" Well, even though God was predicting such thorough, inescapable catastrophe, the thought of remnant never escaped Him. In Amos 9:8 there is a big word "except" that screams out hope, light, grace, and redemption.

> 8 Behold, the eyes of the Lord God are upon the sinful kingdom, and I will destroy it from the surface of the ground, except that I will not utterly destroy the house of Jacob," declares the Lord.
> —Amos 9:8

God will destroy, but not "utterly destroy" the house. In fact, his destruction will not be indiscriminate. Instead, his judgment will be more like a sieve, in which all sinners will die, but not one pebble will fall to the earth.

> 9 For behold, I will command, and shake the house of Israel among all the nations as one shakes with a sieve, but no pebble shall fall to the earth.
> 10 All the sinners of my people shall die by the sword, who say, 'Disaster shall not overtake or meet us.'
> —Amos 9:9-10

God likens the application of His coming judgment to sifting with a sieve, a tool of discrimination. He is shaking Israel among all the nations where they are banished, just like a sieve is shaken. It is not possible to determine exactly how the sieve mentioned in this verse works. For instance, it is not clear whether the "pebble" is something that should be preserved or thrown away by action of the sieve. The Hebrew word for pebble, *ṣĕrôr*, means a bundle and is used to describe small stones in a wrecked landscape in 2 Samuel 17:13. This leads Motyer to understand the sieve as passing good soil and sifting out rocks, "It is not the sieve's purpose to safeguard the pebbles but to cast them off, leaving the purged soil" (p. 198-199). Other Commentators understand the pebble to refer to a kernel of wheat and see the sieve as saving the kernels and passing the dust and chaff. "But there is always a divine kernel in the nation, by virtue of its divine election, a holy seed out of which the Lord will form a new and holy people and kingdom of God.…The Lord will shake Israel among the nations, as corn is shaken in a sieve; so that the chaff flies away, and the dust and dirt fall to the ground, and only the good grains are left in the sieve" (Keil, p. 219). The ambiguous method of separation may be intentional. The process of sifting is quite a mysterious process. When in a sieve, one may not know what environmental features work to preserve and cast away. It is difficult to point out who will pass the test and who will not. The only thing one knows is that each person is proven before God. Many from Israel were scattered, but only a few found approval from God. For instance, at the time of the Messiah many Israelites were antagonistic towards Him. However, Simeon and Anna were in the temple waiting for the Messiah. God's mysterious sifting worked out all this separation. There was a remnant waiting for the Messiah. This will be God's marvelous work, as He uses the nations to shake His people and the good passes His test.

The coming promise

The remnant is delivered through God's judgment. They are sifted in the context of the nation and become living seeds for God's next step. The remnant is not the end. It is simply a small group of faithful seekers who received grace from God. They become seeds for something much more marvelous. This is what Amos explains in the next verses.

> 11 "In that day I will raise up the booth of David that is fallen and repair its breaches, and raise up its ruins and rebuild it as in the days of old,
> 12 that they may possess the remnant of Edom and all the nations who are called by my name," declares the Lord who does this.
> —Amos 9:11-12

This promise is Amos' most profound declaration. It is quoted by James to confirm that salvation has spread to the Gentiles in the New Testament age (Acts 15:16-17). Here God describes how He will restore a sadly fallen hut, which is a mere shadow of the kingdom of David. He will raise it up, repair it and rebuild it. Eventually, the restored nation will expand to possess territory, which will result in all the nations being called by God's name, sharing the same privileges as members of God's family. The words and thoughts in these verses are full of significance.

Consider first God's description of the sad state of His people; He refers to them as "the booth of David that is fallen," which is in "ruins" and festooned with "breaches." NET translates this as "the collapsing hut of David." A booth is a temporary shelter, pitched where there are few resources and little permanent intention. Isaiah describes the desolate nation as "The daughter of Zion is left like a booth in a vineyard, like a lodge in a cucumber field" (Isaiah 1:8). What a contrast between the "house" that David built and this tent! Not only is it a "hut," but it is "fallen." This word is the same word used to describe the dead concubine in Benjamin, "there was his concubine lying [fallen] at the door of the house" (Judges 19:27). David's grand house has now become a temporary shelter; and even that temporary shelter is beat up and in disrepair. "*Sukkâh*, a hut, indicates, by way of contrast to *bayith*, the house or palace which David built for himself upon Zion (2 Sam. 5:11), a degenerate condition of the royal house of David. This is placed beyond all doubt by the predicate *nōpheleth*, fallen down. As the stately palace supplies a figurative representation of the greatness and might of the kingdom, so does the fallen hut, which is full of rents and near to destruction, symbolize the utter ruin of the kingdom" (Keil, p. 220). Furthermore, the decimated tent is described as "ruins," which is a term used to describe the scattered debris after an enemy has done their destructive work. Elijah sees the Lord's altars in ruins and exclaims to God that His enemies have "thrown down your altars" (1 Kings 19:10). God uses the same word to describe destruction when He tells the Edomites that if they rebuild, "I will tear down" (Malachi 1:4). This sad, destroyed hut is the result of many people tearing it down, just like an army would destroy a wall, a building, or a palace of their enemy. Furthermore, the fallen hut has breaches. These are divisions and tears in the continuity of the people. The word "breach" is used to describe a hole in a stone wall. "And I sought for a man among them who should build up the wall and stand in the breach" (Ezekiel 22:30). It is also used symbolically to describe the divisions among the tribes of Israel, "And the people had compassion on Benjamin because the LORD had made a breach in the tribes of Israel" (Judges 21:15).

   Putting all these words together paints a bleak picture of God's people. They are a hut, some temporary structure, like one you might find in a farmer's field. The hut is fallen, just like that collapsed concubine lying in the doorway. It is in ruins, as if an enemy came and broke down any support that had integrity. Finally, it is full of breaches, deep divisions that have torn the fabric of society apart. It is interesting to think that this is a picture of the remnant that Amos was fighting for in his ministry. It might be more fitting to call them a heap of rubble than to associate them with any semblance of a dwelling.

From the outside it may look like it would be better to burn this fallen hut and start afresh. However, there is something precious to God in this fallen hut which has to do with the lineage of the "ruins." In spite of the terrible condition, the hut is still "of David." The reason God does not abandon this hut is that it is still of David's line, of the line of promise. Even though it may seem insignificant, beat up, ruined, and torn, it is of the right stock and, as such, will receive the sure mercies from God. This surely points to the full work of the Messiah. "The kingdom of David could only be raised up again through an offshoot from David's family. And that this can be no other than the Messiah, was unanimously acknowledged by the earlier Jews, who even formed a name for the Messiah out of this passage" (Keil, p. 221). God doesn't burn the fallen tent and start over. Rather, he raises it up, rebuilds it, and repairs it.

Each of these words shows an aspect of God's wonderful restoring work. Also, each of the words contains some hint of Messiah's marvelous character. First God will "raise it up." The Hebrew word for raise up is used for setting up a ruler, specifically, for setting up Christ, "I will raise up for them a prophet like you" (Deuteronomy 18:18) and, "But they shall serve the LORD their God and David their king, whom I will raise up for them" (Jeremiah 30:9). The same kind of raising

God accomplished for Christ the Prophet and Christ the King will be applied to this fallen hut. Like the shoot that emerges from the felled tree, God, in His gracious, glorious power, will "raise up" the hut. Next God will "repair its breaches." Repair is translated "masons" in 2 Kings 12:12 and is used for building up the stone wall in Ezekiel 22:30. Repair is a masonry word, used for solid stonework. The hut may not be solid, but when God rebuilds it, it will become very substantial. The thought is that God's people have been decimated, divided, and certain members have been taken away. God will now restore those tears using stones. His restoration will be very solid, like masonry work. Finally, God will rebuild the hut. The Hebrew word for "rebuild" is the same word used to refer to God building the woman Eve out of the man's rib (Genesis 2:22). This is the glorious work of God.

Putting these words together gives us a good picture of God's restoration work through the Messiah. He will take the fallen hut, the fallen kingdom of David, and raise it up just as He raised up the Messiah, a root out of dry ground, to be Prophet and King. He will repair the breaches. Just like a mason repairs a tear in a stone wall, God will solidly mend the wall of God's people which previously was wrought with divisions between peoples. In the Messiah, God's people will become unified, whole and solid. Finally, God will rebuild it just like Eve was built from Adam's bone. This is God's marvelous New Creation work. Jesus declared, "I will build my church" (Matthew 16:16) just like this hut will be rebuilt.

It is a general trend in the Bible that when God's people are restored, the next step is that they affect the world. Here is no different. When the fallen hut is restored, then the people of God will "possess the remnant of Edom." The word for "possess" is the same word used for "inherit." It describes Israel gaining their inheritance in the land of Canaan (Deuteronomy 1:39). Edom here symbolizes all the nations of the earth. "Edom was used symbolically by the prophets as an embodiment of the hostility of the world to the kingdom of God…The overthrow of Edom therefore speaks of a real and complete end of all opposition" (Motyer, p. 204). Thus, the possession of Edom by God's people signifies that they will inherit the earth.

Amos does not stop there. The result of Israel's possession of Edom is more than just a subjugation of the kingdoms of the world. God declares that those inhabitants of the earthly nations "are called by my name." This indicates that some from the Gentile nations will become fellow members of God's family. "Consequently the taking possession referred to here will be of a very different character from the subjugation of Edom and other nations to David. It will make the nations into citizens of the kingdom of God, to whom the Lord manifests Himself as their God, pouring upon them all the blessings of His covenant of grace (see Isa. 56:6–8)" (Keil, p. 222). "The verb possess signifies a conquest. The people of God demonstrate a superior power. But the conquest is followed by an equality of citizenship in that it is not their name but the name of their God by which the Gentiles are called" (Motyer, p. 204-205). "*Edom* and *all the nations* are *called by my name*. Isaiah 4:1 shows that this is a piece of marriage terminology. It therefore speaks of intimate oneness….In other words at last the Gentiles *are fellows heirs, members of the same body, and partakers of the promise in Christ Jesus through the gospe*l (Eph. 3:6)" (Motyer, p. 204). The Apostle James saw this same glorious, full participation for the Gentiles in the New Testament promises.

The restoration

Amos concludes his prophecies with a wonderful description of the blessings that pour out after the fallen hut is rebuilt and the nations are called by the Lord's name.

> 13 "Behold, the days are coming," declares the Lord, "when the plowman shall overtake the reaper and the treader of grapes him who sows the seed; the mountains shall drip sweet wine, and all the hills shall flow with it.
> 14 I will restore the fortunes of my people Israel, and they shall rebuild the ruined cities and inhabit them; they shall plant vineyards and drink their wine, and they shall make gardens and eat their fruit.
> 15 I will plant them on their land, and they shall never again be uprooted out of the land that I have given them," says the Lord your God.
> —Amos 9:13-15

This abundance is a result of God's people finally living out God's righteousness. They are now built up by Him, raised up by Him, and called by His name. As such, they have the power of God working within them that allows them to live out the righteousness that Amos has long hungered for. The result is abundant blessing—"the plowman shall overtake the reaper"—implying that harvests are so abundant that the reapers are still reaping at the time when the plowman is supposed to plow again. Mountains shall drip sweet wine and hills shall flow with it. The people who were once fallen and in ruins shall now rebuild cities and plant vineyards. God will plant His people in the land so that they shall never again be moved from their inheritance. "There is one final truth about the citizens of the kingdom: they are set free from the penalty of sin. They cannot ever be robbed of their inheritance (15). The land is theirs forever" (Motyer, p. 207).

CHAPTER FOUR

Obadiah

Obadiah introduces his words in classic prophetic form, boldly declaring what he is about to write as, "The vision of Obadiah" (Obadiah 1:1). In spite of calling his words a "vision," Obadiah doesn't describe a mystical, heavenly scene that he saw while he was in some trance. He is not like Ezekiel in this sense. Instead, he applies his vision, which is his understanding of events from God's point of view, to a series of pictures involving the nations of Edom and Israel. He describes the humbling of Edom due to its pride (Obadiah 2-9), Edom's violence against his brother Jacob (Obadiah 10-14), Edom's punishment in context of the day of the Lord (Obadiah 15-16) and Israel's restoration through the survivors (Obadiah 17-21). Obadiah is very pictorial in his descriptions; for each section he paints an engaging, informative, symbolic picture. Stitched together, all the pictures make up a grand, composite scene, which is "the vision of Obadiah."

The Lord's report concerning Edom

The first nine verses of Obadiah's prophesy are entirely about Edom; Israel is not even mentioned. Today, we might be bored hearing details about Edom, thinking that it is just some obscure Middle East nation that never made a big splash in world history. However, at that time in Israel, the feeling was completely different. Edom was a recent oppressor and a violent persecutor. Israel was currently nursing fresh wounds that had been inflicted by the Edomites. Thus, the people of Israel were intensely interested in any news from Edom, especially any news foreshadowing a calamity that might soon fall upon their angry, violent brother.

Obadiah tells the nation that the Lord Himself is also interested in the very thing that is on their minds—the destruction of Edom. Concerning Edom, Obadiah says, "We have heard a report from the LORD" (Obadiah 1). "The prophet includes himself in the nation (Israel), which has heard the tidings in him and through him. This implies that the tidings were of the greatest interest to Israel, and would afford it consolation" (Keil, p. 351). The news from God reports that messengers are traveling to many surrounding nations, stirring them up to attack Edom, saying, "Rise up! Let us rise against her for battle!" (Obadiah 1).

Edom's situation and meaning

In verses two and three, Obadiah describes some of Edom's history with God and their current prideful disposition.

> 2 Behold, I will make you small among the nations; you shall be utterly despised. (Or Behold, I have made you small among the nations; you are utterly despised)

> 3 The pride of your heart has deceived you, you who live in the clefts of the rock, in your lofty dwelling, who say in your heart, "Who will bring me down to the ground?"
>
> —Obadiah 2-3

In the quoted verses, I included the ESV note on verse two, which gives an alternative reading. The alternative reading indicates that God had in some past time made Edom small, not, as the main ESV text says, that God will in some future time make Edom small. In the context of the book, I consider the past tense, as described by the note, to be a better fit here.

These verses paint a picture of Edom. At their beginning, God made their nation small, giving it a small inheritance and ordaining that they would always be despised among their peers. Edom settled around Mt. Seir, a mountainous, rather inhospitable, rocky region southeast of Israel's land. Today, this area contains the ruins of the city of Petra in the modern-day nation of Jordan. There the people of Edom lived "in the cleft of the rocks" (Obadiah 3), which is literally where they lived—in caves carved into the rocky cliffs. Because their houses and cities were naturally fortified, they felt very safe. They felt so safe, that they began to swell with pride, deceiving themselves into thinking that they were invincible, even to the point of boasting, "Who will bring me down?" (Obadiah 3). This pride was a springboard for Edom's incessant desire for more. Edom was never satisfied with the inheritance or place God ordained for them. They constantly sought to expand, take more than what they inherited and occupy a place higher than the place God had in mind for them.

John Calvin sees in this a deeper significance to the nation of Edom. Edom is a picture of an entity who is not satisfied with the place given him by God. Edom received his inheritance from God, yet still wanted the inheritance God gave to Jacob. Calvin explains, "when he says, 'Lo, little have I set thee.' To me it appears probable, that the Prophet reproves the Idumeans, because they became arrogant, as it were, against the will of God, and in opposition to it, when, at the same time, they were confined to the narrow passes of mountains. It is said elsewhere, (Malachi 1:2,) 'Jacob and Esau, were they not brethren?' "But I have given to you the inheritance promised to your father Abraham; I have transferred the Idumeans to mount Seir." Now it is less bearable, if any one be elated with pride, when his condition is not so honorable. I therefore think that the Idumeans are here condemned because they vaunted so much, and arrogated to themselves more than what was right, when they yet were contemptible, when their condition was mean and obscure, for they dwelt on mount Seir" (Volume 2, p. 424)

The punishment of Edom

Verses four through nine describe how the prideful Edom will be punished. "Though you soar aloft like the eagle, though your nest is set among the stars, from there I will bring you down, declares the LORD" (Obadiah 4). He describes how their judgment will be complete and utter. If thieves ravished the nation, they would only take what they wanted, not everything. If grape gatherers harvested the nation, they would at least leave some gleanings on the vines. However, in the coming destruction, Esau will be completely pillaged. All his treasures will be taken away (Obadiah 5). Edom's allies, which he had formerly relied upon will drive them to their borders and completely deceive them. The nations, with whom Edom had formerly shared bread, will set a trap beneath them (Obadiah 6). As these old alliances crumble, Edom will have no understanding of what is happening (Obadiah 7). Formerly,

Edom had prided itself on wisdom. In fact, even one of Job's friends "Elaphaz the Temanite" (Job 4:1) was from a main city in Edom, Teman (Obadiah 9). In Edom's destruction, all their wisdom will not avail. God will "destroy the wise men out of Edom, and understanding out of Mount Esau" (Obadiah 8).

In the end, Esau will be brought low in the most humiliating way. Their alliances will crumble. Former friendly nations will turn against them. Their wisdom, which enabled them to wield an effective foreign policy, will be useless to lessen the blow. They will not even understand what is happening. They will be utterly plundered. All the wealth hidden inside the fortresses of Edom will be searched out, found out and pillaged. In the end, there will be absolutely nothing left.

Edom's violence toward their brother Jacob

What did Edom do to deserve this harsh, severe treatment? In short, they committed violence to their brother. "Because of the violence done to your brother Jacob, shame shall cover you, and you shall be cut off forever" (Obadiah 10). One would think that because Esau was Jacob's brother, he should have shown compassion to Israel, especially after Israel had been attacked by enemies. Instead, Esau used an enemy's attack upon Israel, as opportunity for persecuting Israel even more. "And he calls him his brother, not for honor's sake, but, on the contrary, for the purpose of showing forth more fully the cruelty of the Idumeans; for consanguinity had had no effect in preventing them from raging against their own brethren, and as it were against their own bowels. It was therefore a proof of barbarous inhumanity, that the Idumeans, forgetting their common nature, had been so inflamed with hatred against their own brethren: for, as it is well known, they had descended from the same common father, Abraham, and also from Isaac, and had the symbol of circumcision" (Calvin, Volume 2, p.438).

In verses eleven through fourteen, Obadiah paints a picture of what Edom did when Jerusalem was attacked by foreigners. As the city was being attacked, Edom sat idly by, watched, and waited aloof for the disaster to be complete (Obadiah 11). When the strangers carried off the wealth of the city, Edom rejoiced, as if he himself received that treasure; he made himself like "one of them" (Obadiah 11). He gloated over his unfortunate brother, rejoiced in the day of his ruin and boasted in the day of his distress (Obadiah 12). "The prophet shouts as if in the grip of a nightmare. He feels afresh the emotions of resentment and loathing as in his mind's eye he sees again the leering, loutish folk of Edom" (Allen, p. 156). Edom didn't stop at merely gloating over Jacob's distress. He himself entered the conquered city and looted its wealth (Obadiah 13). Furthermore, as the fugitives ran away from the destruction, Edom waited at the cross roads, cut them off and handed them over to the victors (Obadiah 14), presumably for a price.

The fact that Esau was a brother to Jacob makes his violent, uncaring, self-serving, greedy actions especially appalling. "The consciousness that the Israelites were their brethren, ought to have impelled the Edomites to render helpful support to the oppressed Judaeans. Instead of this, they not only revelled with scornful and malignant pleasure in the misfortune of the brother nation, but endeavored to increase it still further by rendering active support to the enemy. This hostile behaviour of Edom arose from envy at the election of Israel, like the hatred of Esau towards Jacob (Gen. 27:41), which was transmitted to his descendants, and came out openly in the time of Moses, in the unbrotherly refusal to allow the Israelites to pass in a peaceable manner through their land (Num. 20)" (Keil, p. 360).

The coming day of the Lord

Up to this point, Obadiah has been hyper-focused on Edom. Verse fifteen marks a great expansion of Obadiah's view, because he zooms out to talk about "all nations," not just Edom, and "the day of the Lord," not simply a single event—the coming destruction of a small nation inhabiting rocky cliffs near the Dead Sea. He exclaims, "For the day of the Lord is near upon all the nations" (Obadiah 15). The day of the Lord mentioned by Obadiah is greatly developed by other prophets. It is a day when all the nations will be judged according to their deeds and when God's kingdom will be established on the earth through the restoration of His people. For Obadiah to introduce such a wide-ranging theme in context of Edom, shows the power of "vision." A person without vision can talk about Edom. However, a person with vision can go beyond Edom alone. Vision allows Obadiah to link the judgment of Edom to the day of the Lord, God's future work, which will encompass all nations and will establish a heavenly kingdom on earth.

Obadiah understands that the day of the Lord means all nations will receive just recompense from God for their deeds. He uses this fact to look at the world in a just and far-reaching context. He applies that far reaching fact to what he has just seen concerning Edom, declaring to the nation, "As you have done, it shall be done to you; your deeds shall return on your own head" (Obadiah 15). This reveals how Obadiah's vision informs his understanding of current events. "Obadiah passionately believed in God's providence as a powerful factor, which would eventually right wrongs or at least compensate in some way for wrongs committed" (Allen, p. 160). In a sense, Obadiah, did not have to seek God particularly for a definite speaking about Edom. Instead, Obadiah saw a vision—the day of the Lord—and could apply the truth of that vision to Edom. Thus, Obadiah's grand vision affected his daily life. "For Obadiah the orientation of judgement was centered firmly in this world and this life upon earth. Therefore, God's moral sovereignty meant that God had so ordained the constitution of the world and the movement of its history that the principle of retribution was written into life" (Allen, p. 160).

Obadiah can also use events in Edom's narrative to further clarify details of the vision he sees. He looks at Edom and prophesies concerning all the nations, "For as you have drunk on my holy mountain, so all the nations shall drink continually; they shall drink and swallow, and shall be as though they had never been" (Obadiah 16). Obadiah paints the picture of Edom reveling at a drinking party in Jerusalem as they are celebrating the sack of the city and helping to loot it. Just like Edom drank down the wine as they participated in their drunken revel, all the nations will drink the wine of God's wrath. The nations will cease to exist under the righteous judgment of God. We see here how Obadiah, a man with vision, can observe a current event and use it to illustrate the heavenly vision he sees. For Obadiah, his daily life and his vision, were inextricably linked. Sometimes his vision informed his understanding of current events; other times, current events served to illustrate his vision.

The escapees in Zion

In the last section of the book, we will see that Obadiah's vision does not stop simply with pronouncing judgment on one errant nation or even on all errant nations. It also includes the restoration of God's people through the instrumentality of those who escape the calamity. If Obadiah would have stopped before this point, his vision would have been merely negative. Because his vision goes farther, he has opportunity to minister hope to God's people. He declares, "But in Mount Zion there shall be those who escape" (Obadiah 17). "The Jews might indeed have objected, and said, "What is it to us, though the Lord may avenge our wrongs? Should the Idumeans be destroyed for our sake, what profit will that be to us? We are in the meantime destroyed and have no hope of deliverance." The Prophet here meets this objection, and says, *In mount Zion shall be escape* Though then the Idumeans had attempted to intercept all outlets, as it has been before mentioned, yet God promises here that there would be an escape in mount Zion: he says not, from mount Zion, but in the very mountain. What does this mean? even that God would restore those who might seem then to be lost. Then Obadiah clearly promises that there would be a restoration of the Church" (Calvin, Volume 2, p. 448).

"Those who escape" refers to people who remain after some calamitous event. Interestingly, it is first used by Jacob when he is considering how to arrange his family as they return to meet Esau, "thinking, "If Esau comes to the one camp and attacks it, then the camp that is left will escape"" (Genesis 32:8). Joseph also uses this word to describe the remaining few who are saved by the food he can supply from Egypt, " And God sent me before you to preserve for you a remnant on earth, and to keep alive for you many survivors" (Genesis 45:7). The word "escape" implies something of God's intervention. "Those who have escaped do not owe their survival to simply fortuitous circumstances or luck. Their survival is only of God's mercy. As a matter of fact, *pĕlêṭâ* means not only "escape" but also "deliverance," as in II Chr 12:7. "In a little while I will grant them deliverance"" (Harris, p. 725).

Obadiah is asking his readers to turn their attention to those who are still on Mount Zion and who have escaped.

This means that they remained after the calamity devastated Jerusalem and that they were delivered by the working of God. They survived the attack of the city from the foreign power and even survived the violence that Edom unleashed upon them. Their survival is because God is merciful. "That Obadiah is thinking in terms of the survivors of the earlier conflict rather than of some distant event in the future is suggested by his taking up the term of v. 14. The survivors are invested with theological significance as those who inherit the old prophetic promises concerning the remnant" (Allen, p. 164). Obadiah as visionary uses these escapees to not only encourage the Israelites that some survive the sack of the city, but also to further elucidate his vision of the restoration of God's people for His kingdom. Obadiah considers the survivors on Mount Zion to be examples of the first step God will take to restore His people. First, God will mercifully protect a few, "those who escape." These will become the seeds who will one day inherit the earth and establish God's kingdom.

The remnant reversing Edom's gains

According to Obadiah's visionary understanding, those survivors change everything. Previously, foreigners had cast lots for Jerusalem (Obadiah 11) and Mount Zion was the scene of a heathen drinking revel (Obadiah 16). In the presence of the escapees, Mount Zion, "shall be holy and the house of Jacob shall possess their own possessions" (Obadiah 17). Edom, in the pride of his heart, sought to expand their territory so that they might possess the possessions of Jacob. They wanted to expand from the place God had given them to lay claim to parts of Judah. In the presence of the survivors, Edom will be kicked out and God's people will once again possess the land God had given them. As Jacob possesses their rightful inheritance, Edom will be burned by the very people they previously gloated over and opened their mouth at as they witnessed their misfortune. "The house of Jacob shall be a fire and the house of Joseph a flame, and the house of Esau stubble, they shall burn them and consume them" (Obadiah 18). Here Obadiah sees both the houses of Jacob and Joseph—Israel united as one nation—working in concert to burn Edom, that the proud, violent nation might be consumed.

Possessing the nations

Verses nineteen and twenty emphasize the growth of the inheritance God's people will occupy. God's people will not merely occupy the lands conquered by David and settled by Solomon. The nation will go beyond. Unlike Edom, who desired to possess more than God gave him and failed, Israel will possess even more than what he was initially allotted. In describing the details of Israel's expanded possessions, God's message is that His inheritance is bountiful, expanding, rich, supplying and good.

Obadiah says this by detailing who will possess what. We will look at each possession and try to appreciate the expansion God is promising. "Those of the Negeb shall possess Mount Esau," means that the Jews who are living in the southern portion of Judah would move to the east side of the Dead Sea and possess Mount Esau, the former the land of Edom. "Those of the Shephelah shall possess the land of the Philistines" (Obadiah 19). The Shephelah is in the southwest portion of land allotted to Judah. "Historically it formed an important line of defense for Judah with regard to attacks from the west. Until the Philistines were finally subdued under David it formed a buffer zone between them and Judah" (Harris, p. 951). The people living in this lowland, southwest region will move west, to possess all the lands of the Philistines. The people of Judah "shall possess the land of Ephraim and the land of Samaria," means that the people of Judah shall restore to rightful possession the areas given by God to Ephraim, including the Judean hill country, and Samaria, the region southwest of the Sea of Galilee. "Benjamin shall possess Gilead" means that those who live in the land of Benjamin, which is in the south, surrounded by the inheritance of Judah, shall move to the land of Gilead, which is northeast of the sea of Galilee. "Hengstenberg has rightly shown that we have here simply an individualizing description of the promise in Gen. 28:14, 'thy seed will be as the dust of the ground; and thou breakest out to the west and to the east, to the north and to the south,' etc.; i.e., that on the ground of this promise Obadiah predicts the future restoration of the kingdom of God, and its extension beyond the borders of Canaan" (Keil, p. 371).

Obadiah sees beyond even this glorious expansion. He sees a great return of exiles, who will possess even more land. The returnees will "possess the land of the Canaanites as far as Zarephath" which is a city situated on the Mediterranean between Tyre and Sidon, to the north-west of the land of Canaan. More exiles will return from "Sepharad" (Obadiah 19) and possess the Negev. The exact location of Sepharad is not known. Keil speculates that it might be Sparta, in southern Greece (p. 374). Allen ventures a guess that it is Sardis, in modern-day Turkey (p. 171). In either case, it represents captive Israelites returning from far-off exile to possess the regions of the Negev, the southern region of the traditional area occupied by Judah.

The overall impression given by the details of these two verses is that God's peoples' inheritance will expand and grow. God's blessing is not meager, nor is His allotment stinted. He expands His inheritance to His people. The escapees who were the seeds of restoration have grown to become the nation possessing God's rich and growing inheritance.

Saviors spreading the kingdom on earth

The final verse in Obadiah lifts us beyond considering how God's people will possess God's inheritance to seeing the way God's authority will be established on earth. It introduces God's people as "saviors" who will rule so that the kingdom will be the Lord's. This verse might be the pinnacle of Obadiah's visionary seeing.

> 21 Saviors shall go up to Mount Zion to rule Mount Esau, and the kingdom shall be the Lord's.
> —Obadiah 1:21

Here Obadiah describes God's people using the term, "saviors," which in Hebrew is *moshi'im*. The word means deliverer or savior. Historically this term has been applied both to God and to God's people. There is no question that God Himself is the Savior, "But I am the Lord your God from the land of Egypt; you know no God but me, and besides me there is no savior" (Hosea 13:4). What may be surprising, however, is that this word also applies to God's people. It was used for the judges, who God raised up to deliver the nation, "The Lord raised up a deliverer for the people of Israel, who saved them, Othniel" (Judges 3:9). Obadiah is describing God's people as "heroes, resembling the judges, who are to defend and deliver Mount Zion and its inhabitants, when they are threatened and oppressed by enemies" (Keil, p. 250-1). "These deliverers spoken of are, no doubt, instruments that Jehovah will employ in the day that is coming, for He means to put great honour on His ancient people when brought to Himself; He promises to make the feeblest among the inhabitants of Jerusalem like David, and the house of David as God, like an angel of Jehovah before them, as said Zechariah" (Kelly, p. 203). Obadiah describes that these saviors will "rule Mount Esau." The word rule is the Hebrew word, *Shâphat*, which is most often translated "judge." "*Shâphat* is not to be restricted in this case to the judging or settling of disputes, but includes the conduct of the government, the exercise of dominion in its fullest extent, so that the "judging of the mountains of Esau" expresses the dominion of the people of God over the heathen world" (Keil, p. 251).

The title (saviors) and function (ruling) of the people of God in this verse is surely impressive. It implies much about the equipping, edification and maturity of God's people. Here God does not say He is the Savior, although that is true. Instead, God says that His people are saviors. This implies that they have experienced Him, learned from Him, been supplied through Him and have been perfected by Him so that they can be saviors worthy of God Himself. God delivers His people indirectly through the saviors that He has raised up. Maybe they can deliver the people based on their rich experience of God delivering them as they had grown with God. It is the same with ruling. Here God does not say that He rules in Mount Esau, although that is true. Instead, the saviors rule in Mount Esau. This means that God has worked on His people to educate them, equip them with His judgment and make them mature in their discernment, wise in their evaluation and firm in their decisions. He raised them up so that they can rule on Mount Esau. Maybe they rule the nations in the same manner as God has ruled in their lives as they were growing with and learning from God. This is an impressive picture of God's full-salvation working on His people so that they may serve Him.

The end result of these saviors ruling over Mount Esau is that "the kingdom shall be the Lord's" (Obadiah 21). This is a picture of how God and man, man and God work together. God raises up the saviors. The saviors rule, but the kingdom is the Lord's. This indicates that the saviors are not centered on themselves, but on the one Lord and Savior. When they deliver the people, they do it in a way that the people understand that God has delivered them. Similarly, when they exercise authority as they rule, they do it in a way where people understand that God is, in fact, ruling. Only with this kind of union with God, can these saviors truly affect the kingdom's expansion so that "the kingdom will be the LORD's." "Under the saviours, as Hengstenberg has correctly observed, the Saviour *par excellence* is concealed" (Keil, p. 251). Obadiah's view of the covenant community in action, God with His people, shines through in this picture. Allen likens it to a picture of how David interacted with his generals and others in his government. "Just as David did not rule in his own right, so again true theocracy would be manifested, with the community of God serving as the agents of his will. The nation would be a window through which the power and presence of the divine Monarch could be glimpsed." (Allen, p. 166) Thus, Obadiah's last verse leaves us with an impressive view of God's people cooperating with God Himself to spread His kingdom on earth. How glorious God's people will become! This might be considered the pinnacle of Obadiah's application of his vision. Obadiah's entire prophesy shows how he advanced to see more and more profound items in God's work. First, his vision showed him what would happen to Edom. Second, he progressed to see the day of the Lord, when all nations would be righteously judged according to their deeds. Third, he went further to see the hope of those who are escaped in Zion, especially how they will make the mountain holy.

Fourth, Obadiah's saw how the escapees would expand their footprint to possess the possessions given them by the Lord. Finally, he sees God's people as saviors who will deliver His people and rule Mount Esau so that the kingdom will be the Lord's. Putting this together indicates how Obadiah saw God's people grow from stage to stage. They were oppressed by Edom, escaped the oppression, enjoyed God's inheritance and eventually became God's mature co-workers, ruling with Him, so that God's authority and kingdom may spread to the whole earth. The book of Obadiah is truly a vision worthy of God.

CHAPTER FIVE

JONAH

Act 1: God's Call and Jonah's Flight

The story of Jonah begins with God telling the prophet, "Arise, go to Nineveh, that great city, and call out against it, for their evil has come up before me" (Jonah 1:2). In spite of this charge being unusually specific and unmistakably divine, Jonah disobeys it. Instead of heading east towards Nineveh, Jonah goes west, to Joppa, a seaport which is now in the modern city of Tel Aviv. There he boards a ship intending to sail to Tarshish, which is a Phoenician port located of the southern coast of modern-day Spain. "The ship on which Jonah traveled was most likely a merchant ship and probably of Phoenician registry. The Phoenicians were responsible for most of the sea traffic in the Mediterranean during this period of time. They pioneered exploration and trade by sea" (Smith, p. 228).

Jonah later gives the reason he fled, saying to God, "That is why I made haste to flee to Tarshish; for I knew that you are a gracious God and merciful, slow to anger and abounding in steadfast love, and relenting from disaster" (Jonah 4:2). Essentially, "He refused to go [to Nineveh] because he was afraid God's message would be successful among them" (Feinberg, p. 135). God's great mercy on underserving people is not a new idea for Jonah. He had grown up in the northern kingdom of Israel and had seen much of God's gracious dealings. Even though the kings of Israel were so evil, God had mercy on them time and time again. Jonah had seen God's grace poured out on undeserving Israel and Jeroboam II. He learned that this is who God is and what God does. He simply did not want this grace to spread to a Gentile city, like Nineveh.

Jonah's fleeing from God's presence and from God's service, shows that it is indeed possible for a prophet of God to disobey God. Actually, every prophet had the *opportunity* to not obey the command of the Lord. Jonah's demonstration of disobedience highlights even more how wonderful the instances were when prophets did, in fact, obey. It gives us a window into their lives, showing us that they were real human beings like us. "The prophets were not machines. They had power to resist the word of God. However, this is the instance on record where a prophet refused to carry out his commission" (Feinberg, p. 135).

Act 2: The Ship and the Storm

After the ship left the land, "the LORD hurled a great wind upon the sea, and there was a mighty tempest on the sea, so that the ship threatened to break up" (Jonah 1:4). All the sailors cried out to their gods because of the storm. However,

Jonah was fast asleep in the inner part of the ship. The sailors wake him, find out that he is a Hebrew prophet who is fleeing from the presence of the Lord, and realize that the storm rages because of him. They ask Jonah, what they should do with him. He replies, "Pick me up and hurl me into the sea; then the sea will quiet down for you, for I know it is because of me that this great tempest has come upon you" (Jonah 1:12). The sailors, afraid of innocent blood that might be on their hands if they throw Jonah overboard, try to row back to port, yet to no avail. Finally, these Gentile sailors call out to the Lord to not let innocent blood be upon their head and then they throw Jonah overboard. As soon as he was overboard, the storm stopped. The Gentile sailors feared the Lord exceedingly, offered a sacrifice to Him and made vows to Him.

The fact that Jonah was asleep in the storm might show just how much anxiety he was under in running away from the Lord. "The shock of being called to Nineveh and the journey to the coast have taken toll of his nerves and physique, and he is glad to relax, safe on the ship that would carry him far away, as he thinks, from the appalling experience" (Allen, p. 207). He was asleep, just like Adam slept in the garden. "The same root (*rdm*) is used in Gen 2:21 for the sleep of Adam that allowed for "surgery." Even through the roaring of the wind and the tossing of the ship, Jonah remained asleep, as dead to the world as he was to God (cf. 1 Thess 5:6)" (Smith, p. 230).

The Gentile sailors seem much more alive to the things of God than God's prophet Jonah in this scene. "There is extreme irony here: a "heathen sea captain" pleaded with a Hebrew prophet to pray to his God. It is sobering to see one who might be termed an "unbeliever" pleading for spiritual action on the part of a "believer." The "unbeliever" saw the gravity of the situation while the prophet slept. It is a sad commentary when those who are committed to the truth of God's word have to be prodded by a lost world into spiritual activity" (Smith, p. 231).

Jonah realized his guilt and also accepted the consequences: he simply asks the sailors to throw him into the sea. "The answer of Jonah reveals him in a better light than anywhere else in the book. It took real courage to advise them as he did. Note that he did not throw himself into the sea, for there is a vast difference between an awakened conscience and a despairing conscience. Jonah confesses he is worthy of death and is willing to endure the punishment. These are noble words of a true servant of God. He was willing to sacrifice himself to save those who are about to die" (Feinberg, p. 137).

When the sailors tried to avoid this by rowing back to shore, they realized the futility of their efforts in the face of the move of God. "They resort to their own efforts to escape the peril of the sea. "All these aids had to be shattered, all solutions blocked and man's possibilities hopelessly outclassed by the power of the challenge"" (Allen, p. 211). Exhausting all possibilities, Jonah calmly accepts his fate. "As Jerome says, "He does not refuse, or prevaricate, or deny; but, having made confession concerning his flight, he willingly endures the punishment, desiring to perish, and not let others perish on his account"" (Keil, p. 267). In doing so, Jonah perfectly portrays the future death of the Messiah at the hands of those around him, "Herein Jonah is a type of Messiah, the one man who offered Himself to die, in order to allay the stormy flood of God's wrath" (Jamieson et al, Vol. 1, p. 684).

Act 3: A Prayer from the Fish's Belly

After Jonah was thrown overboard, he sank deep into the heart of the seas (Jonah 2:3). Waters closed in over him to take his life. Sea grasses wrapped around his head, entangling him, as he sank to the very foundation of the mountains, which imprisoned him, just like a bar on a gate (Jonah 2:5-6). He realized that his current plight was fully arranged by God, praying to God from the depths of the sea, "you cast me into the deep, into the heart of the seas…all your waves and your billows passed over me" (Jonah 2:3). He said to God, "I am driven away from your sight" (Jonah 2:4). However, in that deep darkness something within him rose up. It was as if he turned and changed right there. He declared, "yet I shall again look upon your holy temple" (Jonah 2:4). As Jonah's life was fainting away, he remembered the Lord and his prayer came to the Lord and to His holy temple (Jonah 2:7). Out of such distress, he "called out to the Lord" (Jonah 2:1). The Lord heard him as he cried from the belly of Sheol and the "Lord answered" him by bringing up his life from the pit (Jonah 2:6). Jonah victoriously praises God from the belly of the fish, confident that God had saved him from the pit and that, even though he was in a fish, God would fully deliver him from all his calamity. Jonah rejoices in God, proclaims the vain life of all who hope in idols, who have forsaken the steadfast love of the Lord (Jonah 2:8), and boldly declares that he will sacrifice to the Lord with his voice of thanksgiving and will pay his vows to the Lord. He concludes his praise with a marvelous, transcendent declaration, "Salvation belongs to the LORD!" (Jonah 2:9).

Jonah's praise, uttered from the fish's belly, is the highlight of his walk with God. "The entire prayer breathes an atmosphere of deliverance in spite of the recital of the dire circumstances in which the prophet of God was found" (Feinberg, p. 140). It is not a prayer pleading for deliverance. Rather, it is a praise for victories already attained. From the fish's belly, Jonah realized that everything he went through was because of God. "Martin Luther said: "Jonah does not say the waves and the billows of the sea went over me; but thy waves and thy billows, because he felt in his conscience that the sea with its waves and billows was the servant of God and of His wrath, to punish sin'"' (Smith, p. 246). In such a state, he did the right thing—he turned to the one who was the Author of his calamity and who alone could be the Savior. "The prophet of God, though disobedient to the command of God when it did not meet his own desires, knew who to turn instinctively when in trouble" (Feinberg, p. 139). The victory Psalm came to him when he realized God saved him from the deep. "When Jonah had been swallowed by the fish, and found that he was preserved alive in the fish's belly, he regarded this as a pledge of his deliverance, for which he praised the Lord" (Keil, p. 269).

Jonah's Psalm is actually a compilation of many Psalms, showing that Jonah was a person full of the Word of God, which came alive within him, as he passed through the experience of death and resurrection. "The chapter is full of reminiscences of passages from the Psalms, and these reveal how well versed Jonah was in the Holy Scriptures and how full his mind and heart were of the Word of God....The prophet had stored up these words in his heart, and, now in the time of greatest distress, he is able to draw comfort from them" (Feinberg, p. 140). Compared with the Jonah who ran from the presence of the Lord in chapter one, the Jonah of chapter two is a different person. He has passed through the depths, realized God bringing his life up from the pit, and is profoundly aware of the extent of the salvation that belongs to the Lord. Jonah has advanced with the Lord. "While it is obvious from a reading of the entire Book of Jonah that the prophet had not reached spiritual maturity, there were some significant advances in his life. This prayer clearly shows him turning back to the Lord" (Smith, p. 250). "Jonah is now supremely a saved man who has tasted the grace of Yahweh, and who has been delivered from the just reward of his disobedience. It is in this radically new role that he is soon to be addressed by Yahweh again" (Allen, p. 219).

God then commanded the fish to vomit Jonah out upon dry land. "In all probability the dry land upon which Jonah was cast was the coast of Palestine near Joppa" (Feinberg, p. 141). "Jonah has been brought back to his point of origin—in place but not in experience. He is now "a new man, a new creature like the one who has passed through baptism"" (Allen, p. 220). "The Jonah in chap. 3 is somewhat different from the person found in chap. 1. Much had happened, and many lessons were learned, but the process of discipleship obviously was not yet complete" (Smith, p. 254). When God's command comes again, "Jonah needs no urging: with open ears he listens to the commission he shunned before" (Allen, p. 220).

Act Four: Nineveh's Repentance

After Jonah was vomited out of the fish's mouth, probably back in Palestine near Joppa, the word of God came to Jonah again. "Arise, go to Nineveh, that great city, and call out against it the message that I tell you" (Jonah 3:2). This time Jonah obeys God, travels the five-hundred miles to Nineveh, went a day's journey into the city and began calling out against the city. He declared, "Yet forty days, and Nineveh shall be overthrown!" (Jonah 3:4), using the same Hebrew word for "overthrown" that was used by God to describe the overthrow of Sodom and Gomorrah (Genesis 19:25). Jonah's preaching was electric. "Nowhere do we read in the Bible or outside of it, that one message from a servant of God was used of God to so great an extent" (Feinberg, p. 144). "The people of Nineveh believed God. They called for a fast and put on sackcloth, from the greatest of them to the least of them" (Jonah 4:5).

The effect of Jonah's preaching spread like wildfire. It began with the common people, who were most probably the ones who heard Jonah's preaching directly. Soon word spread to the king himself, who arose from his throne, covered himself with sackcloth and sat in ashes. Furthermore, the king issued a proclamation to Nineveh "Let neither man nor beast, herd nor flock, taste anything. Let them not feed or drink water, but let man and beast be covered with sackcloth, and let them call out mightily to God. Let everyone turn from his evil way and from the violence that is in his hands. Who knows? God may turn and relent and turn from his fierce anger, so that we may not perish" (Jonah 3:7-9). The entire city, from the young to the old, even to the beasts, participated in this repentance. "This king seems to have a sense that even the brute creation is involved in man's sin" (Coates, p. 27). "There lay at the foundation of it this deep truth, that the irrational creature is made subject to vanity on account of man's sins, and sighs along with man for liberation from the bondage of corruption (Rom. 8:19ff.). We cannot therefore take the words "cry mightily unto God" as referring only to the men, as many commentators have done, in opposition to the context; but must regard "man and beast" as the subject of this clause also, since the thought that even the beasts cry to or call upon God in distress has its scriptural warrant in Joel 1:20" (Keil, p. 277).

Jonah's preaching was fitting in every way. First, he preached from his own experience of being guilty and rescued by God. It wasn't mere theory. "He himself had been saved from death and thus could give the guilty city of Nineveh its needed hope in the Lord Himself" (Feinberg, p. 144). Second, he used words and names that would resonate with the Gentile population. The people believed in Elohim, not in Yahweh (Jonah 3:5). This leads Smith to conclude, correctly, that "Jonah did not mention the name *Yahweh* for God at this point. He used the word *Elohim*. The obvious purpose was to bring home that Jonah had not been proclaiming Yahweh to those who did not know him but that the supreme God, whatever his name, was about to show his power and judgment" (p. 261).

The end result of this short stint of preaching was that the city repented and God relented of the calamity that He had threatened. "When God saw what they did, how they turned from their evil way, God relented of the disaster that he had said he would do to them, and he did not do it" (Jonah 3:10). "The story of the sparing of Nineveh in chap. 3 parallels Jonah's own experience. He too had been the object of divine anger and later experienced God's miraculous redemption. So too was the experience of the Ninevites" (Smith, p. 270).

Act Five: Jonah's Angry Reaction to Nineveh's Repentance

Any normal gospel preacher, who invested a few days in announcing judgment and repentance to a city and then got the result that Jonah witnessed would be overjoyed. However, this is not the case with Jonah. When he saw that God repented of the calamity, he became angry. "it displeased Jonah exceedingly, and he was angry" (Jonah 4:1). Here is where we realize that the Bible does not sanitize the lives of its subjects. "If man, unaided by the Spirit of God, were writing this account, it would probably have concluded with the close of chapter 3....Why does the record not close here?...Because God must teach His servant (and us through him) certain truths about the narrowness of his heart, as well as the boundless greatness of God's own blessed heart" (Feinberg, p. 148). Jonah's problem is that he did not want this Gentile city to receive the grace of God, which was exactly what they had just received. "Jonah begrudged the heathen Ninevites the abundant mercy of God" (Feinberg, p. 148).

Jonah explains himself here, showing that he truly does understand God and at the same time vehemently disagrees with what he understands to be true of God. "And he prayed to the Lord and said, "O Lord, is not this what I said when I was yet in my country? That is why I made haste to flee to Tarshish; for I knew that you are a gracious God and merciful, slow to anger and abounding in steadfast love, and relenting from disaster" (Jonah 4:2). "He flings in Yahweh's face an orthodox summary of his attributes of patience and mercy, which appears in a basic form in Ex. 34:6" (Allen, p. 228). "At the very worst we see a prophet with a shocking disregard for human life and a bitter hatred toward those who had experienced mercy. At the very best he was a prophet who misunderstood God's mercy and had a limited view of God's plan for the redemption of his own people. While there may have been some reasons for Jonah's displeasure, it is sad to see him place limits on the same grace that saved him" (Smith, p. 272).

Jonah continues to pray, which is good. However, he prays for God to simply end his life, which is not so good. "Therefore now, O Lord, please take my life from me, for it is better for me to die than to live" (Jonah 4:3). "The prayer which follows, *"Take my life from me,"* calls to mind the similar prayer of Elijah in 1 Kings 19:4; but the motive assigned is a different one. Whilst Elijah adds, "for I am not better than my fathers," Jonah adds, *"for death is better to me than life."* This difference must be distinctly noticed, as it brings out the difference in the state of mind of the two prophets" (Keil, p. 278). Whereas Elijah was concerned for the besieged and attacked honor of God. Jonah feels that it is better "for him" to die than live. They are in different realms. With Jonah, "It is still a man of God praying but surely not in conformity with the will and plan and heart of the infinite God" (Feinberg, p. 149).

Act Six: God's Further Lesson for Jonah

After Jonah became so angry, he left the city, went up onto a nearby hillside, built a booth out of branches and watched the city to see what might become of it. This might have been before the forty days had expired. Jonah, therefore, may have thought that God might still destroy the city. If He did destroy it, Jonah wanted to see it from a good vantage point.

While Jonah was up there, God didn't leave him alone, just like he didn't leave Jonah alone when he was on the ship or sinking into the ocean. When Jonah was sinking, God appointed a fish to swallow him. Here, using the same word "appoint," God appointed a plant to quickly grow over Jonah so that it might shade him from the sun and save him from his discomfort. The plant was a gift from God to Jonah. For the first time in the book, Jonah was happy, "Jonah was exceedingly glad because of the plant" (Jonah 4:6). This was lesson number one from God: the lesson is that people can be glad about something God gives.

The next day, however, God appoints more things that do not make Jonah happy. God appoints a worm to attack the plant so that the plant withers. He also appoints a hot east wind, which caused Jonah to greatly suffer from heat as the sun scorched him. As Jonah's comfort withered, so did his gladness. Again, he selfishly prays that he might die, saying, "It is better for me to die than to live" (Jonah 4:8).

In this state, Jonah was now ready for God's final lesson. He first tries to get Jonah to realize the self-interest that is at the root of his anger. "God said to Jonah, "Do you do well to be angry for the plant?" And he said, "Yes, I do well to be angry, angry enough to die"" (Jonah 4:9). When Jonah reaffirms his self-interest, God connects with him according to the pity he felt for the plant and tells him that God pities the people in the city, just as Jonah pitied the plant. "And the Lord said,

"You pity the plant, for which you did not labor, nor did you make it grow, which came into being in a night and perished in a night. And should not I pity Nineveh, that great city, in which there are more than 120,000 persons who do not know their right hand from their left, and also much cattle?'" (Jonah 4:10-11). Here, with this final lesson, the book ends.

God's dealing with his curmudgeon prophet, who hated people and disagreed with the characteristics of God that he understood, provides a wonderful picture into how God keeps working with us. He uses Jonah to teach us. "Yahweh now has a rebel on his hands: his agent of salvation, though compelled to do his will, is by no means convinced of its correctness....By exposing him to a series of overwhelming experiences, Yahweh conditions the prophet to a point where he can hear the question afresh, and is given the opportunity to use his own self-centeredness as a window upon the very heart of God" (Allen, p. 230). God doesn't cause a lightning bolt to fall from the sky. "There is no word of rebuke or upbraiding or punishment. God tries to draw Jonah out of himself to view his anger and sinful displeasure in their true light" (Feinberg, p. 149).

In comparing God's feeling for Nineveh with Jonah's feeling for the plant, God seeks to give his prophet a living lesson. "Your concern was dictated by self-interest, not by genuine love....And this is how I feel about Nineveh, only much more so. All those people, all those animals—I made them" (Allen, p. 234). God even uses the same verb used by Joel to denote His concern for Israel to described God's concern for this Gentile city. "By borrowing the verb "show concern" (hus) from Joel 2:17 the narrator makes blatantly obvious his insistence that Yahweh cares not only for Israel but for all men" (Allen, p. 234). This entire scene shows God's amazing breadth and love for all mankind. "The tender voice of God is telling forth the love of God for all the nations, for all His needy creatures" (Feinberg, p. 151).

We need the message of Jonah, because in the deep parts of our being, we are also Jonah, "A Jonah lurks in every heart, whimpering his insidious message of smug prejudice, empty traditionalism, and exclusive solidarity. He that has ears to hear, let him hear and allow the saving love of God which has been outpoured in his own heart to remold his thinking and social orientation" (Allen, p. 235). For this reason, it is so good to have the book of Jonah, an Old Testament missionary book, tug at our selfish heartstrings. "This book is the greatest missionary book in the Old Testament, if not in the whole Bible. It is written to reveal the heart of a servant of God whose heart was not touched with the passion of God in missions" (Feinberg, p. 151).

The fact that we do not know how Jonah responded, is as if the book leaves us with a question, "How would I respond?" "Would my heart change?" "Would I allow God to align my heart with His?" "Would I stay in my anger and insularity?" "Lord, have mercy on me!" It surely is true that, "the seeming abruptness of the close of the book is intentional and much more forceful than if the thought had been carried out in further detail" (Feinberg, p. 151).

CHAPTER SIX

MICAH

Micah's prophecy can easily be divided into three sections, each beginning with a word "hear." There is a surprising uniformity of views among commentators in favor of this division. Each section declares some unrighteousness in God's people and presents a prophecy of the Messiah or God's kingdom. In Micah's first section (Micah 1:1-2:13), Micah wails and laments because of Israel's idolatry, wickedness, greed, and debauchery. After the majority will be judged, Micah prophesies that the Messiah as "Breaker" will gather a remnant and lead them out as His flock. In the second section (Micah 3:1-5:15), Micah is full of the Spirit to declare the transgressions of Israel and reveals the corruption of the priests, prophets, and leaders. However, the Spirit who filled Micah doesn't stop there. Micah reveals his clearest picture of God's restored kingdom, the coming of the Messiah, the future shepherding of the Messiah and the process which God will make His people pass through to ready them for the future. The third section (Micah 6-7) is an appeal by God for His people to join in the vision Micah unveiled. When the majority refuse to join, Micah sets himself to wait and look for the Lord. Then he describes the pathway of such a servant, his prayer, and the coming salvation.

Looking at these three sections can give us a snapshot of Micah's message. The first section says, "There is a problem, but Christ the Breaker will come and save the remnant." The second section says, "Yes, there is a problem, but look at the grand vision of the coming Messiah and kingdom." Then, the third section says, "Here is how you may participate in that grand vision of God's move." This is Micah in a nutshell. Now we will look at it in more detail.

Idolatry and fornication amongst God's people

Just like Amos begins his prophecy with God roaring at unrighteousness, Micah starts out with God emerging from His dwelling place to address the wrongs of the nation. Micah declares, "behold, the Lord is coming out of his place, and will come down and tread upon the high places of the earth" (Micah 1:3). Micah begins his list of woes by highlighting the capital of each nation, "What is the transgression of Jacob? Is it not Samaria? And what is the high place of Judah? Is it not Jerusalem?" (Micah 1:5). In pointing out Samaria, Micah is drawing attention to the idolatrous worship that has been happening there ever since Jeroboam established a corrupted way of worship in Bethel. In pointing out Jerusalem and calling it a "high place," Micah is declaring that Jerusalem is just like any other "high place," which was used to worship idols or to worship God in an errant manner apart from His unique Jerusalem altar. Micah opens his prophecy by declaring the sins inherent in the two capitals of God's people. He rails against them for their idolatry and for the prostitution, which often accompanies idol worship. God declares through Micah, "All her idols I will lay waste, for from a fee of a prostitute she gathered them, and to the fee of a prostitute they shall return" (Micah 1:7).

Micah's passionate cry for the sad state of Israel

After the grand introduction of God's judgment, Micah pauses to reveal his first hint of who he is as a prophet. He gives a personal testimony about the passion with which he conveys his message.

> 8 For this I will lament and wail; I will go stripped and naked; I will make lamentation like the jackals, and mourning like the ostriches.
> 9 For her wound is incurable, and it has come to Judah; it has reached to the gate of my people, to Jerusalem.
> —Micah 1:8-9

When Micah says he will lament and wail, he uses strong words to denote the passion he feels for God's people who are about to receive God's judgment. The Hebrew word for lament, *sāpad*, is mainly used for the mourning that takes place at someone's death. Abraham lamented at the death of Sarah (Genesis 23:2). Joseph lamented at the death of Jacob (Genesis 50:10). This word is employed by Isaiah and Jeremiah to denote the sadness they feel because of the profligate nation and the coming judgment (Isaiah 32:12; Jeremiah 4:12). Micah also wailed, Hebrew *yālal*, which is a word used when destruction falls upon a nation or a city. "Wail, for the day of the LORD is near; as destruction from the Almighty it will come!" (Isaiah 13:6). Micah felt as though he were attending a funeral and gazing at the wreckage of a demolished city.

These words give us a window into the passions and personality of the prophet. As Micah vividly saw the reality of what he was speaking concerning the nation's sinfulness and coming judgment, he had a deep sense that he was looking at a deceased friend or relative. He saw the nation, a cold corpse lying there lifeless, and felt a deep loss. As he saw the outward prosperity of the nation with his physical eyes, he saw the inward desolation and destruction with his spiritual eye more clearly. He wailed out loud, even sounding like jackals and ostriches. "Wailing like jackals and ostriches is a loud, strong, mournful cry, those animals being distinguished by a mournful wail" (Keil, p. 292). His wailing showed that he didn't just repeat God's message and hope the people would be affected; Micah first felt the message himself. Far from simply doing his prophesying job for a paycheck, Micah was emotionally involved in his message. "Micah's unflattering description of himself in such terms indicates something of the depths of his agony on behalf of the people of Samaria" (Prior, p. 117).

Micah's emotional involvement had a purpose. He wanted to communicate his message on as many levels as possible. "The prophet first shows how the coming judgment affects himself, in order that he might affect the minds of his countrymen similarly" (Jamieson et al, Vol. 1, p. 688). It was as if he set his whole person to become a reflector of the feelings and sensitivities that the nation should feel at the sound of his words. "Prompted by the declaration of the coming disaster, Micah first indulges in a display of unrestrained grief which reinforces emotionally the severity of the catastrophe and gives a cue for the reaction he expects from the audience" (Allen, p. 274).

Even Micah's clothes conveyed the message he was giving. He goes about "stripped and naked," which Keil understands to be "the costume of a prisoner, not that of a mourner" (Keil, p. 292). Micah is dressed in a way that reminds his onlookers of a prisoner. As a member of the nation, he is sharing the fate of the nation in his words, feelings, dress and even voice. "Micah's intention is not only to exhibit publicly his mourning for the approaching calamity of Judah, but also to set forth in a symbolic form the fate that awaits the Judaeans. And he can only do this by including himself in the nation and exhibiting the fate of the nation in his own person" (Keil, p. 292).

Micah addresses his message to small towns

Surprisingly, after he describes how he is wearing a prison uniform and wailing like wild animals, Micah does not descend to become an uncontrolled, emotional wreck. Instead, he proceeds in the next section to speak reasonably to many small towns in the Judaean countryside. As he addresses the eleven towns around Jerusalem, it is not unusual for Micah to use word plays, assonance or, what we might call, puns. Here, the wailing lamenting prophet switches gears to become the incisive, quick-witted prophet, who is seeking any way to wake up the spiritually sleepy nation. It should be noted how unique this section is in prophetic warnings. It is not unique merely in Micah's use of wordsmithing. It is unique in that it directly addresses the countryside, the small towns which form so much of the backbone of the nation's society. In contrast to some prophets, like Isaiah who counsels kings, Micah addresses the inhabitants of Zaanan, Achzib, and Beth-ezel, so-called "nobodies" in small towns.

Micah proceeds to address eleven different small towns in Judah (Micah 1:10-16). All of his prophecies here make use of colorful wordplay, which I will attempt to briefly highlight. "Tell it not in Gath," means that the news of destruction should not be told in Gath, a city of the Philistines, who would rejoice over the destruction of Israel. "Tell," Hebrew nagad, sounds a little like "Gath," thus Micah colorfully exclaims "taggidu bgat." The inhabitants of the small town of Beth-le-aphrah, which means "house of dust" should "roll themselves in dust," which in Hebrew is Aphrah. Inhabitants of Shaphir, which means beauty, will not be beautiful at all. They will be in "nakedness and shame." The inhabitants of Zanaan will not "come out." The Hebrew word for Zanaan, "saanan" resembles the sound of the word for "come out," yasah. The people who live in Beth-ezel, which means "a place of nearness" will be taken away and, therefore, won't be near. The inhabitants of Maroth, which means "bitterness" will wait anxiously for any good to be there. They will surely be bitter. The inhabitants of Lachish should harness their "rekhesh," steeds, to their chariots so that they can escape. Lachish and rekhesh rhyme. Inhabitants of Moresheth-gath will get parting gifts, even though their name sounds like "betrothed" which would warrant a gift in celebration of a husband joining a wife, not parting. The residents of Achzib, which means to deceive, will indeed become an achzab, a deceptive thing. Mareshah, which means "that which is at the head" will not fulfill the meaning of its name. God will bring a conqueror to her to possess her. Finally, the glory of Israel will come to Adullam, a small town, which is only noted for possessing a cave in which to hide.

These words constitute a wake-up call to the countryside. It is like Micah is saying to them, "Look at me, I'm lamenting, wailing, naked, stripped, and I sound like a couple of different wild animals. You, yes you in Achzib, you. I'm talking to you who works that farm over there in Maroth. You should look at me, listen to my message and eventually feel the way I feel. You in Lachish should feel like you are at a funeral. You in Gath should feel like your field and barn and house are all devastated. You should wail like me. I hope that you will sound like an ostrich, just like I do. I hope the countryside containing Moresheth-gath and Beth-le-aphrah will be full of the sounds of jackals and ostriches, because our situation is that serious."

The wickedness of the people

After Micah's warnings of coming judgment, he proceeds to expose the true state of sinfulness and hardness of heart among the people of the nation, especially among those who are wealthy. Micah describes the people as those who are occupied with wickedness and greed. "Woe to those who devise wickedness and work evil on their beds! When the morning dawns, they perform it, because it is in the power of their hand. They covet fields and seize them, and houses, and take them away" (Micah 2:1-2). Such greed and wickedness will justly incur God's judgment, which will come and take away all the fields and houses of these wicked inhabitants.

These inhabitants have very selective hearing when it comes to which prophets they listen to. If any true prophet comes who speaks judgment and truth to them, they say to them, "Do not preach….one should not preach of such things; disgrace will not overtake us" (Micah 2:6). Micah warns them specifically about quenching the true speaking of God's words. He warns them, saying, "Do not my words do good to him who walks uprightly?" (Micah 2:7). In other words, if any of these people walk uprightly, they would respond to the genuine words of God and allow those words to do them good. However, with the wicked people of the nation, there is a hardness of heart that shuts down the preaching of the pure word of God. As this wicked group continues to strip robes off of soldiers who just fought for them and drive women out of delightful houses and oppress the poor children, they seek for a prophet who can tickle their ears with what they want to hear. Micah mocks them, "If a man should go about and utter wind and lies, saying, "I will preach to you of wine and strong drink," he would be a preacher for this people" (Micah 2:11). A prophet of mixed drinks and fine wines would surely please this generation of greedy, debauched, and wicked oppressors who have no regard for the word or thought of God.

The great assembly and the breaker

However, in spite of this hardened condition all is not lost. Micah concludes this section by speaking about a future and a hope for all God seekers. God will not rain His salvation on the whole nation. However, He will assemble a small part that is left over after the great scourging. This small part, called by Micah, a remnant, is the seed for future blessing, expansion, and advancement of the kingdom of God.

> 12 I will surely assemble all of you, O Jacob; I will gather the remnant of Israel; I will set them together like sheep in a fold, like a flock in its pasture, a noisy multitude of men.
> 13 He who opens the breach goes up before them; they break through and pass the gate, going out by it. Their king passes on before them, the Lord at their head.
> —Micah 2:12-13

In order to understand these verses, it is helpful to rephrase them and consider the picture they paint. These verses describe how God will assemble the entire nation of Jacob and will gather together the small, remaining portion—the remnant—of Israel. After gathering them, He will join them together more strongly, setting them together like sheep in a fold. They will be likened to a flock in the middle of their pasture and will be a noisy, large group of men. The one who goes before them is a "breaker"—he opens a breach or a doorway in front of them. Because He broke through, they also break through as they follow Him. They don't exit their place by the breach. Rather, they pass through the gate and exit by the gate. The result is a grand procession—a whole group on the move. Their King goes on in front of them. The Lord, Yaweh, is at their head.

Commentators differ on what this picture means. One group, including and greatly supported by John Calvin, sees here a description of God's future judgment of His reprobate nation. The other group of commentators reads the same words and sees a completely different picture.

To them, these words shine out God's salvation for the faithful remnant of Jacob. Here is their picture. After the nation has been scattered to various places and has experienced severe judgments, God will turn the tide from scattering to assembling. He will assemble all of Jacob, which amounts to simply a remnant, a small residue of Israel, which has survived God's harsh judgments upon the reprobate nation. He will gather this faithful remnant, join them together into a fold, a safe place, and lead them to be like a flock in rich pastures. Because they are gathered together and are so bountifully nourished, they multiply into a great number of men. They make a joyful noise of praise to God for their rich salvation. Their leader—called affectionately their "breaker"—acts marvelously to include them in God's move. This group of sheep was not intended to stay in their own world—in the fold that God made for their restoration. Instead, their leader as the breaker, breaks the walls down to widen the gate due to the great multitudes of men that have multiplied the flock. The Captain of their salvation makes a breach in their fold, widens their gate, causes each of them to break out, and then leads them out through the gate as their King and Leader. God, Yahweh, also goes before them, as they participate in God's great move throughout the entire earth. This is a marvelous picture of how God will assemble, multiply, protect, and eventually free His people to follow Him as their King.

We will look at two aspects of this process in order to understand it in more detail. First, we will look at how God assembles the remnant. Then, we will look at how the Breaker helps them break out.

Assembling, gathering, and being set together

Micah describes how this remnant will be gathered like sheep in a fold using three wonderful words, which convey how God treasures the flocking aspect of His sheep. God will first "assemble," Hebrew ʾāsap, then He will "gather," Hebrew qābaṣ, then He will "set them together," Hebrew yaḥad. Each of these words highlight an aspect of God's thought about His people gathering together. Assemble, ʾāsap, is a general word used for the gathering of many different things. Sheep are assembled into a flock to be watered (Genesis 29:3). Food is assembled for storage or harvest (Genesis 6:21; Leviticus 23:39). This is a very general word and denotes here the general gathering of God's people as if they are a harvest collected or a flock assembled from scattered parts of the wilderness. God doesn't stop at merely assembling, ʾāsap; He goes on to "gather" or qābaṣ, them. This verb "refers primarily to gathering people into one place" (Harris, p. 783), and is thus more specific. It is almost as if God first classifies the people, acknowledging that, "Yes, they are one group. I consider them as part of the one flock." However, they are not yet face to face with one another in the same room or space. When God gathers them, He takes those people, the individuals of the remnant, and puts them into one physical place. It is a closer, more specific gathering. It is if a person is a member of a "cancer survivor club," but has never met anyone from that club face to face. They are "assembled" but not "gathered." Then, they all attend a reception where they can actually sit across the table from the others and hear stories of how each one survived. They see facial expressions. They see body movements. They can even feel the warmth of a touch. They are not just assembled; they are gathered.

Then, God takes one more step, He "sets them together." This step, described by the Hebrew word *śîm*, "describes the community in action, doing things together. In Ps 34:3 [H 4]; Isa 52:9, the community extols the praise of God together" (Harris, p. 373). If Saul would receive David, he would be "joined," with Saul in heart (1 Chronicles 12:12). When the kings of the earth take counsel together they are joined in this way (Psalm 2:2). Thus, when God "sets them together," they are brought into one mind, one united action. Maybe they praise God together. Maybe they are brought into one mind concerning His kingdom.

These three words probably would be a true balm to the ears and souls of the remnant who were scattered among the nations, in the midst of the debauchery and stiff-necked people of God. They might feel alone, separated from other God seekers. They might yearn for a community life centered around God and His purpose. Micah's description would be music to their ears. Not only would they be assembled like a harvest, but they would also be gathered, so that they could have a genuine community with other God seekers. And even more, God would bring in a harmony among them, so that they think together, aiming for God's purpose, His glory and seeking to love God together. Coates understands these words to be a spiritual picture of a practical church life, where there is real gathering and feeding in the pasture God supplies. "In *assembling* His people God has the positive side of their blessing before Him. He would have His saints to take up together their relations with Him according to His own thoughts of grace and love. *Gathering* the remnant of Israel is not quite the same thought; it views them as having been scattered. "That he should also gather together into one the children of God who were scattered abroad", John 11:52. Gathering has reference to a previous scattering, but assembling is to the positive blessedness of our divine relations. Indeed, there are three thoughts in this verse 12 of chapter 2; assembling, gathering, and putting together. The latter term is used of God's people in the character of a flock of sheep, "in the midst of their pastures". It is an important feature of God's way that He puts His people together to feed. One of His first thoughts is that we should all be satisfied by feeding on the same spiritual food. Later in this book we learn wonderful things about the Shepherd who leads and feeds His flock, but here it is seen to be God's work to put the flock together in the midst of their pastures" (Coates, p. 34).

Such assembly in the midst of rich pastures, nourishing and gladdening the flock is good reason for multiplying and praise. God's assembled remnant will be a joyous, "noisy multitude of men" (Micah 2:12).

The Breaker breaking out

However, that is not all God's Shepherd does for the sheep. After gathering, He breaks them out. This is the only verse in the entire Bible that speaks about the Messiah being a "Breaker," one who opens the breach. The Hebrew word translated "breaker", *pāraṣ*, is used for breaking out of many different situations. *Pāraṣ* can be a breaking out, as in birth, "And she said, "What a breach you have made for yourself!" Therefore his name was called Perez" (Genesis 38:29). *Pāraṣ* can be a victory over enemies, "And David came to Baal-perazim, and David defeated them there. And he said, "The LORD has broken through my enemies before me like a breaking flood."" (2 Samuel 5:20). *Pāraṣ* can be the tearing down of a wall, as when Jehoash "came to Jerusalem and broke down the wall of Jerusalem for four hundred cubits" (2 Kings 14:13). *Pāraṣ* can mean spread abroad, as when God promised to Jacob that his "offspring shall be like the dust of the earth, and you shall spread abroad" (Genesis 28:14). It can also describe increasing to the extent of overflowing, "your vats will be bursting with wine" (Proverbs 3:10). All these are instances of the verb *pāraṣ*, "to break." If we consider the Messiah to be a Breaker, we could imagine many scenarios in which His breaking out is brought to bear.

When the leader opens the breach, then the followers also break out. This is special. If anyone is bound behind walls that are hard, high and thick, they need to see that Messiah, the leader is also a Breaker. There is no barrier too great, no problem too daunting, no weakness too severe, no sin so strong, no flesh so wicked and selfish, no hold so great, that limits this Breaker. Sin will never have the final say. Death will never give the last word. Pride will never conclude the remarks. All will be broken through. If a person has not experienced this, then they don't know what it is like and they don't know the absolute power of the Messiah as Breaker. He can break addiction, selfishness, pride, sin, rebellion, weakness, and death. He is the Breaker.

When did the Breaker do his work? Was it before God's people were gathered, when they were in captivity, and bondage of exile? Or, was it after they came into the fold? Actually, the Hebrew and the picture presented in Micah 2:13 do not tell us definitively. It could have been either before or after they are gathered. On the one hand, people in exile are in bondage, not free to serve God, worship Him, and collectively praise Him. Messiah as the Breaker breaks those bonds and leads them out. On the other hand, God's gathered remnant could be in a wonderful setting, which is prepared by God for their preservation. However, this fold can become their bondage and prison. Any Christian who is part of a wonderful corporate move of God, will know the joys of the pasture found in that move, and the dangers that the very move of God could be. The move of God one year, could become the prison the next year. This can be a fold that has become a prison. Messiah is able to break out of anything. Just as He was able to break His people out of the bondage of exile, He can also break His people out of the fold of the Law.

I will conclude this section with a list of quotes showing what commentators have speculated the Breaker breaks the people out of. Hopefully, this will give us light and enable us to trust that the Breaker can break what is in front of us. He can break that and allow us to go farther with Him, move more with Him, be freer in Him, and enjoy more of God's wonderful move.

"The breaker—Jehovah-Messiah, who *breaks* through every obstacle in the way of their restoration: not as formerly *breaking forth* to destroy them for transgression (Ex 19:22; Jdg 21:15), but breaking a way for them through their enemies." (Jamieson et al, Vol. 1, p. 690). ""The three verbs, they break through, they march through, they go out, describe in a pictorial manner progress which cannot be stopped by any human power" (Hengstenberg)" (Keil, p. 304). "Through the gate of the foe's city in which they had been captives. So the image of the resurrection (Ho 13:14) represents Israel's restoration" (Jamieson et al, Vol. 1, p. 690). "The Lord's action enables his people to break through the city gate and exit the place of their confinement" (Barker, p. 71). "In v. 13 the redemption of Israel out of exile is depicted under the figure of liberation from captivity. Was Egypt a slave-house (Mic. 6:4; cf. Ex. 20:2); so is exile a prison with walls and gates, which must be broken through" (Keil, p. 303). "He it is who will break the siege. The barricade of men and armaments will be swept away with irresistible might. The refugees will be able to sally forth with heads high *through the city gate*" (Allen, p. 303). "Jehovah will break through every barrier that hinders His remnant from following Him in a future day, and He has done so in this day. It was a breaking through of everything conventional when the Lord led many of His saints to see that they need not remain identified with national systems, or with anything sectarian. He was making a way for the true assembling and gathering and putting together of His own. It needed faith to break forth from all that had the sanction of long usage just as it needed faith to break forth from Judaism at the beginning of our period" (Coates, p. 35). "The fulfilment of this prophecy commenced with the gathering together of Israel to its God and King by the preaching of the gospel, and will be completed at some future time when the Lord shall redeem Israel, which is now pining in dispersion, out of the fetters of its unbelief and life of sin" (Keil, p. 304).

Whatever the barrier, the Breaker is able to break it. The result is that the people are free in a corporate setting to participate in the grand move of God Himself. "Their king passes on before them, the LORD at their head" (Micah 2:13). This image paints a picture of the King—God Himself—leading

His people. The word for "passes" is another word indicating stepping over barriers and passing through boundaries. The Lord broke them out. Now the Lord is leading them as a group as He moves for the fulfillment of His plan. If anyone asks what freedom is, this picture may provide the best answer. Freedom is being led by God along with His people as He moves to fulfill His plan. May our eyes and hearts be opened to see God's mighty power that operates toward us who believe!

Part 2—Micah's most profound vision

Overall, Micah's first section presents a picture of encouragement. Even though Micah passionately presents the degradation of the people at the beginning of the section, the end shows a glorious, gathered and freed remnant following their King. Micah's second section shows a similar trend. The beginning reveals even more details about the corruption of the people. We will even see how Micah is filled with the Spirit to announce these transgressions. However, Micah advances is this section as well. He eventually unveils a grand vision of God's dream for the restoration of His people. These are surely Micah's most profound visions.

The degraded leaders, prophets and priests

Micah's begins this section by declaring how the leaders, prophets, and priests are all corrupt. To the leaders Micah declares, "Hear, you heads of Jacob and rulers of the house of Israel!" (Micah 3:1). They do not know justice. They ruthlessly oppress the people; they "break their bones in pieces and chop them up like meat in a pot, like flesh in a cauldron" (Micah 3:3). Micah warns them that, one day, they will cry out to the Lord in distress, but He will not answer. The prophets are also corrupt. If someone gives them food or a present, then the prophesy "Peace." However, if they are not offered a gift, then they declare a holy war (Micah 3:5). Micah warns these "prophets" that darkness will come to them. They will be disgraced and, just like the rulers, God will not answer them when they call.

All levels of leadership are defiled, involved in financial corruption and spiritual hypocrisy.

> 11 Its heads give judgment for a bribe; its priests
> teach for a price; its prophets practice divination
> for money; yet they lean on the Lord and say, Is not
> the Lord in the midst of us? No disaster shall come
> upon us."
> —Micah 3:11

The judgment that will result will be that Zion, Jerusalem, and even the whole mountain of the Lord will be become a wasteland.

> 12 Therefore because of you Zion shall be plowed as a
> field; Jerusalem shall become a heap of ruins, and
> the mountain of the house a wooded height.
> —Micah 3:12

Micah's testimony of being full of the Spirit

In the midst of pointing out the leaders' corruption, Micah interjects his own testimony, which stands in great contrast to those who are pretending to be prophets. Micah unveils what motivates a true servant of God and, in turn, the effect that a true servant of God can produce.

> 8 But as for me, I am filled with power, with the Spirit of the Lord, and with justice and might,
> to declare to Jacob his transgression and to Israel his sin.
> —Micah 3:8

Micah testifies that he is filled with the Spirit of the Lord. Here we see the crucial role that the Holy Spirit plays in any true servant of the Lord. "Yahweh's spirit was the medium by which his will was communicated to the prophets…It was the spirit that kept the prophet in personal touch with his God and gave impulse, direction, and authority to his oracles" (Allen, p. 314). It was the Spirit who brought Micah into close fellowship with his Lord, who searched the depths of God, revealed them to Micah and gave Micah the capital with which to prophesy. Only such a vital, living, present, real, true, holy filling of the Spirit can give any servant of God effectiveness in ministry.

Micah was also filled with justice and might. "*Mishpât* [justice]…is the divine justice which the prophet has to proclaim, and *gᵉbhûrâh* strength, manliness, to hold up before the people their sins and the justice of God. In this divine strength he can and must declare their unrighteousness to all ranks of the people, and predict the punishment of God (vv. 9–12)" (Keil, p. 307). "He was a powerful voice for justice: that was the impact of the Spirit" (Prior, p. 143). Micah, therefore, could declare the sins and transgressions of the people. To declare means "to place a matter high, conspicuous before a person" (Harris, p. 549). What Micah essentially did was to highlight the sins that were downplayed, hidden, and maybe forgotten, and, by the power that he was filled with, bring those sins and transgressions into conspicuous notice.

It is important to see that the Spirit within was the source of Micah's power. Thus, he could boldly testify, "as for me, I am filled with power" (Micah 3:8). "The Hebrew preposition 'et- ("with") should perhaps here be read with the preceding clause in the sense, "I am filled with power by the help of the Spirit" (cf. Gen 4:1)" (Barker, p. 78). Possessing true power before God is not a small thing. Without power, words sound hollow and actions are weak. The power Micah is talking about is, "Capacity to act…but more commonly it expresses potency, capacity to produce" (Harris, p. 437). God is willing to bestow just such power, "He gives power to the faint" (Isaiah 40:29). Power means that the servant possesses the ability to alter his environment in a way that is towards God and His purpose. Without power, words fall emptily. Without power, a ministry is completely ineffective. It is simply a waste of energy and time. Real power comes from the Spirit within and fills a servant on the inside. With power, the situation is infused with God's presence and changed towards God's interests. Power opens a pathway to God for any who might be seeking. Micah did not just emptily repeat words that he had studied. Rather, he poured out words that were poured into Him by God. This is a servant who has real power from the Lord.

Here it is worth noting a contrast between the false prophets and Micah. The false prophets received input from the people to whom they prophesied. If the people gave them food, their words were "peace." If the people didn't offer anything, their words were "war." This meant that the so-called "prophets" only spoke based on what the people offered. Micah, however, was different. He spoke according to what he was filled with by God. God filled him with justice and with the manliness required to speak that justice. This allowed him to speak according to God and not according to man's wishes.

This honesty, combined with him being genuinely filled with the Spirit, resulted in Micah having true spiritual power. This is the key for a servant of the Lord. He speaks what he is filled with by God, and not merely what the people want to hear or what gives him advantage. In chapter three we have seen that the Spirit within Micah testifies powerfully concerning the sins of the people. In the next chapter, we will see how this same Spirit within Micah uplifts his message to convey heavenly scenes of Christ and His kingdom.

The mountain of the house of the Lord will be lifted up

Micah ends chapter three speaking about the judgment of Jerusalem. Micah declared that, because of the leaders' corruption, the mountain of the house will become a wooded height (Micah 3:12). This means that the mountain upon which the temple and Jerusalem sit will become so desolate that it will revert to a forest, just like it was before any inhabitants were there. This is a picture of the complete destruction of God's house and city. Immediately after predicting this desolation, Micah takes a grand turn in his prophecy. The same Spirit within Micah that prophesied of the destruction turns in him to unveil a great restoration for that same mountain.

> 1 It shall come to pass in the latter days that the mountain of the house of the Lord shall be established as the highest of the mountains, and it shall be lifted up above the hills; and peoples shall flow to it,
> 2 and many nations shall come, and say: "Come, let us go up to the mountain of the Lord, to the house of the God of Jacob, that he may teach us his ways and that we may walk in his paths." For out of Zion shall go forth the law, and the word of the Lord from Jerusalem.

> 3 He shall judge between many peoples, and shall decide disputes for strong nations far away; and they shall beat their swords into plowshares, and their spears into pruning hooks; nation shall not lift up sword against nation, neither shall they learn war anymore;
> 4 but they shall sit every man under his vine and under his fig tree, and no one shall make them afraid, for the mouth of the Lord of hosts has spoken.
>
> —Micah 4:1-4

Here Micah portrays a vision of a glorious future. That same mountain that was once a forest due to the ravages of God's judgment will one day be placed higher than the hills and even higher than the highest mountain. This means that God's house will be given the highest place in the estimation of all who dwell on the earth. Because God's house is on top of that mountain, nations of the earth will stream up to it, just like a river that flows against gravity and rushes up a mountain. "The Hebrew for the verb "stream" has the same root as the Hebrew word for "river." The picture is that of people from "many nations" (v. 2) rushing like a great river toward Jerusalem" (Barker, p. 84). "Stress is laid on the mountain as the place of the house of the Lord, and the nations will flow to it because the Lord's house is there, not simply because of its location or its loftiness....The flow of the nations to the new Jerusalem is nothing less than a spontaneous pilgrimage" (Prior, p. 149).

Zion, which is upon this mountain, will become the source of justice and righteousness throughout all the earth. In chapter three, Micah described how justice was unknown by the current inhabitants of Zion due to their corruption. However, in this vision, what was formerly the seat of corruption will become the seat for right judgments. This will bring true peace to the entire earth. People will no longer learn war, not because a strong nation will overpower all the weaker ones and establish its will by force, but because God's just rule from His mountain will prevail. War will no longer be an option that a nation must consider in order to solve conflicts. This will truly be a glorious setting. People will be joyful and peaceful, sitting under their "vine" and their "fig tree" (Micah 4:4).

The great assembly

Micah next declares how God will work to bring about this wonderful transformation. He will assemble His people. Concerning verses six through eight, Allen writes, "This present message provides a necessary intermediate link between a present state of despair and the attainment of future expectation" (p. 329). In a show of the wonderful power of His salvation, God reveals that He will begin working with the least expected group of people: the lame, the afflicted and those who have been driven off.

> 6 In that day, declares the Lord, I will assemble the lame and gather those who have been driven away and those whom I have afflicted;
> 7 and the lame I will make the remnant, and those who were cast off, a strong nation; and the Lord will reign over them in Mount Zion from this time forth and forevermore.
> 8 And you, O tower of the flock, hill of the daughter of Zion, to you shall it come, the former dominion shall come, kingship for the daughter of Jerusalem.
> —Micah 4:6-8

This picture shows the amazing power of God's salvation. He gathers people who are lame, driven off, and afflicted and makes *them* a remnant and a strong nation. How did the people get into the sorry state in which they begin in these verses? How did they become lame, driven off and afflicted? The Bible relates each of these conditions to certain experiences God's people have had with God or with leaders of God's people. Jacob became "lame" after wrestling with God (Genesis 32:31). From the time God touched his thigh, he walked with a limp. God's people became "driven off" by bad shepherds, as Jeremiah relates, "Therefore thus says the LORD, the God of Israel, concerning the shepherds who care for my people: "You have scattered my flock and have driven them away, and you have not attended to them"" (Jeremiah 23:2-3). God's people become "afflicted" under the disciplining judgment of God Himself. God's "infliction of pain on people is not due to viciousness; it is the just judgment of sinners who do not respond to his call for repentance" (Harris, p. 885). We could imagine that this group of people has had a rocky history with God. Maybe some of them wrestled with God and were so stubborn that God had to "touch their thigh" so they would limp the rest of their lives. Maybe others suffered under wicked rulers among God's people. Maybe others were rebellious towards God and suffered under His loving, but harsh, disciplinary hand. The result was that this group had become battle scarred and wounded. They were lame, driven off and afflicted.

Unlike a truly stiff-necked, heart-hearted people, however, this group was different. They allowed those interactions with God, even though they might have been harsh, to do their work and eventually bring them to genuine repentance and restoration. What happened to them could be understood in terms of the way Micah described God's judgment on the nation. Referring to God's judgment, Micah says, "Zion shall be plowed as a field" (Micah 3:12). These people allowed God's "plowing" to do its work, so that their "soil" could become fruitful. They allowed the dislodging of the soil to loosen it so that good things could eventually grow.

When the good things will grow, it will be truly marvelous. God will make His strong nation out of a sorry looking group of people who may only find in themselves enough strength to rely on God. "His hearers present a pitiable spectacle: they are like limping sheep which have strayed from the flock. The community has disintegrated, and they have lost that sense of solidarity and security which is the foundation of normal living….The injuries afflicted by God are just retribution, tokens that the people must themselves own responsibility for their present state. But the God who has demonstrated his power to break and mar has also the power to mend and make anew…The depleted nation is eventually to constitute a dynamic nucleus, a sturdy stock from which to breed and develop with new strength" (Allen. P. 330). Their restoration, then, provides a wonderful, powerful picture of God's salvation.

Micah poetically describes His restored people in Micah 4:8. God powerfully refers to them as "tower of the flock" and "hill of the daughter of Zion" (Micah 4:8). The tower of the flock describes a high tower that is built for the purpose of watching over the sheep—the nation of Israel (see, for example, the towers in the sheep fields built by Uzziah in 2 Chronicles 26:10). This tower is most likely the same as the tower associated with the prison in the complex of king David's palace, "the tower projecting from the upper house of the king at the court of the guard" (Nehemiah 3:25). It is a powerful, solid, armory that is an imposing structure for the exercise of kingly rule and authority, "Your neck is like the tower of David, built in rows of stone; on it hang a thousand shields, all of them shields of warriors" (Song of Songs 4:4). Furthermore, the people of Israel are likened to "the hill of the daughter of Zion." The word for "hill" here, is actually "ophel," which was a substantial mound on the south-eastern border of the city of Zion, upon which a strong wall was built by Jotham (2 Chronicles 27:3) and made high by Manasseh (2 Chronicles 33:14), as a crucial element for the defense of the city. Putting these two items together gives a picture of where God has brought the remnant. They have become a strong tower, like the one housing the armory near the prison in David's palace complex. They have become like the Ophel, built substantially out of strong stones and set for the defense of the city. To this built up edifice has come the former dominion, just like David ruled in his time. This dominion will allow them to rule with authority and power over the daughter of Jerusalem and beyond.

The necessary travail

The next six verses, Micah 4:9-5:1, retreat from the glorious picture of God's restored remnant and the tower of the flock to review three coming calamities that God will allow the nation to pass through on their road to glory. Through these calamities, we will see examples of the discipline God administers to His people, the deliverance He gives, and the colorful pathway God's people will walk. They will eventually emerge from this path as lame, cast-off and afflicted people, who now trust in God and are fit to receive His full restoration.

The first calamity is the nation's coming exile to Babylon (Micah 4:9-10). Micah prophesies, "for now you shall go out from the city and dwell in the open country; you shall go to Babylon" (Micah 4:10). In Babylon the nation will learn many lessons, have time to consider their past unfaithfulness and eventually witness God's great deliverance. In Babylon, God declares, "you shall be rescued; there the LORD will redeem you from the hand of your enemies" (Micah 4:10). The second calamity is a future siege of Jerusalem, where all the nations gather around the city to destroy it, saying, "Let her be defiled, and let our eyes gaze upon Zion" (Micah 4:11-13). During this siege, which refers to the final, future siege of Jerusalem (Zechariah 12:2; 14:2), God's people will repent from their past rejection of the Messiah and call upon Him. God will then enact a great deliverance. He will make the besieging nations like sheaves of wheat and Judah like a threshing sledge and then command Judah, "Arise and thresh, O daughter of Zion" (Micah 4:13). The third calamity describes a siege against Jerusalem in which the besiegers will "strike the judge of Israel on the cheek" (Micah 5:1). The deliverance from this calamity will be through the birth of the Messiah, the Ruler who will be born in Bethlehem (Micah 5:2).

These cycles of trial and deliverance surely have an effect on God's people. For those who are seeking God, each trial, whether it is the Babylonian captivity or the Jerusalem siege or the striking of the judge, gives opportunity for some lesson to be learned and some repentance to be exercised. God's many-faceted deliverance in each instance teaches of His grace, redemption, power, and glory.

In addition to the difficult, yet edifying, effects of these experiences, Micah also directs his readers to see two other aspects of these calamities. Seeing these aspects may help any God seeker face any loving discipline God may lay in front of him. The first item to see is that God considers the calamities to be labor pains, saying to those facing the Babylonian exile that pain has seized them "like a woman in labor" (Micah 4:9). He then charges them to "Writhe and groan, O daughter of Zion, like a woman in labor" (Micah 4:10). The pain associated with childbirth is different than any other pain, like that of an injury or illness. Birth pangs carry with them an inherent hope for new birth, new life and continuation. "Her travail will result eventually in her bringing forth a seed for blessing in the earth" (Coates, p. 39). For an enlightened Israelite, the Babylonian captivity is not merely pointless suffering of the nation as a consequence of sins. Micah's message is that the captivity is like labor pains. "The message is one of substantial hope: these sufferings will not be endless or meaningless. Something better, something new awaits" (Prior, p. 155).

The second lesson Micah teaches is that the calamities and deliverance work themselves out according to God's untraceable, wonderful thoughts. God declares that the nations who are besieging Jerusalem "do not know the thoughts of the Lord; they do not understand his plan" (Micah 4:12) and then describes how the tables will be turned on the besiegers. The siege is a picture of the mind bogglingly wonderful thoughts and plans of God. We might think, "Oh, no! It's a siege. This is really bad for the Lord's people and for the Lord's testimony." However, God changes the situation, flips it, and shows that His thoughts are higher than ours. The word translated "thoughts" here is used by Isaiah, "For my thoughts are not your thoughts" (Isaiah 55:8). This word is also used to describe artistic work, as when the tabernacle workers were "to devise artistic designs, to work in gold and silver and bronze" (Exodus 35:32), or the development of new machines, as when Uzziah "made machines, invented by skillful men" (2 Chronicles 26:15). The siege and deliverance are pictures of God's thoughts. As His thought is being worked out, it may appear like pointless pain. However, at the end we find that they were actually labor pains, the birth of something wonderful. Every stroke, which formerly seemed so random, now holds it perfect place in the picture God is laying out on the canvas. We "do not know the thoughts." We cannot fathom the "counsels." However, God is ever the Master. He turns the siege into a victory and helps us as we give birth to something new and grand.

The birth in Bethlehem

Maybe the greatest example of God's untraceable thoughts and His people's most wonderful birth pangs appears in God's response to the situation where the judge of Israel is struck on the cheek (Micah 5:1). God's response is that the Messiah, Christ, will be born in Bethlehem to be the genuine ruler of His people. "But" is a wonderful way to begin the announcement of the Messiah. Micah 5:1 reports that the judge of Israel has been struck on the cheek, BUT….

> 2   But you, O Bethlehem Ephrathah, who are too little
>   to be among the clans of Judah, from you shall
>   come forth for me one who is to be ruler in Israel,
>   whose coming forth is from of old, from ancient
>   days.
> —Micah 5:2

The Ruler will be born in a small, seemingly insignificant town, "too little to be among the clans of Judah," Bethlehem Ephrathah. The name itself is full of poetic meaning, "'*Ephrâth* and *Ephrâthâh*, i.e., the fertile ones, or the fruitfields, being the earlier name; by the side of which *Bēth-lechem*, bread-house, had arisen even in the patriarchal times: see Gen. 35:19; 48:7; Ruth 4:11" (Keil, p. 323). The name means the house of bread by the fruitful field. It speaks of fertility, sustenance, nourishment and goodness. It is small, but very nourishing. From that town will come for a ruler "for me," that is for God. "The coming Messiah is a provision not so much for Israel as for the LORD himself. He will fulfill all his purposes, not simply the people's deepest longings" (Prior, p. 158).

Micah calls Him a "ruler," in Hebrew *māšal*, which emphasizes how the Messiah will be a capable, fitting leader for the people of God's nation. This word is used of Joseph when Pharaoh made him "ruler of all his possessions" (Psalm 105:21). It is used by Abraham to describe his servant Eliezar, "who had charge of all that he had" (Genesis 24:2). It is used to describe how Solomon "ruled over all the kingdoms from the Euphrates to the land of the Philistines and to the border of Egypt" (1 Kings 4:21). Each of these uses emphasizes the capability, effectiveness and dexterity of the ruler. This word does not necessarily denote a king. Rather, it emphasizes leading, ruling and administrating. Messiah will be in charge not simply because He is appointed King. He will rule, because He is a good Ruler. As such, He meets God's need for a worthy Ruler for His people. In this sense, God can declare that the Ruler is "for me." He will tenderly and firmly shepherd God's people, thus meeting God's need.

"His coming forth is from of old, from ancient days" (Micah 5:2) is a mysterious and rich phrase describing the Messiah. His goings forth are described as being from two sources, the first "of old" and the second "from ancient days." These two phrases use different Hebrew words. "Of old" uses the Hebrew word, *qedem*, which means antiquity. It is used by Micah to denote the time of the fathers, when God pledged His covenant to them, "You will show faithfulness to Jacob and steadfast love to Abraham, as you have sworn to our fathers from days of old" (Micah 7:20). Based on the word *qedem* many commentators understand that the ruler proceeds from Bethlehem, as is fitting for a ruler in the line of David who will assume the throne of David. This word is rarely, if ever, used to denote an eternal measure of time. The other phrase, "from ancient days" employs a different Hebrew word, *ʿōlām*, which is used to refer to a much broader range of times. This word is sometimes used to describe the time of a simple historical event. However, ʿōlām, is also used to denote eternity. "Before the mountains were brought forth, or ever you had formed the earth and the world, from everlasting to everlasting you are God" (Psalm 90:2). "Then the LORD God said, "Behold, the man has become like one of us in knowing good and evil. Now, lest he reach out his hand and take also of the tree of life and eat, and live forever [ʿōlām]"" (Genesis 3:22). It even refers to the eternal beginnings of the Son, "Ages ago I was set up, at the first, before the beginning of the earth" (Proverbs 8:23). This word, then, conveys the eternal beginnings of the Messiah. Together, these words describe the Ruler in the most marvelous way. On the one hand, He is from the town of Bethlehem, according to the line of the man David. He is a real man, indicated by the word *qedem*. On the other hand, He is divine, from eternity past, and as such is a Ruler of a very different caliber than any ruler who had gone before. As God, His beginnings are from eternity, indicated by the word ʿōlām. Jamieson et al. summarize this well, "The plain antithesis of this clause, to "come forth out of thee" (*from Beth-lehem*), shows that the eternal generation of the Son is meant. The terms convey the strongest assertion of infinite duration of which the *Hebrew* language is capable (compare Ps 90:2; Pr 8:22, 23; Jn 1:1). Messiah's generation as man coming forth unto God to do His will on earth is *from Beth-lehem;* but as Son of God, His goings forth are *from everlasting*" (Vol. 1, p. 692).

Put together, this verse describes a marvelous picture of the Messiah. If one only had these words with which to know Him, that person would be blessed. This verse describes how He will come from humble, yet nourishing beginnings. He is born in the smallest of towns, yet, in a fruitful place that is a source of bread. The Messiah will be first and foremost pleasing to God and focused on the fulfillment of God's purposes. He will be a just, firm, fair, and good Ruler to the nation. He will be man, just like David was a real man, and He will also be God, having His beginnings in eternity. What a picture this verse paints! What a Messiah we have!

Another birth

The remaining verses of Micah chapter five paint a picture of what the earth will look like after the Messiah's birth. Not surprisingly, the coming of His rule will not look like what one might imagine. A person might think that after the Ruler is born, everyone listens to Him and He cleans up the world. This would be too simple, and it is not what happened after Jesus' birth. Instead of enacting a quick, outward change on the earth that would make Israel the center of government, God actually gives up His nation, until *another* birth occurs.

> 3   Therefore he shall give them up until the time when
>   she who is in labor has given birth
>   —Micah 5:3

The exact meaning of the birth mentioned here is debated among commentators. Some, including Keil, understand this birth to refer to the birth of the Messiah and "she who is in labor" to be Mary (p. 327). Many others, including Govett, Jamieson, Calvin, see "she who is labor" to represent the travail of God's people after Messiah is born. "The Church's throes are included, which are only to be ended when Christ, having been preached for a witness to all nations, shall at last appear as the Deliverer of Jacob, and when the times of the Gentiles shall be fulfilled, and Israel as a nation shall be born in a day (Is 66:7–11; Lu 21:24; Rev 12:1, 2, 4; compare Ro 8:22)" (Jamieson et al, Vol. 1, p. 692). This group of commentators, including Govett, sees two births here, one of the Messiah and one of the man-child described also in Revelation 12, "The former verse of Micah [5:2] celebrates the birth of Jesus at Bethlehem, as the destined ruler of Israel....The preceding verse [5:3] foretells the restoration of the kingdom to Israel" (Govett, Vol. II, p. 3).

I understand Micah 5:3 to be the travail of God's people after the coming of the Messiah, thus supporting the many New Testament references to God's people being in travail. Jesus likens His death to the disciples experiencing sorrow, like labor pains (John 16:20-22). Paul travailed as if he were giving birth when he was ministering to the Galatians (Galatians 4:19). Finally, there is a great birth announced in Revelation 12, where all God's people are in labor to bring forth the man-child (Revelation 12:10). Here, Micah is prophesying this same thing. After Jesus is born in Bethlehem, God gives up the nation of Israel until God's people travail in labor to bring forth the man-child. Right now, all God's people should be participating in this travail, which will eventually end the age in which we are living and bring God's kingdom to earth, as described in the remainder of Micah chapter five.

The result of the second birth

Micah 5:3-15 announces the great changes that come about on earth after that birth happens. We will list the marvelous results. "Then the rest of his brothers shall return to the people of Israel" (Micah 5:3). The rest of his brothers are the remaining part of God's people who will return again to their nation. Israel will be thus be regathered and restored. Furthermore, the Ruler, who was born in Micah 5:2, "shall stand and shepherd his flock in the strength of the LORD" (Micah

5:4). This means that the Ruler, Christ, will finally be a received, active, and effective Shepherd to Israel, which formerly had so many bad, evil, selfish shepherds during the period when God had given them up (Micah 5:3). "As David was a shepherd (Pss 23; 78:70–72), so his antitype, the royal Shepherd, will lead, feed, protect, and exercise authority over his own. As a Shepherd, he will be invincible: David protected his flock from the lions and bears; the ruling Shepherd will be endowed *bĕ 'ōz yhwh* (with the strength of Yahweh), exercising divine strength to protect the flock. The Lord himself will enable the Shepherd-King to do his work "in the strength of the Lord"'" (Barker, p. 100).

This shepherd will bring in a marvelous situation to the sheep. They will dwell securely in their land under His abundant and loving protection. "For now he shall be great to the ends of the earth" (Micah 5:4). This means that there is no threat that will be able to overcome the sheep under His care. He is greater than all. Furthermore, "he shall be their peace" (Micah 5:5). Their peace is personal. It is fully involved in the presence of the person of the Ruler. If He is there, they have peace. It is as if they are small children under the care of their loving father. As long as the kids can see their father, they are peaceful. The father could be defending them from many things, from want, from thieves, from harmful weather, from those that might harm them. However, they may not even know that he is doing that. They just see their father and they have peace. Peace continues as long as they are under the influence of that father. It is the same with the Shepherd. As long as the sheep see the Shepherd, they have peace. Their peace is personal. He Himself is their peace.

What that peace and security look like is described in the remaining verses of chapter five. First, it means that Israel will have good rulers, who can genuinely protect them from attacks. "When the Assyrian comes into our land and treads in our palaces, then we will raise against him seven shepherds and eight princes of men" (Micah 5:5). The seven shepherds and eight princes indicate the abundance of able rulers who will be able to stem the attack and even take their rule to the enemy's lands, "they shall shepherd the land of Assyria with the sword" (Micah 5:6). Good leaders are a sign of God's blessing and smile (Isaiah 3:1-4).

The second fruit of the Ruler's fine shepherding is that the remnant of Israel will become a blessing to the entire earth. "Then the remnant of Jacob shall be in the midst of many peoples like dew from the LORD, like showers on the grass.... like a lion among the beasts of the forest, like a young lion among the flocks of sheep" (Micah 5:7-8). As the remnant spreads out to the nations, they live among the nations and bring blessing to those they live with. Micah describes this blessing as dew, showers and lions. "Dew is here, as indeed everywhere else, a figurative expression for refreshing, stimulating, enlivening (cf. Ps. 110:3; 133:3, and 72:6; Hos. 14:6; Deut. 33:2). The spiritual dew, which Jacob will bring to the nations, comes from Jehovah, and falls in rich abundance without the co-operation of men. Without the spiritual dew from above, the nations are grass (cf. Isa. 40:6–8)" (Keil, p. 330). They are showers, which speak of spiritual refreshment and as a source of growth and encouragement. There is also something fierce about this remnant—they are lions. "The people of God show itself like a lion, trampling and rending the sheep among the nations of the world which oppose its beneficent work. And over these may it triumph" (Keil, p. 330).

The point with all these images is that when the people of God are under a proper shepherding from the Messiah, then they are able to go forth and be a two-fold blessing to the nations. On the one hand, they water what may grow and bear fruit for God and, on the other, they "weed the garden" by opposing and tearing what opposes God. "Micah sees the remnant, not as a holy huddle gathered together for mutual protection and mere survival, but a force in the midst of many peoples…among the nations (7,8). They will, moreover, be a force both for refreshment and for rending: like dew from the Lord (7), and like a lion among the beasts of the forest, like a young lion among the flock of sheep (8). These two contrasting images point up the double impact of a people united and committed to the Lord's Messiah; to some they are a fragrance from life to life, to others 'a fragrance from death to death' (2 Cor. 2:16)" (Prior, p. 162).

Finally, the Ruler being peace to the flock looks like a genuine, pure, thorough cleansing of all defilement that was formerly in the nation. "I will cut off your horses" (Micah 5:10) means that they will no longer rely on other things for protection. "I will cut off sorceries from your hand…your carved images…and you shall bow down no more to the work of your hands" (Micah 5:12-14). Here God purifies the nation from any other worship, from all idolatry, and from all efforts at bowing down to idols. Under proper shepherding the nation is solely to rely on Him. His influence even extends to touch the authority of all the nations. "In anger and wrath I will execute vengeance on the nations that did not obey" (Micah 5:15). Thus, the entire earth—God's people and the nations—is purified for God.

Part 3—An invitation to participate in God's move

After portraying a profound vision of the coming Messiah with His kingdom in the second section of his prophecy, Micah drastically switches gears in his third section. He no longer focuses on declaring the sins of the nation by making sounds like a jackal or an ostrich. He is no longer striving to speak about what will be. He no longer paints pictures of future graces, births, rulers and restorations. Instead, Micah simply pleads with the nation to come before the Lord. When the majority of people don't return, Micah returns himself and shows a pathway that a returned person must take.

It is almost as if this section shows Micah travailing in birth so that the nation might participate in God's plan. Micah spoke about travail in chapters four and five, but did not give examples of how a God seeker might participate in that. In chapters six and seven Micah gives a living example of his travail on behalf of the nation. As he lives out his travail, he pleads that the people would come before God, join with God, and receive God's salvation. Micah's first section, chapters one and two, is a declaration of the sins of the people; his second section, chapters three through five, is a display of God's restoration. His third section, chapters six and seven, is an invitation to participate in that glorious restoration.

God's open-air court

Micah begins by describing how God wishes that He and the nation both present their arguments with one another in an open-air court.

> 1 Hear what the Lord says: Arise, plead your case
> before the mountains, and let the hills hear your
> voice.
> 2 Hear, you mountains, the indictment of the Lord,
> and you enduring foundations of the earth,
> for the Lord has an indictment against his people,
> and he will contend with Israel.
> —Micah 6:1-2

Here, God is holding court in front of the mountains, hills and fountains. He is asking Israel to "plead" her case against Him and follows that by laying out His own "indictment" against them. Both these words are actually the same Hebrew word, *rîb*, which is used to represent a complaint. This word often describes an instance where one party of an existing relationship has an issue that violated the boundaries or expectations involved in the initial agreement. For instance, God never pleads, *rîb,* with the nations, nor do they quarrel, *rîb,* with God; there was no agreement between them. However, as recorded in the writings of Moses, the Psalms and the prophets, God often pleads, *rîb,* with His people and His people also contend, *rîb,* with Him. The use of this word here in the open-air court indicates two things. First, it implies that God has a formal relationship with His people. Second, it indicates that the boundaries of that relationship have been violated. Therefore, in front of the mountains and hills, these violations should be brought out into the open.

God's indictment against His people

God presents His indictment in a surprisingly tender and loving way.

> 3 "O my people, what have I done to you? How have I wearied you? Answer me!
> 4 For I brought you up from the land of Egypt and redeemed you from the house of slavery, and I sent before you Moses, Aaron, and Miriam.
> 5 O my people, remember what Balak king of Moab devised, and what Balaam the son of Beor answered him, and what happened from Shittim to Gilgal, that you may know the righteous acts of the Lord."
> —Micah 6:3-5

God opens His indictment with the words, "O my people" (Micah 6:3), which show His tender feelings towards His wayward nation. He does not begin by saying, "You have sinned," although he could have easily done that. Nor does He begin, "I will destroy you," although this would have also fit. Rather, He begins with these affectionate words and, in doing so, changes the tone of the book. "These are the words of the Lord himself by the prophet, expressing his strong affection to the people of Israel, of which his goodness to them was a full proof" (Gill, on Micah 6:3). "The entire mood of his case against Israel has changed. This is shown by the LORD's opening form of address: 'O my people' (3), which is repeated for emphasis (5). If the whole passage evokes the atmosphere of a lawcourt, the language here is personal and passionate, far more like a father's pleas to his child or a husband pleading with his wife" (Prior, p. 170).

With such touching, emotional, opening words, God seeks to touch His peoples' conscience in order to make them realize how wrong their thoughts of Him are. He proceeds to ask, "What have I done to you?" and, "How have I wearied you?" "In a touching appeal to their heart and conscience He asks what they could have against Him" (Darby, p. 576). They may have had in the back of their minds some vague feeling that God had wronged them or that He was asking drudgery of them. If they would be asked, "Has God wronged you?" they might have felt, "Yes, of course." However, if the questioner would continue and say, "How has God wronged you?" they could not come up with one instance. If they were asked, "Is God's relationship wearying?" They might have answered automatically "Yes," thinking of all the endless sacrifices and repetitious temple rites. However, if they were asked, "Did God actually command you to perform those rites perfunctorily and mindlessly repetitiously?" They would have to say,

"No." Micah shows us that they could not come up with one instance demonstrating their vague, errant feeling of being wronged.

Instead God reminds them of instances to the contrary. In verses four and five God lists examples of His care and help throughout their history. He brought them up from the land of Egypt. Was that wearying to them? He redeemed them from the house of slavery. Was that an offense to them? He sent Moses, Aaron and Miriam to them to help them. Was that tiring to them? It is as if God is saying, "When you are in vital relationship with Me, this is the kind of thing that happens. You get brought up from Egypt, redeemed from slavery, and you receive very good leaders. You know, there was no reason for this to stop. Why did you turn me into a wearying religion? I'm the most vibrant, exciting, and real Husband that you can imagine." "God's people were bored stiff with the mechanics and the routine of worship…They have lost the plot and passion…But the Lord wants his people to concentrate on his saving acts (5), because he is aware that the only adequate motivation for a restored and renewed relationship between them is gratitude for all that he has been and done for them over the years" (Prior, p. 171).

Then God reminds them of Balak, Balaam, and what happened from Shittim, the last station where they rested before they crossed the Jordan, to Gilgal, the first station they visited after they crossed that river. "The period of Israel's journeying from Shittim to Gilgal embraces not only Balak's advice and Balaam's answer, by which the plan invented for the destruction of Israel was frustrated, but also the defeat of the Midianites, who attempted to destroy Israel by seducing it to idolatry, the miraculous crossing of the Jordan, the entrance into the promised land, and the circumcision at Gilgal, by which the generation that had grown up in the desert was received into the covenant with Jehovah, and the whole nation reinstated in its normal relation to its God. Through these acts the Lord had actually put to shame the counsel of Balak, and confirmed the fact that Balaam's answer was inspired by" (Keil, p. 334).

The fact is that they lost sight of who God was. If the true God is on the other side of the relationship, then there is no weariness. It is ever new, ever fresh, ever different, ever growing, ever increasing, ever becoming more lovely, ever growing richer and more glorious. Why? Because God is the source of life and the ever living One!

We can see from God's argument here that as He pleads for them to return, He reminds them of events from their history with Him. This shows how important vital remembrance is to a God seeker. When God moves in a nation's or person's life, that move becomes a landmark in a spiritual journey. If the landmark is forgotten, then moving onward becomes difficult. However, if the landmark is appreciated, then the person or nation has a way to go forward in the present. History with God is powerful and crucial for the person who is seeking God. "Israel are summoned to remember an episode in their salvation history. Their remembering is not at all the type of memory work necessary in studying for a history examination. It marks rather the impact of God's past work for Israel on the life of the present generation" (Allen, p. 367). Remembering is far from a merely mental exercise. It opens the door for participation. "Remember in the Bible is not merely a matter of calling to mind, but of 'actualizing the past into the present.' Remembrance equals participation." (Prior, p. 173).

A faulty response to God's care

The next verses show that God's open-air courtroom definitely stirred up something in the people. After they listened to God's indictment, they had a resolution in their hearts. It is as if they began to think, "Yes, I do love God. Yes, I do want to come to God and give everything to Him. Yes, let's go." The only question is "How real is their turn to the Lord?" Micah speaks in a very interesting way on behalf of these emotional, passionate people.

> 6 "With what shall I come before the Lord, and bow myself before God on high? Shall I come before him with burnt offerings, with calves a year old?
> 7 Will the Lord be pleased with thousands of rams, with ten thousands of rivers of oil? Shall I give my firstborn for my transgression, the fruit of my body for the sin of my soul?"
> —Micah 6:6-7

This response begins wonderfully—it starts out with the thought of coming before the Lord. This is exactly what God desires. He wishes that His nation would come before Him. Then, the response goes farther, asking what a person should bring when he or she comes to the Lord. This is also not a bad thought. In fact, a reasonable thought for an Israelite, especially one who had a sinful past, is to come to the temple bringing something to offer the Lord. This is very good. At first, Micah asks if he should bring some legitimate sacrifices. Should he come to the Lord with burnt offerings? Or with calves a year old? Then, Micah surprisingly begins to venture into the absurd. How about bringing thousands of rams and rivers of oil with me as I approach the Lord? Then he goes even farther. Should I sacrifice my firstborn son? "The series of hypothetical questions rises to a hysterical and ghastly crescendo in the ultimate offer of a child sacrifice" (Allen, p. 370). Some speculate that the hysterical crescendo is the result of a misinformed, emotional public responding to an appeal from God. Prior thinks it paints a picture of misaimed "religious" duty. "But as is usually the case when people with a religious background resolve to take God seriously again, the individual concerned begins by wanting to step up his acts of piety" (Prior, p. 175). These verses show that the people's intention was good—coming to the Lord with something in their hands. However, they do not have a clear understanding of what would be an appropriate response to God. Micah is then ready to tell them.

In the next verse, Micah reminds the people of exactly what God demands of them. His demands don't require burnt offerings, calves, rivers of oil, thousands of livestock, or even their firstborn.

> 8 He has told you, O man, what is good; and what does the Lord require of you but to do justice, and to love kindness, and to walk humbly with your God?
> —Micah 6:8

"The prophet therefore proceeds in v. 8 to overthrow these outward means of reconciliation with God, and reminds the people of the moral demands of the law" (Keil, p. 336). Here Micah voices the real demand of God, involving people's actions, loves and spiritual walk. God's requirements are to do justice, love kindness and walk humbly with your God. "In other words, God wants our very selves, our lives and our love" (Prior, p. 176).

This verse is a beautiful picture of the relationship God is seeking. It doesn't involve offering sacrifices. Rather, he requires and delights in our adherence to what He says and our relationship with Him. "Doing righteousness and exercising love. These two embrace all the commandments of the second table, of whose fulfilment Israel thought so little, that it was addicted to the very opposite,—namely, injustice, oppression, and want of affection (vid., Mic. 2:1, 2, 8; 3:2, 3, 9 ff., 6:10 ff.). There is also a third: humble walk with God, i.e., in fellowship with God, as Israel, being a holy priestly nation, ought to walk" (Keil, p. 336). Justice, kindness and walking with God are a package, which goes together, each part relying on the others. "Micah's threefold requirement cannot, therefore, be conveniently dissected, packaged and labelled. The three qualities hold together. It is only by applying ourselves to the third (to walk humbly with your God), that we can begin to practice the first two (to do justice, and to love kindness).... Justice and kindness are, in fact, essential qualities in the nature of God himself. They do not come down from heaven wrapped in parcels. They are expressed in and through people who walk humbly with their God" (Prior, p. 177).

The sad result

If the people truly had taken God's admonition here, then we might imagine Micah advancing to describe the glorious fruit of the renewed relationship, like he described in Micah 5:10-15. We are hoping to ascend to great heights of fellowship and justice with God. However, verses 9-16 fall like a thud. God just made an emotional, vivid plea for the people. The people responded, wanting to come to him, and realizing their sin. Micah voiced what God required, how he desired them to walk with Him and thus live out His virtues. However, it is as if the whole thing was a hollow exercise. They were touched emotionally, but it didn't translate into their life. The people might have been willing to give rivers of oil to God. However, to walk humbly with God was an order too tall for them to fill. They didn't exhibit the virtues God requested. Thus, Micah reverts to speaking again about the wickedness existing in society. "Because Israel is altogether wanting in these virtues, the Lord must threaten and punish. V. 9. *"The voice of Jehovah, to the city it cries, and wisdom has thy name in its eye; hear ye the rod, and who appoints it!"* With these words Micah introduces the threatening and reproachful words of the Lord" (Keil, p. 336).

Instead of walking humbly with their God, Israel presents a very sad scene. There are "treasures of wickedness in the house of the wicked" (Micah 6:10), "wicked scales" (Micah 6:11) meaning corrupt business dealings, "rich men", people "full of violence," "lies," "deceitful" tongues (Micah 6:12), those who hold the statutes of Omri and the works of the house of Ahab (Micah 6:16). Instead of God enjoying the relationship His people have with Him as they walk with Him and love kindness and justice, He will strike the nation with a grievous blow (Micah 6:13). They will eat and not be satisfied. They will sow and not reap (Micah 6:14-15). God will severely punish them, making them a desolation and their inhabitants a hissing (Micah 6:16).

The depths of Micah's disappointment

Faced with this sad result, Micah appears to fall into a deep depression, crying out "Woe is me!" (Micah 7:1). He had just ridden the roller coaster of chapter six. He voiced God's appeal to the nation, conveyed God's tender care through the years, witnessed a response of the people, heard God's clear demands, and witnessed God's demands ringing hollow in the lives of the nation. The people he had been pouring his life out to help had not followed through on their return to God. Maybe Micah is thinking that the illness lies deeper than he ever imagined. Maybe now he realizes the extent of their fall and disease. Maybe, after he himself was affected by God's appeal and after he thought they were also affected, he wakes up and realizes that their response was a sham. In this woeful state, he cries out, "Woe is me! For I have become as when the summer fruit has been gathered, as when grapes have been gleaned: there is no cluster to eat, no first-ripe fig that my soul desires" (Micah 7:1). When Micah looks at the nation, he sees no cluster of grapes to eat and no desirable figs—out of the masses of the nation there is no person who is walking with God.

While some commentators consider that Micah is speaking here the words of a future remnant of Israel, many read the first person in this section as an expression of the more personal feelings and sentiments of the prophet. They read these words as a sign that a crisis is unfolding in Micah the prophet and man. He has come to the end of some internal reserve and now exclaims "Woe is me," as he realizes that no fruit can be found in the nation. "But now he feels woe deep within his inner being. In the authentic tradition of Israel's prophets, the impact of God's holy judgment on sin—his own, or particularly that of his contemporaries—sears Micah through and through" (Prior, p. 188-189). The fact that Micah feels this way is not a sign of his weakness or failing. Rather, Micah's personal feelings convey God's feelings as well. Micah cannot find fruit to satisfy himself. Neither can God find fruit among the nation to satisfy Him. "This lament fulfils both functions, relieving before God his feelings of despair and trust and also making plain to the people the divine view of their corruption, a view the prophet fully shares as God's representative" (Allen, p. 384).

Micah proceeds to detail the sad state of Israel that has left him without a first-ripe fig or a cluster of grapes. "There is no one upright among mankind" (Micah 7:2). Instead "they all lie in wait for blood" (Micah 7:2), "their hands are on what is evil" (Micah 7:3), "the prince and judge ask for a bribe" (Micah 7:3), and "the best of them is like a briar" (Micah 7:4). In such a corrupt setting, the foundations of society are collapsing. Neighbors, friends, even family members are no longer able to be trusted. Micah warns, "put no trust in a neighbor, have no confidence in a friend…a man's enemies are those of his own household" (Micah 7:5-6).

Micah's resolution towards God

Verse seven begins a drastic turn in the focus of Micah's prophecy. From here to the end of the book, Micah glories in God, rejoices that God's building work will be accomplished, prays in faith, receives answers to prayers and pours out his whole being in praise. All of this begins with Micah's strong, firm resolution.

> 7 But as for me, I will look to the Lord; I will wait for the God of my salvation; my God will hear me.
> —Micah 7:7

This verse is refreshing, like a cool glass of water after an arduous journey or like finding grapes growing in the shade of a hot desert crevice. Here Micah declares how he will look to the Lord, how he will wait for the God of his salvation, and how God, who is his God, will indeed hear him. This is glorious!

The English translation of the Hebrew in this verse waters down the intensity of Micah's resolution that is evident in the original Hebrew. When Micah says "I will look" he is using the Hebrew word, *sāpâ*, which is a word for intensive watching. "*Sāpâ* conveys the idea of being fully aware of a situation in order to gain some advantage or keep from being surprised by an enemy" (Harris, p. 773). The participle of this word is translated "watchman." It is used to denote the intensity with which Eli watched for the precious ark to return from battle, "Eli was sitting on his seat by the road watching, for his heart trembled for the ark of God" (1 Samuel 4:13). After Habakkuk asks God a question, he sets himself to intensely watch for an answer, "I will take my stand at my watchpost and station myself on the tower, and look out to see what he will say to me" (Habakkuk 2:1). Here Micah uses a Piel stem of the verb, which may further emphasize the intensity of his looking. He also uses the imperfect tense, indicating that his watching is an ongoing activity, not a one off. Micah is saying here that his eyes are fixed, as if he were a watchman, as if he were looking to protect something so precious and so vital to him. He is looking to the Lord.

When Micah says, "I will wait," he uses the Hebrew word, *yāḥal*, which "is used of "expectation, hope" which for the believer is closely linked with "faith, trust" and results in "patient waiting"" (Harris, p. 373). This word conveys not merely the idea of delaying action until an event occurs. Rather, it conveys the expectant hope that the event will occur based on solid evidence. In places in the Old Testament it is translated "hope," as in "But I will hope continually and will praise you yet more and more" (Psalm 71:14). Such waiting is sometimes accompanied by great encouragement, "Be strong, and let your heart take courage, all you who wait for the Lord!" (Psalm 31:24). The Septuagint translates *yāḥal* here into the Greek word, "hupomeno," which is similar to the word translated "abide" in the New Testament. This may indicate that as Micah is hopefully waiting, he is enjoying the intimate presence of his God.

This declaration is a wonderful statement concerning a servant of God stepping forward to trust in God. Micah looks to the Lord continually, as if he were a watchman protecting the city or looking for any indication of vital approaching messenger. That is how he is with his Lord. Furthermore, he is full of trust and faith and expectation that the God of his salvation will act and will be. He has an attitude of waiting for expectant hope, because he knows his God and his God's saving power. "But further, the verse reflects not only the ground of faith, the Lord himself, but the saving activity of his God. In short, that which is hoped for is not some desideratum arising from one's imagination, but in God himself and whatever he should propose to accomplish" (Harris, p. 374).

  Furthermore, here Micah calls God "my God" and declares that "he will hear me." These are the words of an intimate friend. God is not someone else's God. God is very personal to Micah. He is so close to him that he can call the One he is looking for, hoping for and waiting for, "my God." Micah doesn't have to plea for his God to hear, nor does he fear that God will not answer him, as he predicted for some of the prophets (Micah 3:7). He knows God, expects God's salvation to come, possesses God, and is sure of an intimate conversation and open communication. While the people around Micah are scorning God, making hypocritical vows to return to Him, and being scorned by Him, Micah has found a refuge and an oasis. He is looking at One, hoping for One, talking to One, and enjoying the riches of the One God, his God.

There is some debate about if Micah is speaking for himself in this verse or if he is speaking for some future remnant. One thing is clear, whether it is Micah's personal experience or him speaking for a future group, this verse demarks a clear differentiation between the one who looks to God and the vast majority of people at the time. "The word "but" (a Hb. adversative *waw*) draws a sharp contrast between faithful Micah and his unfaithful contemporaries (cf. 3:8). "Watch" provides a link with v. 4 ("watchmen"), where the same Hebrew root occurs. There, however, the watching was for judgment; here it is for salvation" (Barker, p. 124). Keil sees this as representing a group of faithful, who are light to the dark situation. "Even though all love and faithfulness should have vanished from among men, and the day of visitation should have come, the church of the faithful would not be driven from her confidence in the Lord, but would look to Him and His help, and console itself with the assurance that its God would hear it, i.e., rescue it from destruction" (Keil, p. 323). Others see the verse as coming from Micah personally, who also may represent the remnant. "Micah—perhaps speaking for the righteous, faithful remnant—brings some relief to his own dark times by the light of his trust and hope in God" (Barker, p. 124).

Others see this verse as an intentional separation that Micah inserts between himself and the unfaithful nation. "Micah makes his own stance plain" (Prior, p. 192). "The tone of the lament changes from general pessimism to personal optimism" (Allen, p. 389). "The prophet, like any other saint not immune to attacks of doubt, here strengthens himself in his God and bears bold witness to divine reality beyond the dark clouds of human discord….His pessimism did not drive him to despair, but into the arms of the God to whom he was personally related" (Allen, p. 390). Coates sees such a separation as the only pathway for a faithful servant of God in a dark day, "The effect of all this is to isolate anyone who really fears God from the state of things which surrounds him, and to shut him up to God. He comes to realize that nobody can be trusted….it is a detaching and sanctifying exercise. In an evil day it is impossible to find a divine path without taking it up" (Coates, p. 49-50).

Darby sees Micah's stand here as being a beacon of light to the entire nation. Yes, God's judgment is surely coming for the masses. However, Micah's ministry is not merely to declare sins and announce judgment to them. It is also to intercede for the people based on what God will do. "The Spirit of God declares judgment indeed on God's part, but, because God loved the people, becomes a Spirit of intercession in the prophet for the people" (Darby, p. 576). Micah becomes a beacon of hope, a person who has blazed a trail of faithfulness to God. Such a trail could be followed in the future by any seeker of God.

The life of a person looking to God

Micah proceeds to outline a pathway that a servant of God may take as he follows the Lord. What may surprise many is that Micah's pathway contains falling and darkness. The pathway the Lord gives His servant is not void of pitfalls. Rather, in the Lord's pathway, a fall will be met by a rising up. In the Lord's pathway, a servant sitting in darkness finds the Lord as light. It is not a pathway where there are no enemies, but one in which the enemies will eventually be conquered. It is not a pathway free from sin, but one in which sins are righteously dealt with by God until He is satisfied and His child is brought into freedom. Micah boldly declares his expectation for the pathway he will walk as he looks to and waits for the Lord.

> 8 Rejoice not over me, O my enemy; when I fall, I shall rise; when I sit in darkness, the Lord will be a light to me.
> 9 I will bear the indignation of the Lord because I have sinned against him, until he pleads my cause and executes judgment for me. He will bring me out to the light; I shall look upon his vindication.

> 10 Then my enemy will see, and shame will cover her who said to me, "Where is the Lord your God?" My eyes will look upon her; now she will be trampled down like the mire of the streets.
>
> —Micah 7:8-10

Micah begins with commanding his enemy not to rejoice over him. Evidently either Micah's personal enemy or an enemy of the nation was mockingly taunting, "Where is the Lord your God?" (Micah 7:10). While this taunt was going on, Micah possibly was fallen or sitting in darkness or beset by some sin that he had committed against the Lord. Maybe, Micah was at that very time experiencing all three. He was a fallen person, sitting in darkness, full of sins against His Lord. At that very low point, the enemy approaches, looks and mocks, "Where is the Lord your God?" and begins rejoicing over him.

Here Micah, after declaring how he will look to God with expectant hope, and that God is his God, unveils the power of the salvation God brings to bear for those who look to Him. Yes, Micah may be fallen. However, he will rise, because God's salvation is such. Yes, Micah may be sitting in darkness right now. However, God can still hear him, and furthermore, God Himself in His full saving ability can be light to Micah. How sweet when we sit in darkness, when the Lord Himself is light. We have the quiet, confidence of the presence of the Lord. It makes all the difference.

Furthermore, Micah has sinned against the Lord. He is not perfect, nor even close. The Lord is wrathful due to these sins. However, Micah is full of trust in the Lord's dealings. Thus, he can proclaim trustingly that he "will bear the indignation of the Lord" (Micah 7:9). Then, just like David chose to fall into the hand of God for his sin instead of into the hand of his enemies because he knew God is merciful, Micah is able

Micah 219

to do the same. Why can he say this? Because he knows God, knows the righteousness *and* kindness of God, and knows that whatever is measured to him is out of love. God will discipline until God begins to "plead his cause" (Micah 7:9). At this point, the discipline is enough. It is over and has not gone too far. Then, God will bring him out to the light and Micah will look upon the vindication, the righteousness of God.

This is the pathway of a servant of God who is walking humbly with God and enjoying the salvation He is dispensing. An enemy may come in the midst of this process and tauntingly mock, saying, "Where is the LORD your God?" However, the enemy doesn't know the ways of God. The pathway with God is that of perfection, but it involves a person who is imperfect who knows the salvation, light, comfort and resurrection of his Savior. This is the wonderful pathway Micah is cutting. This is the trail he is blazing. The enemy will one day experience shame and eventually be trampled down, like the mire of the streets. However, Micah is in the light, has had his sins fully dealt with, and has been raised up after being fallen. Micah thus paints a picture of a person following God that is applicable in any age and any setting.

> "Once Micah again focuses his attention on the LORD, my God', everything begins to get into another perspective. Most of all, he begins to see aspects of God's character and activity which he has been in danger of forgetting amid all the personal trauma caused by the wickedness around him. He became buoyant and upbeat....The enemy is not actually named. Whoever or whatever the enemy, whether it is Micah's personal enemy or the nation's, the message is: Rejoice not over me, O my enemy....Micah is not presumptuous enough to say that he will not fall. He knows that he can and will. But the Lord will pick him

> up. Neither is he naïve or triumphalist, to the point of thinking that life with the Lord will be all sweetness and light. There will be darkness, and the darkness will not be a passing cloud. He will find himself sitting in darkness and in the shadow of death. But there the LORD himself will be a light to him. He will not need human sources of light, however pleasant and positive they might be. The LORD will be enough"
> — Prior, p. 193-4

Keil sees Micah's experience as representing more than just an individual man. He is representing the faithful group of God's people who become a testimony to their dark age by their experience of their God. "The church is here supposed to be praying out of the midst of the period when the judgment has fallen upon it for its sins, and the power of the world is triumphing over it. The prophet could let her speak thus, because he had already predicted the destruction of the kingdom and the carrying away of the people into exile as a judgment that was inevitable (Mic. 3:12; 6:16). Sitting in darkness, i.e., being in distress and poverty (cf. Isa. 9:1; 42:7; Ps. 107:10). In this darkness the Lord is light to the faithful, i.e., He is their salvation, as He who does indeed chasten His own people, but who even in wrath does not violate His grace, or break the promises which He has given to His people" (Keil, p. 343). "Micah's crucial function at this point is to articulate his own quiet confidence in the LORD on behalf of his people and in spite of his people's sad condition. As the prophet discovers the LORD to be light in the darkness, hope is kindled for the people" (Prior, p. 195).

A firm restoration, like stone walls

Micah next speaks of the restoration that will result from walking such a pathway with God. The enemies will be trampled down like the mire of the streets. However, God's people will be solidly built up and edified.

> 11 A day for the building of your walls! In that day the boundary shall be far extended.
> 12 In that day they will come to you, from Assyria and the cities of Egypt, and from Egypt to the River, from sea to sea and from mountain to mountain.
> 13 But the earth will be desolate because of its inhabitants, for the fruit of their deeds.
> —Micah 7:11-13

Micah describes the restoration. The daughter of Zion's walls will be built up and her boundary extended far. There will be a gathering of God's people from all over the earth, from Egypt, Assyria, from between the seas and the mountains. All the wicked of the earth will be judged because they will receive just recompense for their evil deeds.

The words Micah uses for "walls" and "boundary" shed light on details of this restoration. Micah uses the Hebrew word *gādēr* for the wall which will be built. This word is used to denote a stone wall that is usually built around a vineyard (Numbers 22:24). When God portrayed the kingdom of Israel as a vineyard in Isaiah chapter five, He announced that He will "will break down its wall" (Isaiah 5:5) as He judged His rebellious kingdom. Now, that same wall will be rebuilt around the vineyard. The restoration of a stone wall around God's vineyard indicates the kingdom of God will be restored in strength. "The unusual use of *gādēr* for "walls" may point toward a metaphorical use to speak of the restoration of the Jews to Judah and Jerusalem" (Barker, p. 129). The word for boundary is also full of meaning. Micah uses the Hebrew word *chōq*, which is many times translated as statute or law. "*Chōq* is apparently used here for the ordinance or limit which God has appointed to separate Israel from the nations; not a land-boundary, but the law of Israel's separation from the nations" (Keil, p. 344). Darby translates it, "on that day shall the established limit recede"; NKJV, "*In* that day the decree shall go far and wide"; ASV, "in that day shall the decree be far removed." It gives the sense of expansion, inclusion, not only physically, but also culturally, racially, nationally, and tribally.

Thus, Micah's restoration picture here is of the kingdom of God symbolized by the wall around the vineyard, being strongly and solidly edified. At the same time, the boundary of the kingdom becomes more inclusive and broader. "This expansion could have a double reference: to Israel's returning exiles, and to the gathering-in of the Gentiles under the rule of the new shepherd king. For them all, 'Zion's walls will be expanded to embrace all the elect from the ends of the earth'" (Prior, p. 195).

Micah's prayer and God's answer

After Micah sees the glorious vision of God's restored kingdom, he cries out to God in a powerful, learned and accurate prayer. His prayer is informed by his experience of waiting on God, being delivered by God and seeing the vision of God's coming restoration. In light of all that experience, Micah cries out to God:

> 14 Shepherd your people with your staff, the flock of your inheritance, who dwell alone in a forest in the midst of a garden land; let them graze in Bashan and Gilead as in the days of old.
> —Micah 7:14

Micah opens his prayer by asking God to shepherd His people. This is a marvelous prayer, because the request is very much on God's heart—He wants to shepherd His people—and it is also very much in all the people's best interest—they sorely need shepherding. To pray that God would shepherd His people is to pray that God would fulfill His deep desire, counsel and plan for His flock. Asking God to shepherd is like asking a famous basketball player to lead his team well to the championship. It is what he wants to do, and it is also what the players and fans want to happen. God Himself spoke through Micah that the ruler who is coming forth from Bethlehem "shall stand and shepherd his flock in the strength of the Lord" (Micah 5:4). Now Micah is praying for God to do what He already promised He would. A prayer like this is full of revelation and appreciation for what God wishes and what God is planning and intending to do. It is a model prayer and an example of a transcendent plea for God to accomplish His plan.

The Hebrew word for "shepherd" is very close to the meaning "feed" or "pasture." In fact, the Darby version translates this imperative, "Feed thy people with thy rod." Micah is here realizing how important it is for God's sheep to have food and find proper pasture. This shows the dire need and crucial importance of food for God's people. When Micah requests that God shepherd His people "with his rod" he is referring to God's discipline in His leading. Such discipline leads his sheep to real food. It is thus a comfort to His people, as David testifies, "Your rod and your staff they comfort me" (Psalm 23:3). "In Ps 23:4 it is used metaphorically of the Lord's protection of his servant as he walks in paths of righteousness" (Harris, p. 897). God's rod could be His direct dealings or His indirect working through the nations. "Metaphorically, the Lord used Assyria as his instrument to correct Israel (Isa

10:15) and the nations to correct his wayward king (II Sam 7:14)" (Harris, p. 897). God's rod will work in the lives of His people. Micah prays that this rod will lead them to food, their real need and God's true desire. Maybe after the nations like Assyria and Babylon have done their work, God's people will humbly wake up and say the simplest of phrases, "Lord, I'm hungry for spiritual food." Then, they will be ready to receive God's rich provisions.

Micah asserts what God already knows—that His people are "the flock of his inheritance" (Micah 7:14). Here Micah shows his high, transcendent view of God's people. They are His inheritance, which means He is working on them and with them, so that they will have a great future with Him. He will fully own them and be proud of them as His glorious possession for all the future. Micah describes God's people as those who "dwell alone in the forest in the midst of a garden land." These are very positive statements. Dwelling alone indicates that they are separate from the nations. Balaam prophesies that Israel would enjoy this separateness, "behold, a people dwelling alone, and not counting itself among the nations" (Numbers 23:9). Moses also prophesies the riches of being separate "Jacob lived alone, in a land of grain and wine, whose heavens drop down dew" (Deuteronomy 33:28). Living in a forest is also wonderful thing, a sign of the Lord's protection, "I will make with them a covenant of peace and banish wild beasts from the land, so that they may dwell securely in the wilderness and sleep in the woods" (Ezekiel 34:25). They are also living in a garden land (Hebrew, "Carmel") which signifies that they are in a fruitful, productive field.

In Micah's mind, as he prays, Israel is not in a bad situation. They are God's people, God's inheritance, and are separated from the nations in the protection of the woods enjoying the fruitful produce of a garden. However, Micah prays that God would shepherd them so that they would rise to an even higher level. They would not simply be separated in the woods and in a fertile garden. He wants God's rod to shepherd them so that they might feed in richer pastures. "Let them graze in Bashan and Gilead, as in the days of old" (Micah 7:14). Both Bashan and Gilead are known for being rich pasture lands, the best that the land of Canaan can provide for the hearty and substantial growth of the flocks of Israel (Numbers 32:1, Deuteronomy 32:14).

Keil reinforces how this prayer echoes God's promises and wishes, "The prayer is related to the promise in Mic. 5:3 ff., viz., that the ruler coming forth out of Bethlehem will feed in the strength of Jehovah, and involves the prayer for the sending of this ruler. "With this staff," i.e., the shepherd's staff (cf. Lev. 27:32; Ps. 23:4), is added pictorially; and as a support to the prayer, it designates the people as the sheep of Jehovah's inheritance" (p. 346). Additionally, he sees it as a prayer made by a future, godly, believing remnant for God to shepherd them, so that they may become the inheritance He desires. "The question in dispute among commentators, whether this prayer is addressed to the Lord by the prophet on behalf of the nation, or whether the prophet is still speaking in the name of the believing church, is decided in favour of the latter by the answer addressed to the church in v. 15" (Keil, p. 346). This indeed may be the case. However, Micah could also be placing himself as a member of that future remnant, as one of "them." In this case he utters the prayer himself on behalf of God's inheritance. This prayer is a cry that the Lord would do more, shepherd more, feed more, so that God's inheritance would not merely be alone, but would be richly fed to reach the full glory befitting God's inheritance.

God's marvelous answer

God answers the prayer in full and in a truly marvelous way. When Micah declared "as for me, I will look to the LORD" he also declared "my God hears me" (Micah 7:7). This answer to prayer shows that yes, it was really the case. God heard Micah and responded to his prayer.

> 15 As in the days when you came out of the land of Egypt, I will show them marvelous things.
> 16 The nations shall see and be ashamed of all their might; they shall lay their hands on their mouths; their ears shall be deaf;
> 17 they shall lick the dust like a serpent, like the crawling things of the earth; they shall come trembling out of their strongholds; they shall turn in dread to the Lord our God, and they shall be in fear of you.
> —Micah 7:15-17

In response to Micah's prayer, God will act again, renewing wonders like He enacted when Israel was coming out of Egypt. "He refers to the time when his people came out of Egypt, and he showed them his "wonders" (supernatural occurrences; see Ps 114 for the highlights of those miraculous wonders). His future mighty saving acts for them in a kind of new exodus and restoration will include numerous similar displays of his redemptive grace and power in their behalf" (Barker, p. 131). Just like the exodus caused Egypt to witness a great lesson concerning God's power, the nations will similarly be amazed. They will lay their hands on their mouths in awe. Their ears will be deaf because of the wonder. They will come trembling out of their strongholds.

Concluding New Testament Praise

After such a magnificent answer to prayer, the only thing left for Micah to do is praise, which is exactly what is recorded in the last three verses of the book.

> 18 Who is a God like you, pardoning iniquity and passing over transgression for the remnant of his inheritance? He does not retain his anger forever, because he delights in steadfast love.
> 19 He will again have compassion on us; he will tread our iniquities underfoot. You will cast all our sins into the depths of the sea.
> 20 You will show faithfulness to Jacob and steadfast love to Abraham, as you have sworn to our fathers from the days of old.
> —Micah 7:18-20

Micah's praise starts by focusing on God and His interest in the remnant (Micah 7:18). In the middle, he focuses on how God will cleanse His people from sin (Micah 7:19). He ends by focusing on God's faithfulness to His people as He has shown faithfulness to His called-out people throughout history (Micah 7:19). Putting these items of praise together, gives a pretty decent *New Testament* picture of God and His people.

First, Micah appreciates God, exclaiming, "Who is a God like you?" (Micah 7:18). What makes God so unique is His boundless mercy, "pardoning iniquity and passing over transgression." He will pour out forgiveness, overlook the worst infraction and pardon the most habitual iniquity for the sake of His remnant, because, as Micah says, this remnant is "the remnant of his inheritance" (Micah 7:18). God mentioning His inheritance here, indicates that God looks at His people and sees His own inheritance. If they will be inherited by

God, He must work with them, in order to make them fully fitting for Him. "What he could not and would not do for the criminals in the city (see 6:11) he delighted to do for the remnant of his inheritance (18), for those who, in the midst of his visitation (7:4), respond to his leadership" (Prior, p. 200).

The root of God's forgiveness and commitment to His people is that "he delights in steadfast love" (Micah 7:18). This is the Hebrew word, chesed, which a common word in the Minor Prophets, especially in Hosea, and which expresses the deep commitment God has toward His people in context of a covenant relationship. He takes pleasure in this kind of strong commitment to His covenant people. It is this commitment, which makes Him unique. "To behave in a kind, merciful and compassionate way is a sheer delight for the LORD our God....What marks the LORD out from all other gods is his steadfast love (hesed, 18, 20), a love located in the will which stresses mainly unchanging commitment; and also his compassion (19), a love that is mainly emotional" (Prior, p. 199).

In verse nineteen Micah considers the blessings that will come to God's people. God will have compassion on His people, tread their iniquities under His feet, and cast their sins in the sea. The Hebrew for "compassion" suggests a tender, maternal love such as a mother would have for her child. The Hebrew for "tread underfoot" also could be rendered "subdue." Sin is pictured as an enemy that God conquers and liberates His people from. "God overcomes sin and sets his people free. Fausset adds, "When God takes away the guilt of sin, that it may not condemn us, He takes away also the power of sin, that it may not rule us"" (Barker, p. 134). As if this were not glorious enough, Micah poetically portrays the great gulf that God will open between us and our sins. "You will cast all our sins into the depths of the sea" (Micah 7:19). Our sins are truly, really, absolutely, truthfully gone, just as if they have been thrown into the depths of the sea and will never be returned. "So he will hurl all "our" sins into the depths of the sea. This, of course, speaks of the complete forgiveness of sin and the removal of its guilt forever (see Jer 50:20). "God not only puts our sins out of sight [Isa 38:17]; he also puts them out of reach (Mic 7:19; Ps 103:12), out of mind (Jer 31:34), and out of existence (Isa 43:25; 44:22; Ps 51:1, 9; Acts 3:19)"" (Barker, p. 135).

Micah concludes his praise in verse twenty by linking God's future care for His people to the way God has worked in the past. God's coming care will be according to the faithfulness He showed to Jacob, the steadfast love He showed to Abraham and the promises He spoke to the fathers. Micah is transcendent, looking from past promises to future blessings, seeing God's eternal workings and praising Him for those things. "God had sworn to Abraham (Gen 22:17) and Jacob (Gen 28:14) that their descendants would be as numerous as the stars in the sky, the dust of the earth, and the sand on the seashore; and he had promised Abraham that he would be the father of many nations (Gen 17:5; cf. Luke 1:54–55). All believers are ultimately included in this promise (Rom 4; Gal 3:6–29; Heb 11:12)" (Barker, p. 1326). In short, Micah sees God's New Covenant, having begun with Abraham and being consummated with His people in the future. From this grand vantage point, Micah ends his words. There is really no better way. "It is a monument to the faith of men who transcend their earthly woes and climbed to a spiritual vantage point. From there they could survey the present in the reassuring light of God's past and future dealings with his covenant people" (Allen, p. 404).

CHAPTER SEVEN

NAHUM

I find it easiest to understand the book of Nahum by sectioning it into four different parts. The first section (after his introductory verse) is Nahum's vision of God, who is jealous and good, and his application of that vision (Nahum 1:2-11). Sections two through four each begin with God's direct, first-person speaking and end with Nahum's development of God's message. The second section begins with God announcing how He will free Judah from Assyria and ends with Nahum's vivid detail of Israel's freedom (Nahum 1:12-2:12). The third section begins with God cutting off Nineveh's messengers and concludes with Nahum's description of Nineveh's destruction (Nahum 2:13-3:4). The final section relates how God will judge Nineveh as a harlot and ends with Nahum describing how the earth will rejoice over that judgment (Nahum 3:5-19). As a visionary, Nahum expands God's messages in each of these sections and makes them striking to his readers. Put together, the sections convey a glorious vision of a jealous God (section one), the freedom God will give Israel (section two), the destruction of Nineveh (section three) and the earth's rejoicing over Nineveh's judgment (section four).

We know almost nothing about the biography of Nahum, beyond the fact that he is from the small town of Elkosh. Although the location of this town in uncertain, many commentators, including Jerome, think it is a small town in northern Galilee (Jerome, p. ??). Most likely, Nahum moved from that town to Jerusalem to prophecy. His prophecy mostly focusses on the city of Nineveh, which is the capital of the Assyrian Empire located on the site of the modern-day city of Mosul, Iraq. Nahum was not from a noble background, a grand family or an important city. He did, however, have a vision, which makes his contribution to God's word so important. He boldly claims that what he sees is a "vision" and what he writes is an "oracle," thus placing himself with other visionary prophets, such as Isaiah and Obadiah. He begins the book, "An oracle concerning Nineveh. The book of the vision of Nahum of Elkosh" (Nahum 1:1).

The jealous, avenging and good God

Nahum opens his prophecy with a powerful vision of God Himself. Nahum sees both God's jealous, avenging side (Nahum 1:2) and His good, protective side (Nahum 1:7).

> 2 The Lord is a jealous and avenging God; the Lord is avenging and wrathful; the Lord takes vengeance on his adversaries and keeps wrath for his enemies.
> 3 The Lord is slow to anger and great in power, and the Lord will by no means clear the guilty. His way is in whirlwind and storm, and the clouds are the dust of his feet.

> 4 He rebukes the sea and makes it dry; he dries up all the rivers; Bashan and Carmel wither; the bloom of Lebanon withers.
> 5 The mountains quake before him; the hills melt; the earth heaves before him, the world and all who dwell in it.
> 6 Who can stand before his indignation? Who can endure the heat of his anger? His wrath is poured out like fire, and the rocks are broken into pieces by him.
> 7 The Lord is good, a stronghold in the day of trouble; he knows those who take refuge in him.
> 8 But with an overflowing flood he will make a complete end of the adversaries, and will pursue his enemies into darkness.
>
> —Nahum 1:2-8

Nahum's initial description of God is universally true. He refers to no specific incident where God pronounces judgment. He provides no context for God's actions. Nahum begins his book by saying, "Here is God in truth. Look at Him. Understand His characteristics. The solution to any problem starts from understanding God. Any move that God makes will be consistent with His true, eternal, real character. Here He is." Before Nahum speaks about what God will do, he paints many characteristics of God so that his readers can understand who God is.

The jealous God

The first and foremost characteristic Nahum ascribes to God is that He is jealous. Nahum's clarion call begins "The Lord is a jealous and avenging God" (Nahum 1:2). In ascribing jealousy as God's first characteristic, Nahum is highlighting a fundamental feature of God's person, which God

Himself reveals in the second commandment, "You shall not bow down to them or serve them, for I the LORD your God am a jealous God" (Exodus 20:5). Even God's name is "Jealous," "You shall worship no other god, for the LORD, whose name is Jealous, is a jealous God" (Exodus 34:14). Later, we will see how Nahum's oracle describes God's wrath falling upon Nineveh. However, wrath is not the fundamental characteristic that God is displaying as Nineveh is destroyed. God doesn't delight in the death of the wicked. No, the underlying motivation for God's destruction of Nineveh is His jealousy for His people. God's jealousy is His motive for why His wrath falls. It is God's deep concern for something very dear to Him—His people and His righteousness.

Jealousy is often used in the Bible to describe an inappropriate feeling that causes a person to transgress. Joseph's brothers sold him into slavery because "his brothers were jealous of him" (Genesis 37:11). God's jealousy, however, is not inappropriate. Instead it shows His possession. The Hebrew word for Jealousy, *qannô'*, "expresses a very strong emotion whereby some quality or possession of the object is desired by the subject….The central meaning of our word, however, relates to "jealousy" especially in the marriage relationship" (Harris, p. 802). As the Husband of Israel, He will fiercely act in order to guard His most prized possession, His people as His bride. This feeling is similar to Solomon's intense feelings for the Shulamite. When Solomon considers his love for her, he links his love with his jealousy, "for love is strong as death, jealousy is fierce as the grave" (Song of Songs 8:6). "The Lord is jealous in the sense that he demands an exclusive relationship, zealously protects that relationship, and desires the worship that belongs to him alone" (Barker, p. 169).

As we consider the remainder of Nahum's description of God, especially his description of God's wrath and vengeance, we must keep in mind the fundamental driver of these wrathful actions is His jealousy, which is deeply rooted in His love. Because of God's jealous love, He will move to deliver His people from oppression. In the process, He will deliver the entire world from tyrannical rule and evil oppression. "God is jealous, and Jehovah revengeth. It is a solemn thought that, however great His patience, a day is coming which will prove that He does not bear with evil. Yet it is a comforting thought; for the vengeance of God is the deliverance of the world from the oppression and misery of the yoke of the enemy and of lust, that it may flourish under the peaceful eye of its Deliverer" (Darby, p. 579).

The Lord is avenging and wrathful

It is truly fearful to experience the wrath of the living God. Anyone who opposes God will one day taste this wrath, "The LORD takes vengeance on his adversaries and keeps wrath for his enemies" (Nahum 1:3). Nahum portrays that nothing will be able to stand in the way of God exercising His full power to pour out His wrath. First, Nahum makes it clear that God is able to go anywhere to administer His wrath. His way is in the whirlwind and storm (Nahum 1:3). Just as a ferocious wind rips apart dwellings and levels fortresses, God in His wrath overpowers all barriers. Clouds are like the dust that His feet walk upon (Nahum 1:3). Wherever a cloud can reach, the wrathful God can travel there and pour out His horrible judgment. Second, any barrier can be broken by God. A sea or river is no barrier to Him, as evidenced by His breaking through the Red Sea and Jordan River (Nahum 1:4). Third, no earthly provision provides protection from His wrath. Bashan and Carmel, places known for abundant produce can be dried up by Him in an instant. Lebanon, known for its strong Cedars, will wither at His will (Nahum 1:5). Fourth, no place in the earth or under the earth will be safe. No mountain, hill, rock or cave can inhibit the pouring out of the great wrath of God (Nahum 1:6). The wicked should be warned by this fierce description. They can't go anyplace where God will not reach. They cannot be protected by a river, a sea or a rock. No fruitful field or abundant wealth will mitigate the severe power of His vengeance. Even if they burrow deep in the mountains of the earth, they will not avoid His wrath. Only one place will offer any protection from this terrible wrath. That place is in God Himself. The underlying message is, therefore, "Get to God."

God is good, a stronghold in the day of trouble

"The LORD is good, a stronghold in the day of trouble; he knows those who take refuge in him" (Nahum 1:7). Almost every word of this verse shows how good and rich God is to those who seek Him. The Hebrew word for stronghold, *mā ʿôz*, is used to describe the protection of many different things in the Old Testament. *Mā ʿôz* describes a mountain, a harbor, a city, a temple, even a great world-power like Egypt. All these things may be a stronghold for protection against some trials. However, none of these strongholds protect against God's wrath. For that, we must realize that the strongest stronghold is God Himself. It is man's job to discover just how strong God's stronghold is as compared with the other strongholds. "See the man who would not make God his refuge [*mā ʿôz*], but trusted in the abundance of his riches" (Psalm 52:7). "By far the most common use of this word is the figurative one, designating God as the refuge of his people" (Harris, p. 652). While it is true that God is an ever-present stronghold (Psalm 27:1), He is also a particular stronghold, just when His people need Him—in the day of trouble (Nahum 1:7).

Furthermore, God knows those who take refuge in Him. Barker comments on the Hebrew word for "know." "The Hebrew term *yd'* (NIV "cares for") means literally "to know." God wants a personal relationship with his people in which they know him as a person, and he knows everything about them. Such knowledge is the basis of a relationship in which he can truly show care and concern (Exod 33:12; Pss 31:7; 91:14; Jer 1:5; 12:3)" (p. 178). This word points to the intimate relationship between God and His people when His people truly acknowledge, trust and rely on Him as their stronghold. What a glory it is to rely on God! When one of God's people rely on Him, He "knows" them. That is, He "recognizes as His own (Ho 13:5; Am 3:2); and so, cares for and guards (Ps 1:6; 2 Ti 2:19)" (Jamieson et al, p. 697) them.

Seeking refuge is a genuine sign of trust. The Hebrew word for "seek refuge" is *ḥāsâ*, which means *"seek refuge, flee for protection and thus figuratively put trust in* (God), *confide, hope in* (God or person)" (Harris, p. 307). To seek refuge is an active term, denoting more than simply trust. One actively seeks shelter from a rainstorm (Job 24:8). "The root is probably to be distinguished from *bāṭaḥ* "rely on," "take refuge in" as denoting more precipitate action" (Harris, p. 307). To seek refuge means that that person needs God. ""To seek refuge" stresses the insecurity and self-helplessness of even the strongest of men. It emphasizes the defensive or external aspect of salvation in God, the unchanging one in whom we "find shelter"" (Harris, p. 308). No one who seeks refuge in God is cursed. There is only advantage, blessing, strength and as Nahum mentions here, the knowledge of God. "The result of taking refuge in God is to be "blessed" (Ps 2:12) and be "saved" (Ps 17:7). Such a person should rejoice (Ps 5:11 [H 12]), find goodness (Ps 31:19 [H 20]) and "possess the land" (Isa 57:13)" (Harris, p. 308).

It is a fair question to ask what such a positive description of God is doing in the book of Nahum. "The Lord is good" (Nahum 1:7) is stuck between descriptions of "the heat of his anger" (Nahum 1:6) and "he will pursue his enemies into darkness" (Nahum 1:8). The position that this verse occupies reminds the readers that God is so good. Even though His people pass through "trouble," He is available, near and eager to provide a stronghold equal to no other. For those who show even the slightest inclination towards Him, He is there for them. Just like a person who ducks into a bus shelter to get out of the rain, God is "all in" for that person. Not only does God protect that person, but He also "knows" him in the most intimate way. God does not simply act as a refuge for "His people"—denoting an amorphous mass. He acts as a refuge for "Jim" and "Sally" and "Arnold" and "Peter" and "Nancy." He knows each one.

Another reason this verse is here may be to expand our thought of exactly how God can protect us. His being a stronghold does not end when "the day of trouble" is over. Even after "the day of trouble" God still works to avenge His people from their adversaries. In fact, in the big picture of things, God will not stop until the entire earth is cleared up of all evil, so that His people can live in true peace with Him. When a person says, "God you are my refuge," he receives God as his protection throughout his entire life. He is a stronghold in the day of trouble *and* He will "make a complete end of his adversaries" (Nahum 1:8). This is how Nahum reconciles seemingly irreconcilable characteristics of God: jealousy, wrath, vengeance, goodness, and stronghold. "Nahum described God as jealous, avenging, and good. Though these attributes seem contradictory, Nahum showed the righteousness of a caring God, a God who is zealous for the well-being of his people. After all, what truly good human being could sit idly by in the face of cruel oppression such as that meted out by Assyria? How much less could God allow such wickedness to continue? "At the heart of his message is a recognition of Yahweh as a God of justice who will not let injustice and oppression go unpunished'" (Barker, p. 154).

Judah questions if God is able

After presenting this vision of God, Nahum proceeds to apply the vision to the oppressed people of Judah and to the Ninevites. He asks the people of Judah,

> 9 What do you plot against the Lord? He will make a complete end; trouble will not rise up a second time.
> 10 For they are like entangled thorns, like drunkards as they drink; they are consumed like stubble fully dried.
> 11 From you came one who plotted evil against the Lord, a worthless counselor.
> —Nahum 1:9-11

While many commentators consider the question in v. 9 "What do you plot against the Lord" to be addressed to God's enemies, I agree with Keil, that it fits the context of the section best to consider this question to be addressed to Judah. "Consequently the question, "What think ye with regard to Jehovah?" can only be addressed to the Judaeans, and must mean, "Do ye think that Jehovah cannot or will not fulfil His threat upon Nineveh?" (Cyr., Marck, Strauss). The prophet addresses these words to the anxious minds, which were afraid of fresh invasions on the part of the Assyrians" (Keil, p. 360). The prophet then comforts the oppressed nation, by telling them that God will truly make a complete end of Assyria and that "trouble will not rise up a second time," i.e. Assyria will be so completely destroyed that there is no way that they will be able to rise up again to give you trouble. Although Assyria looks like a tangle of thorns, which is impossible to walk through, and like drunkards with no reason to direct them, they will become like dry stubble and be burned. To the Ninevites, Nahum says, "From you came one who plotted evil against the Lord, a worthless counselor" (Nahum 1:11). Nahum is saying, "Nineveh, from you came a person who was against the Lord. You are on the wrong side concerning God. He will not be a refuge towards you. Rather, His wrath and vengeance are coming."

God's first words—God will break Assyria's yoke off Judah

This second section of Nahum begins with God speaking in the first person. The prophet conveys God's direct claim that He Himself will free His people from affliction, yoke and bondage. To deliver these words of comfort Nahum assumes his most formal, authoritative stance in the book. He utters the words so common to prophets, "Thus says the Lord" (Nahum 1:12). This is "the prophet's guarantee that the predictions that follow are not merely human conjecture but the *dicta* of the infallible God Himself … the prophet's open declaration that his utterances are inspired, that he, as God's mouthpiece, speaks the message of divine, unchangeable truth" (Barker, p. 183). God's direct speaking provides the base for Nahum's later explanation. Nahum will soon apply this word in more detail, explaining it and vividly depicting the consequences of God's message of freedom.

12 Thus says the Lord, "Though they are at full

> strength and many, they will be cut down and pass away. Though I have afflicted you, I will afflict you no more.
> 13 And now I will break his yoke from off you and will burst your bonds apart."
> —Nahum 1:12-13

The Lord comforts Judea by declaring that even though their Assyrian enemies are now at full strength, they will soon be "cut down and pass away" (Nahum 1:12). The word for "cut down" is "taken from the mowing of the meadows, [and] is a figure denoting complete destruction" (Keil, p. 361). It is also used for shearing sheep and cutting hair. God is saying that the enemy Assyria will be cut just like grass, wool and hair. They will come to a complete end.

God also comforts Judah by declaring that He will soon lift their affliction. For discipline's sake, God had put His people under affliction. Now, however, like a loving father, God has realized that the affliction has done its work and should end. The Hebrew word for "affliction" is translated in other places as "impoverished," "violated" and "humbled." It is what God's people experienced in their 400 years in Egypt (Genesis 15:13) and what Jeremiah experienced when God's wrath came, "I am the man who has seen affliction under the rod of his wrath" (Lamentations 3:1). God allows affliction to come upon His people that they may learn to trust in Him, become purified, humble themselves and eventually learn to fight for Him. When His goal for His people is reached, God is happy to lift the affliction, which is an experience of great joy, "The meek [lit. afflicted] shall obtain fresh joy in the LORD" (Isaiah 29:19). This is a reminder that affliction administered by God will never go too far so as to do damage. God will relent when the work is done. "God is the afflicter as well as the deliverer from affliction. Assyria had not had a free hand in gaining control of Judah. God had made them his rod of oppression and discipline. Now Assyria would not have a free hand in maintaining control of Judah. God would intervene and deliver his people from affliction by afflicting Assyria" (Barker, p. 186).

Ending Judah's affliction means that God will break the "yoke" and burst the "bonds" that lay heavily upon His people. Judah's affliction is described as the people laboring under a heavy yoke that was tied to them by bonds. Surely the Assyrians had kept the Israelites under a harsh yoke, imposing a heavy tribute upon Hezekiah and the kingdom, which, tragically, was paid from the temple treasury (2 Kings 18:14-15). The outward bondage involving physical money was surely a picture of their inward, spiritual bondage under God's affliction. This, God declares, will stop. "People in ancient societies unambiguously understood the pictorial language and the meaning of the verse. The yoke referred to the wooden bar placed over the neck of the ox, and the bonds (shackles) indicated the leather straps used to attach the yoke to the ox's neck….Breaking the yoke bar and snapping the bonds allowed the animal to go free" (Barker, p. 186). Freedom from affliction is freedom from the yoke and the bonds of that yoke. "The heavy weight of slaving long hours with excessive burdens will give way to the glorious liberty of the children of God, each person living in freedom to pursue his own labors to the glory of God" (Barker, p. 186).

The next verse records God's commandment to Nineveh, which contains none of the measured discipline that God lovingly metes out to His own people for correction. God corrects His own people for repentance. But God judges the foreigners for elimination.

> 14 The Lord has given commandment about you: "No more shall your name be perpetuated; from the house of your gods I will cut off the carved image and the metal image. I will make your grave, for you are vile."
>
> —Nahum 1:14

Nahum's vivid portrayal of God's speaking

Nahum 1:15-2:2 contain Nahum's exhortation, warning, and explanation based on God's direct words in 1:12-14. He exhorts and encourages Judah (Nahum 1:15), soberly warns Nineveh (Nahum 2:1), and explains God overall purpose for judging Nineveh—the restoration of the majesty of Jacob (Nahum 2:2).

Nahum's strong encouragement to Judah

> 15 Behold, upon the mountains, the feet of him who brings good news, who publishes peace! Keep your feasts, O Judah; fulfill your vows, for never again shall the worthless pass through you; he is utterly cut off.
>
> —Nahum 1:15

In Nahum's encouragement he asks the people to imagine a scene where a messenger is speedily traveling through the mountains. Look at those feet move! Maybe these mountains are the Judean hills north of Jerusalem, which fall along the pathway that a messenger would take coming from Nineveh to Jerusalem. This messenger brings "good news," translated by the Septuagint as *euangelizō*, from which we get the word "gospel." This messenger is proclaiming a wonderful word—peace, which in Hebrew is the word *šālōm*. "God's work has been to proclaim peace *(šālōm)* to all people of all ages" (Barker, p. 190). In Hebrew "peace" is not merely the lack of conflict, but a denotes a wholeness and overall health. "The Hebrew word for 'peace' is one of the most remarkable words in that ancient biblical language. Its meaning is much more profound than simply the cessation of war. It refers to wholeness, completeness, total well-being" (Barker, p. 191).

Good news and peace are wholesome words resulting from lifting the Ninevite yoke. Before their affliction was lifted, Judah had no good news and no peace. Instead, they had been falling away from God, who was then forced to afflict them with the yoke of Assyria for their discipline. This announcement of good news and peace indicates more than simply a return to the state Judah was in before they bore the yoke. It was much better than that. The yoke had done its work to free them from what ailed them. Now, that the yoke was gone *and* the condition of the people was different, good news and peace take on a much richer meaning. This is really good news. It is as if chemotherapy is now finished. Not only is the suffering from the medicine over. The cancer is gone. Thus, the messenger's words, "wholeness, peace, completeness," are very good news indeed.

Nahum next advises the nation about what they should do in this new setting, where affliction is gone, the yoke and bonds are broken and peace is real. They should not turn this occasion into a self-centered celebration where they use their freedom to advance their own selfish interests. Rather, they should celebrate with joyful worship of God their Savior. "Keep your feasts, O Judah. Fulfill your vows" (Nahum 1:15). On the one hand, Nahum's exhortation was because "the feasts could not be properly kept during the oppression by the enemy, or at any rate could not be visited by those who lived at a distance from the temple" (Keil, p. 363). On the other hand, it was a great encouragement to enjoy and thank the Lord. "The great yearly feasts were feasts of thanksgiving for the blessings of salvation, which Israel owed to the Lord, so that the summons to celebrate these feasts involved the admonition to thank the Lord for His mercy in destroying the hostile power of the world. This is expressed still more clearly in the summons to pay their vows" (Keil, p. 363). Nahum's exhortation opens the way for Judah to use this opportunity to renew their consecration to the Lord. "You now have freedom," he proclaims, "now use it to greatly enjoy the Lord." "Nahum called Israel to celebration, a celebration based on the belief that the announced victory had actually occurred. Celebration was not a wild victory party. Celebration was a return to God's house to keep God's worship festivals in the way God commanded. "Neglect of the festivals and the vows was the same as neglecting Yahweh." In this way "they shall respond to redemption by renewed consecration to the Lord"'" (Barker, p. 192).

The vows that Nahum refers to are wonderful, because they are over and above any temple worship requirements that God places upon His people. God requires His people to keep certain feasts throughout the year. All the nation is to gather in Jerusalem to enjoy the Passover, Pentecost, etc. Keeping these yearly feasts is a truly marvelous thing, because they usher the people into a rich enjoyment of God's provision, grace and bounty. God also requires that His people offer some sacrifices. For instance, a sin or trespass offering must be made when a person sins or during certain festival occasions. This is a joyous requirement leading God's people into an experience of God's forgiveness and grace. Vows, as spoken about here by Nahum, are something beyond all these required offerings. A vow is made simply because a person loves the Lord, wishes to thank the Lord or is happy for the Lord's overflowing blessing. It can be made at any time of the year. There is no need to wait for a festival. It is not made because there is a need of forgiveness or restitution. Any person at any time may simply say, "I love God and I want to thank Him. Let's take this bull to the temple and worship the Lord and enjoy Him together." Here Nahum's encouragement is not simply to offer a necessary offering, but to go beyond. It is interesting that the offering associated with vows is the peace offering, just like this messenger proclaims peace to the people. Richly enjoying the Lord is what Judah's freedom is for, what peace is for and what life is for.

A sober warning to Nineveh

Next, Nahum turns to Nineveh and, in a sense say, "get ready, you will soon be attacked." He says, "The scatterer has come up against you. Man the ramparts; watch the road; dress for battle; collect all your strength" (Nahum 2:1).

God's motives for Nineveh's destruction

Then, Nahum explains to the entire universe what God's motives are for this move.

> 2   For the Lord is restoring the majesty of Jacob as the majesty of Israel, for plunderers have plundered them and ruined their branches.
> —Nahum 2:2

This verse is a window into God's motivation and goal for all that Nahum is describing in his book. Previously, Nahum described how God is jealous. Here we see what God's jealousy inspires Him to do—restore the majesty of Jacob. Jacob's majesty could be construed in a very outward way. It could simply be the restoration of the geographical boundaries and economic vitality of the nation. "By 627 B.C. Israel had fallen to the Assyrians almost a century earlier, and Judah consisted of a small area surrounding Jerusalem. The former splendor of the nation now consisted only of ancient memories" (Barker, p. 200). However, Jacob's majesty, or "eminence," is not merely the physical extent of the kingdom. The word can denote the most particular thing about God's people—God's choice of them, His dwelling among them and His involving them in His purpose. Keil considers majesty to mean, "that of which Jacob is proud, i.e., the eminence and greatness or glory accruing to Israel by virtue of its election to be the nation of God, which the enemy into whose power it had been given up on account of its rebellion against God had taken away (see at Amos 6:8)" (Keil, p. 19). God is now restoring Judah's vibrancy of purpose, vitality of relationship, and immediacy of being God's special treasure. This is the true majesty of Jacob that the jealous God is restoring.

This verse shows God's process of restoration. God's restoration follows "the plunderers" who plundered the nation and who ruined the "branches." The word for plunder is also translated "empty." When the Assyrians afflicted the nation, they actually emptied it out. They even "ruined their branches" (Nahum 2:2). To ruin a branch does not mean to destroy the vine. Rather, it means to destroy a branch of the vine, just like the Israelites cut one branch from a grape vine in the land of Canaan, when they "cut down from there a branch with a single cluster of grapes" (Numbers 13:23). Pusey sees a lot in this picture. He sees a vine that has been pruned and a people who have been emptied. After being emptied, God could restore the majesty to the nation giving them their rightful place as God's peculiar treasure and dwelling place. Nineveh is simply a tool in this process. It was used to empty the nation and destroy its branches. When that process was complete, God lays aside Nineveh and restores the majesty of Jacob. If our eyes are on Nineveh, we will never understand what is happening in the world. However, if our eyes are on the jealous God who is restoring majesty to His people, then all things with His people and with the world situation makes sense. Pusey remarks, "Their chastisement is the channel for their restoration. Unlike the world, their emptiness is their fullness, as the fullness of the world is its emptiness" (p. 142). He sees in this hints of the vine described by the Lord, "its fruit-bearing branches, that, as far as in them lay, it should not bear fruit unto God; but to cut the vine is, by God's grace, to make it shoot forth and bear fruit more abundantly" (Pusey, p. 142).

The destruction of Nineveh

The remainder of Nahum's prophesy is straightforward. It concerns Nahum's vivid portrayal of the destruction of Nineveh. As we read Nahum's imagery, we are reminded of one of the functions of a visionary. Nahum presents the direct speaking of the Lord in a vivid way such that his readers feel that they are right there, living in the moment, witnessing with front row seats how the word of God will be fulfilled.

As a sample of Nahum's vivid portrayals of God's speaking, consider an example from the second section of the book. In Nahum 1:14 God speaks directly to Nineveh, saying, "I make your grave." In Nahum 2:3-12, the prophet portrays this word as an exciting story that puts a person on the edge of their seat. Nahum sets the scene of the attacking armies (the Babylonians and Medes), "The shield of his mighty men is red; his soldiers are clothed in scarlet. The chariots come with flashing metal on the day he musters them; the cypress spears are brandished" (Nahum 2:3). He then paints the picture of the chaos in Nineveh as the army begins the siege, "The chariots race madly through the streets; they rush to and fro through the squares; they gleam like lightening; they dart like torches" (Nahum 2:4). As the city falls in the vision, Nahum encourages the plunderers, saying, "Plunder the silver, plunder the gold! There is no end of the treasure or the wealth of all precious things" (Nahum 2:9). Then Nahum zooms out and declares the destruction he sees "Desolate! Desolation and ruin! Hearts melt and knees tremble; anguish is in all loins; all faces grow pale" (Nahum 2:10). "The lion tore enough for his cubs and strangled prey for his lionesses" (Nahum 2:12). After reading this, one can imagine the fear that the well-dressed, highly-trained soldiers produce and the chaos that reigns in the city as it is being attacked.

God's second direct speaking—God will cut off Nineveh's prey and messengers

God's second set of direct, first-person words describe how God will limit Nineveh's effect on many nations, not just its effect on Judah. "Behold, I am against you, declares the LORD of hosts, and I will burn your chariots in smoke, and the sword shall devour your young lions. I will cut off your prey from the earth, and the voice of your messengers shall no longer be heard" (Nahum 2:13). Here, "prey" refers to the nations that Nineveh oppressed and plundered. The "messengers" refer to the people that Nineveh relies upon to communicate with the empire. In speaking these words, God is making Nahum realize the extent to which Nineveh has affected all the nations. No longer is Nineveh simply an afflicter of Judah. God's judgment of her will free many nations, "the prey" who suffered under her weight. God's judgment will limit the influence of the Assyrian king by limiting the messengers that inform him and carry out his orders covering the far reaches of his empire.

In Nahum 3:1-4, Nahum carries out his visionary job by livingly portraying what God has said in Nahum 2:13. Now he looks at the city and sees its oppression, saying, "Woe to the bloody city, all full of lies and plunder—no end to the prey" (Nahum 3:1). He brings the reader into the feeling. "The crack of the whip, and rumble of the wheel, galloping horse and bounding chariot! Horsemen charging, flashing sword and glittering spear, hosts of slain, heaps of corpses, dead bodies without end— they stumble over the bodies!" (Nahum 3:2-3). Nahum explains more of what God meant by "prey." He explains that this severe judgment is because "countless whorings of the prostitute…who betrays nations with her whorings, and peoples with her charms" (Nahum 3:4). "As Assyria was not a worshipper of the true God, "whoredoms" cannot mean, as in the case of Israel, apostasy to the worship of false gods; but, her *harlot-like artifices* whereby she allured neighboring states so as to subject them to herself. As the unwary are allured by the "well-favored harlot's" looks, so Israel, Judah (for example, under Ahaz, who, calling to his aid Tiglath-pileser, was made tributary by him, 2 Ki 16:7–10), and other nations, were tempted by the plausible professions of Assyria, and by the lure of commerce (Rev 18:2, 3), to trust her" (Jamieson et al, Vol. 1, p. 699).

God's third direct speaking—God's judgment of the harlot Nineveh

The last section of Nahum begins with God's direct, first-person speaking about how Nineveh will be judged, and all the earth will rejoice.

> 5 Behold, I am against you, declares the Lord of hosts, and will lift up your skirts over your face; and I will make nations look at your nakedness and kingdoms at your shame.
> 6 I will throw filth at you and treat you with contempt and make you a spectacle.
> 7 And all who look at you will shrink from you and say, "Wasted is Nineveh; who will grieve for her?" Where shall I seek comforters for you?
>
> —Nahum 3:5-7

Here, God declares to the city, "I am against you" and follows His words with a description of shaming fit for a prostitute, saying that He, "will lift your skirts over your face" (see Ezekiel 16:37 as an example of this punishment for prostitutes). Then, God describes the reaction of the nations, "all who look at you will shrink from you and say, "Wasted is Nineveh: who will grieve for her?"" (Nahum 3:7).

In the remainder of the chapter, Nahum brings these words to life with pictures, examples and metaphors. Nahum asks Nineveh "Are you better than Thebes that sat by the Nile, with water all around her, her rampart a sea, and water her wall" (Nahum 3:8). In bringing up Thebes, a city in Egypt that was conquered by Assyria, Nahum is using Assyria's own glorious conquest against a seemingly impenetrable, well-defended city to let Nineveh know that her own defenses are no security. Under the Assyrian onslaught Thebes was devastated, "her infants were dashed in pieces" and "all her great men were bound in chains" (Nahum 3:10). Nahum colorfully describes how Nineveh's defenses will similarly crumble. He says, "All your fortresses are like fig trees with first-ripe figs—if shaken they fall into the mouth of the eater" (Nahum 3:12). Nineveh's leaders will fly away just like locusts who warm up in the morning, "Your princes are like grasshoppers, your scribes like clouds of locusts settling on the fences in a day of cold—when the sun rises, they fly away; no one knows where they are" (Nahum 3:17).

As a finale, Nahum sets the scene for Nineveh's funeral, expanding upon God's words, "who will grieve for her" (Nahum 3:7). Unlike most funerals, this gathering is joyous, because Nineveh was hated by all. "There is no easing your hurt; your wound is grievous. All who hear the news about you clap their hands over you. For upon whom has not come your unceasing evil?" After portraying this final picture, Nahum's job is done. He has conveyed to the best of his ability all the words and thoughts of God. He has fulfilled his claim of having a book of vision. God's words were alive, full of impact and openly portrayed for all who read them.

CHAPTER EIGHT

HABAKKUK

The book of Habakkuk records a conversation between the prophet and God. This dialogue provides the structure for the book. It begins with the prophet asking God a question concerning the violence he sees among God's people (Habakkuk 1:2-4). God answers, saying that He will raise up the Chaldeans, a godless people, to discipline the Judeans (Habakkuk 1:5-11). Habakkuk appreciates God's care, realizes that God is his "Rock" but wonders how God can use such unrighteous people to discipline His nation, which is at least a little more righteous than the Chaldeans (Habakkuk 1:12-2:1). God answers by saying that the righteous will live by faith and that the Chaldeans will indeed be punished (Habakkuk 2:2-20). Habakkuk ends with a prayer, asking God to revive His work, praising Him for His future appearing in context of His many great past works, and declaring how elevated he himself has become because he found strength in God (Habakkuk 3).

How can the holy God bear with unrighteousness in His people?

Habakkuk begins his book in a rather contemplative mood. It is as if he is gazing down from an upstairs window onto a busy square in Jerusalem and considering the iniquity and violence of God's people. He laments that, "Destruction and violence are before me; strife and contention arise" (Habakkuk 1:3) and, "The wicked surround the righteous; so justice goes forth perverted" (Habakkuk 1:4). In this contemplative mood, however, the prophet doesn't merely lament the iniquity he sees in Judah. He allows the iniquity he sees to cause him to question God Himself. He wonders how God, who is holy, can bear with a people so full of iniquity. Habakkuk clearly has a certain understanding about who God is. He considers Him to be a righteous God who cannot bear unrighteousness. However, the situation he sees among God's people does not mesh with this understanding of who God is. Thus, he becomes constricted within. He is torn up inside due to the violence among God's people, the unwillingness of God to do anything about it and the inability of God's law to affect it. He questions God, wondering "why do you look idly at the wrong" (Habakkuk 1:3). He laments that the law is powerless to affect God's people, saying, "So the law is paralyzed" (Habakkuk 1:4).

Iniquity in the nation is by no means a new thing. Many years ago, there was iniquity in Israel. However, at that time, somehow, God did not "see" it. When Israel was about to cross the Jordan River, Balaam prophesied over the nation, saying, God "has not beheld misfortune in Jacob, nor has he seen trouble in Israel" (Numbers 23:21), even though there was much iniquity in Israel at that time. At Habakkuk's time, however, it is different. Now God sees the iniquity yet doesn't do anything about it. God simply looks idly by. This is the contradiction that tears Habakkuk apart. "God not only lets the prophet see iniquity, but even looks at it Himself. This is at variance with His holiness" (Keil, p. 392).

Furthermore, Habakkuk has a history of pleading to God to make the situation right. And he has heard nothing in response to his prayers! He despairs, "how long shall I cry for help and you shall not hear?" (Habakkuk 1:2). He questions God, wondering how long he will "cry to you "Violence!" and you will not save" (Habakkuk 1:2). His long prayed and, as yet unanswered prayers lead the prophet to the brink of despair. Such words provide a window into the prophet's thoughts. Seemingly, he is at a breaking point, in depression and close to despair. "The prophet is at a point where he doubts whether God is interested in sorting out the situation. But he is also nearer to concluding that God is incapable of putting things right" (Prior, p. 211). In despairing moments, he might even question if God *can* save, not simply why He does not. "Behind how long? Is the unspoken cry, 'I have my limits.' Behind why? Is the insistence, 'I must have reasons.' God's silence is impenetrable and intolerable" (Prior, p. 209).

The desperation Habakkuk feels because of this contradiction is palpable. In his prayer he is looking for some glimmer of hope that will allow him to go on with God. "Habakkuk believes that the limits of his tolerance will be extended if he is able to understand why God is acting—or not acting—in a particular way" (Prior, p. 209). He will be attentive to any response God gives, as he desperately seeks light that will enlarge his understanding and give him a pathway forward.

I will send the Chaldeans to judge Israel

God's response to Habakkuk is to ask him to look beyond the borders of Judah. He is to look beyond the square that he may be gazing at from his second story window to the nations far away. If he does this, he will no longer be pining that his eyes are seeing iniquity. Instead, he will be utterly amazed, even to the point of not even believing what he is seeing. "Look among the nations, and see; wonder and be astounded. For I am doing a work in your days that you would not believe if told. For behold, I am raising up the Chaldeans" (Habakkuk 1:5-6). "Habakkuk is thus instructed—he and his people—to turn his eyes away from his own little world and watch God at work on a wider canvas. Like us, the prophet had become preoccupied, if not obsessed, with his own situation. His horizons had narrowed to the limits of his own vision and experience. He could not lift himself above the daily events of his particular circumstances. Because God seemed to be inactive, indeed absent, he was becoming sucked into a downward spiral of doubt and despair" (Prior, p. 212).

God's answer stretches Habakkukk's understanding concerning the grand scale upon which God works. His venue is not just the little nation of Judah. It is the whole earth. "God's raising the Chaldeans showed that he is sovereign over the whole earth. He is not confined to one nation or one people (cf. Amos 9:7). God can work through other peoples to accomplish his purpose. God used the Assyrians as the "rod of his anger" to punish recalcitrant Judah at an earlier time (Isa 10:5–15). He chose Cyrus the Mede to deliver the people of Judah from the exile imposed by the Babylonians (Isa 45:1). In Habakkuk's day God would use Babylon to punish Judah for its rebellion against the Lord" (Barker, p. 305).

God describes to Habakkuk just how terrifying the Chaldeans will be. They are "a bitter and hasty nation" (Habakkuk 1:6) who seizes dwellings that are not their own. "Their horses are swifter than leopards" and "they fly like an eagle swift to devour" (Habakkuk 1:8 cf Deuteronomy 28:49). "They all come for violence" (Habakkuk 1:9). "At kings they scoff, and at rulers they laugh" (Habakkuk 1:10). They are irreverent towards the God of the Hebrews. In fact, they have their own god. God even declares, that their "own might is their god" (Habakkuk 1:11).

Wait! Aren't the coming Chaldeans less righteous than the Israelites?

God's response assures Habakkuk that God will act. He is greatly reassured to know that God is not blindly looking away from iniquity and is still caring for His people. Additionally, even though the coming judgment will be harsh, God will honor His covenant and not go so far as to wipe His people off the face of the earth. Habakkuk states this assurance at the opening of his response, saying, "Are you not from everlasting, O LORD my God, my Holy One? We shall not die" (Habakkuk 1:12). Here, he intimately acknowledges God in three wonderful ways. He calls Him "Lord," using His name, Yahweh. He intimately calls Him "my God," using His name, ʾĕlōhîm. And He reassuringly calls Him "my Holy One," emphasizing God's purity. Yahweh is a term used to denote relationship. Elohim is God's name used to denote the Creator. The Holy One shows his purity and transcendence, even though the nation may be unholy. "The God to whom the prophet prays is *Jehovah*, the absolutely constant One, who is always the same in word and work (see at Gen. 2:4); He is also *Elohai, my*, i.e., Israel's, God, who from time immemorial has proved to the people whom He had chosen as His possession that He is their God; and the Holy One of Israel, the absolutely Pure One, who cannot look upon evil, and therefore cannot endure that the wicked should devour the righteous (v. 13)" (Keil, p. 396). The three names are a balm to the prophet and a firm assurance that the covenant keeping God will not abandon His people. They will not be abandoned to internal rot due to the violence within their own community or to the ravages of the Chaldeans. "It reflects the way his faith is beginning to rise, as he rehearses the attributes of God in prayer. Such growth in faith can come to us also, when we deliberately turn our eyes away from the gods of secular society to the LORD God" (Prior, p. 221). Armed with a new-found, restored and rising faith, Habakkuk declares, "We shall not die." He concludes that God is faithful and will come through for His people.

In the same breath, Habakkuk also acknowledges that he sees how God will work. He understands God's chosen way of dealing with His errant nation by raising up the Chaldeans. "O LORD, you have ordained them as a judgment, and you, O Rock, have established them for reproof" (Habakkuk 1:12) By saying that God is his "Rock" he is affirming his strong faith in God alone. By saying that the Chaldeans are for "reproof" he is affirming that God sees them as a means to discipline the nation, not totally destroy it.

God's response not only assures Habakkuk. It also raises more questions. We will see that some of these questions are challenging and bold. This time, however, Habakkuk can ask his questions from a more secure, assured base of seeing God as his "Rock." "Habakkuk has become free to remonstrate with God at this level only after planting his feet firmly on the Rock (12), on God's eternal changelessness and on his personal commitment in a covenantal relationship between God and the prophet....Paradoxically, his very strong inner security, as a person beloved by and belonging to God, releases him to batter the gates of heaven and berate the living God" (Prior, p. 222). From this strong foundation, Habakkuk can honestly unveil the concerns of his heart to God.

Habakkuk wonders how God could use such unrighteous people as the Chaldeans to punish His own people. He argues that Israel, even though it is full of iniquity, is more righteous than the wicked Chaldeans. He questions how God could stand by idly and let this whole thing play out in the way He has chosen, "Why do you idly look at traitors and remain silent when the wicked swallows up the man more righteous than he?" (Habakkuk 1:13). Furthermore, Habakkuk wonders how God could allow the evil Chaldeans to pillage and oppress many other nations. Not only will the Israelites suffer, but many other peoples will as well. Habakkuk considers the people of the world to be those made in God's image. When he thinks about how the Chaldeans will destroy these people, he questions God about how He made these men, accusing Him, "You make mankind like the fish of the sea, like crawling things that have no ruler" (Habakkuk 1:14). Instead of making man in His own image, it appeared to Habakkuk that God made man like fish, ready to be scooped up in the wicked net of the Chaldeans. Instead of making man after His likeness, who could be organized into a society, it appeared to Habakkuk that God made man like the creeping things of the earth, who had no ruler and no culture.

Habakkuk's second set of challenging questions to God reveals what is in his heart. Just as before, Habakkuk demonstrates that he has a certain understanding of God, what God should do and how God should do it. When he sees a situation that disagrees with his understanding, he accuses God of being inconsistent. "Because Habakkuk knew so much of the Lord, he appeared incredulous concerning God's work among the nations. How could the holy and righteous God use an unholy instrument to punish Judah? Did this fit Habakkuk's understanding of God? (Barker, p. 310). Habakkuk was again tied up in knots because of the inconsistencies he saw. He cried out, argued and desperately prayed to God.

Habakkuk waits for God's response

Habakkuk's next phase is so important. He didn't keep speaking and accusing God. He didn't continue to blurt out his frustrations. He didn't call the elders together to discuss things further. Rather, after finishing his complaint, he set himself to wait for God's answer and prepared himself to listen. "I will take my stand at my watchpost and station myself on the tower, and look out to see what he will say to me, and what I will answer concerning my complaint" (Habakkuk 2:1). Morgan sees this as a defining moment in Habakkuk's interaction, "Then came the great moment in the life of Habakkuk, when he said: I will get me to the watchtower. I will wait to see what it all means" (p. 94). As he waits in quietness, Habakkuk the watchman readies himself for a very different set of actions compared with his past pleading and complaining. From now on, "Habakkuk is to persevere in looking and listening, rather than in pleading and interceding" (Prior, p. 232).

When he declares that he will take his stand at his "watchpost" and station himself on the "tower," he is not saying that he intends to withdraw from the business of society, retreat to some quiet place, and wait for an answer there. Instead he uses these images to describe his inner state. His inner being is waiting, attentive and watchful for the speaking of the Lord. "The words of our verse are to be taken figuratively, or internally, like the appointment of the watchman in Isa. 21:6. The figure is taken from the custom of ascending high places for the purpose of looking into the distance (2 Kings 9:17; 2 Sam. 18:24), and simply expresses the spiritual preparation of the prophet's soul for hearing the word of God within, i.e., the collecting of his mind by quietly entering into himself, and meditating upon the word and testimonies of God. Cyril and Calvin bring out the first idea. Thus the latter observes, that "the watch-tower is the recesses of the mind, where we withdraw ourselves from the world;" and then adds by way of explanation, "The prophet, under the name of the watch-tower, implies that he extricates himself as it were from the thoughts of the flesh, because there would be no end or measure, if he wished to judge according to his own perception'" (Keil, p. 399).

It is especially enlightening to look at the preposition Habakkuk uses concerning God's speaking. ESV translates it as speaking "to me." However, the Hebrew lends itself more to a translation describing God's speaking "in me." Jamieson et al, see this as a picture of Habakkuk's inner life and applies that to believers today, "Literally, "in me," God speaking, not to the prophet's outward ear, but *inwardly*. When we have prayed to God, we must observe what answers God gives by His word, His Spirit, and His providences" (p. 702). Keil also sees this as an exhibition of the inner life of the prophet, "To speak in me, not merely to or with me; since the speaking of God to the prophets was an internal speaking, and not one that was perceptible from without" (p. 399).

Habakkuk's waiting might be a good illustration of the Apostle Peter's description of how the prophets "searched and inquired carefully" (1 Peter 1:10). They sought and search diligently for how the Spirit of Christ in them was making clear concerning the sufferings of Christ and His coming glory (1 Peter 1:11). Maybe part of their inquiry and search was just the sort of inward struggle described by Habakkuk here. Habakkuk stopped, looked within and set himself to receive an answer from within. He laid aside his opinions, any fleshly inclinations, his preconceptions and his fears. He laid aside what he thought he should know. He allowed God, through the Spirit, through His Word, and through His Divine working, to speak to him on the inside. This inward readiness and attention describes Habakkuk at his "watchpost" and at his "tower."

God's inner speaking to the prophet becomes what Habakkuk speaks to others. He says he will look to God for "what I will answer to my complaint" (Habakkuk 2:1). Before Habakkuk will answer his complaint to others, he looks to God to first make it clear to him. "He will wait for an answer from God to this complaint, to quiet his own heart, which is dissatisfied with the divine administration" (Keil, p. 399). The process Habakkuk passes through here demonstrates just how true spiritual ministry is carried out. It begins with the prophet having a problem that he presents to God. Then God speaks to the prophet to meet the need that he presented to God. That answer becomes what Habakkuk ministers to others. True spiritual ministry is not the objective regurgitation of theological principles. It is the result of an active transaction with God as Habakkuk demonstrates here. It is personal, real, vital, interactive, truthful and eminently effective. What God speaks to meet Habakkuk's need becomes his capital to minister to others.

When we consider Habakkuk's interactions with God up to this point, we can see how his faith grows throughout the process. After voicing his first complaint and receiving his first answer, we see that he advanced from his words of despair. He could boldly claim that God was his God and his Holy One. He saw God as his Rock and understood how God's work would discipline but not destroy. After his second complaint, we see that Habakkuk has advanced again. Here he is quiet, restful and waiting in simplicity to find God's inner speaking which would bring the answer he needs. This sets the stage for his next advancement as he progresses to his song. Noticing Habakkuk's process is important, because it conveys how we might also advance with God. Habakkuk "demonstrates the process of how God 'reveals His plan to His servants the prophets' (Amos 3:7). Therefore, Habakkuk serves as revealer, interpreter, and guide, even as he fulfills the traditional function of a prophet (2:1)" (Barker, p. 321).

The righteous shall live by faith

While the prophet waits at his watchpost, God does not disappoint him by not appearing. God speaks to Habakkuk with a glorious vision containing a profound spiritual truth. He tells Habakkuk to blatantly publish what he is about to hear. "Write the vision; make it plain on tablets, so he may run who reads it" (Habakkuk 2:2). God tells Habakkuk to write the coming vision in such an obvious, noticeable way that even a person who is running can read it. God wishes that a person who is bustling along in his daily life might easily read the contents of the vision that Habakkuk received through so much of his desperate effort. God tells him that the vision is for a future time, but that the word spoken hastens towards that time, and therefore will be accomplished.

The first and possibly most important portion of Habakkuk's vision is the central verse of his entire book, "Behold, his soul is puffed up; it is not upright within him, but the righteous shall live by his faith" (Habakkuk 2:4). This one sentence is an answer to all Habakkuk's internal turmoil concerning righteousness and God's plan concerning righteousness. First, the sentence addresses Habakkuk's concern that the unrighteous will prosper. In short, God says, "They won't!" Their soul is "puffed up" and, therefore, "not upright" in God's eyes. The word for "puffed up" is ʻāpal, which means "swell, be lifted up" (Harris, p. 686). is the same word used to describe the arrogance of the children of Israel when they took the ark with them to fight the Canaanites without God's approval (Numbers 14:44). Words like "tumor" or "hemorrhoid" are derivatives of this word. A "puffed up" person indicates that they possess an arrogance that has no foundation in fact and are actually like a tumor or growth in the body. God assures Habakkuk that when He looks at a person in this condition, He proclaims, "Not upright." The Hebrew word for "upright" is *yāšar,* which means "be level, straight, (up) right, just, lawful" (Harris, p. 417). The word is used to denote something pleasing to God or a person. The potter remade the vessel, because it pleased him [*yāšar*] to do so (Jeremiah 18:4). When Saul heard that Michal loved David, it pleased him [*yāšar*] (1 Samuel 18:20). When God sees a puffed-up soul, it does not please Him at all. The prophet can thus understand that God is not sitting idly by, approving of the unrighteous on the earth. This is the first part of God's answer to Habakkuk's complaint.

The next phrase describes God's intended solution for the problem of mankind's righteousness. "The righteous shall live by his faith" is full of profound meaning. It says that a person will be righteous and have life through faith. Each of these words is significant. If a person is "righteous" that means that he is approved by God according to God's standard of righteousness. The only righteousness that is up to God's standard is the righteousness that belongs to God Himself. Here, God declares that through faith a person is regarded as having the same righteousness that belongs to God. Furthermore, faith does not only make a person upright; it also makes a person "live." Life, as described here, is not merely the continuation of the human life we know it to be. It denotes God's divine life, with its eternal aspects, perfect qualities and divine character. Through faith, a person will share the same eternal life as God has it. Faith causes a person to share God's righteousness *and* God's life.

This short phrase reveals that faith is an amazing, wonderful action. It is not merely an objective agreement about the facts of God and His promises. Faith is an organic union with God Himself. In that organic union a person becomes righteous because God is righteous and becomes alive because God is living. The answer to Habakkuk's question about righteousness is that people will touch righteousness and life by the power and virtue of a living faith. This is God's visionary solution to the problem of righteousness among mankind. God is opening the way of faith. When a person has faith, he is brought into an organic union with God, where God's righteousness becomes his and where God's life makes him alive.

This simple phrase "provides Habakkuk with a clear answer to the dilemma he had expressed earlier: 'the wicked swallows up the man more righteous than he' (1:13). No, replies God, the righteous shall live by faith. They will not be swallowed up. They will not merely survive, but flourish. And the quality which produces this outcome is faith" (Prior, p. 239).

Warnings to the Chaldeans

The remainder of chapter two is an announcement of the judgments and woes that will fall on the Chaldeans. Verse five transitions into the woes by likening the Chaldeans to wine. "Moreover, wine is a traitor, an arrogant man who is never at rest…He gathers for himself all nations and collects as his own all peoples" (Habakkuk 2:5). Wine is a fitting likeness for the Chaldeans who were well known for their flagrant drinking bouts (see Daniel 5:1-2). Just like a drunkard can never get enough wine, the Chaldeans can never gather enough nations to satisfy their drunkard-like cravings for power and territory. Eventually, however, the Chaldeans will be judged for all their wicked policies. When judgment comes, all the nations who suffered under their oppression will scoff at them.

God highlights five different Chaldean behaviors that He specifically takes issue with. First, He objects to their selfish collection of plunder, exclaiming, "Woe to him who heaps up what is not his own—for how long?—and loads himself with pledges" (Habakkuk 2:6). God likens the Chaldean's collection of booty to borrowing (taking pledges) and warns the Babylonians that the bankers will eventually come to collect their debts, "Will not your debtors suddenly arise?" (Habakkuk 2:7). Second, God objects to the extreme measures they took to protect their ill-gotten wealth, saying, "Woe to him who gets evil gain for his house, to set his nest on high, to be safe from the reach of harm" (Habakkuk 2:9). The Chaldeans sought to protect their plunder by building safe houses and oppressing the people in their kingdom. God warns them that no protective measure devised in their minds will allow them to keep their wealth. Even the structures they built to house their treasure will cry out against them, "For the stone will cry out from the wall, and the beam from the woodwork respond" (Habakkuk 2:11).

Third, God objects to all the blood they shed in establishing their empire, saying, "Woe to him who builds a town with blood and founds a city on iniquity" (Habakkuk 2:12). The Chaldeans killed many people to establish the towns and cities of their empire. The Lord warns them that the empire they fought so hard to win will eventually be snuffed out, because God will establish His rule upon the earth. "For the earth will be filled with the knowledge of the glory of the Lord as the waters cover the sea" (Habakkuk 2:14). For the earth to be filled with the knowledge of the glory of the Lord means that all rival kingdoms with their glory are to be leveled to make way for the knowledge of the Lord. The Chaldean empire will eventually be erased, so that the earth will only know one glory—the glory of the One God.

Fourth, God objects to the Chaldean's flagrant disregard for the dignity of their fellow human beings, saying, "Woe to him who makes his neighbor drink—you pour out your wrath to make them drunk, in order to gaze at their nakedness" (Habakkuk 3:15). What shame! In return for the outright humiliation of their neighbors, God will turn judgment back on them, "The cup in the LORD's right hand will come around to you, and utter shame will come upon your glory!' (Habakkuk 2:16). The Chaldeans will also suffer judgment for the harm they did to the trees and beasts. "The violence done to Lebanon will overwhelm you, as will the destruction of the beasts that terrified them" (Habakkuk 2:17). The Chaldeans will even pay for doing harm to the environment! Finally, God objects to their flagrant idolatry, "Woe to him who says to a wooden thing, Awake! To a silent stone, Arise!" (Habakkuk 2:19). They will find out that the idol is speechless, breathless, and deceitful.

The Lord is in His holy temple. Keep silent!

After passionately proclaiming all these woes, Habakkuk concludes the prophecy section of his book with a grand statement about God. "But the LORD is in his holy temple; let all the earth keep silence before him" (Habakkuk 2:20). This statement affirms that the Lord in His heavenly temple is totally awesome and completely in control. Considering the Lord in this awe-inspiring place, should make all the earth keep quiet before Him. Previously the Babylonians had a lot to say in their prideful ravaging of nations and in their haughty fortresses where they guarded their wealth. Now the word to them is to be quiet and keep silence. Previously the wicked and lawless people in Jerusalem were very loud in paralyzing the law and perverting justice. Now, they should keep silence.

At the beginning of Habakkuk's book, it seemed to the prophet that God was silent. Now, the tables are turned. God is in His awesome temple. Now it is turn for the earth to be silent. There is nothing more to say. All there is to do is to wait for the execution of the sentence pronounced by the One Judge who matters.

Both Barker and Prior understand that another one also hears God's command to be silent and is, in fact, silent—Habakkuk himself. "The last verse of the chapter serves as a fitting conclusion to the final woe as well as a conclusion to the entire series of woes. Likewise, it points back to a prophet making demands of God, asking questions of God, and retreating to his watchtower to wait for God's answers, impatient at God's silence. Now the prophet hushes himself and all the world, willing to let God act in God's time and willing to wait for God to open his mouth when God chooses" (Barker, p. 349). Habakkuk had complained, God had spoken, now Habakkuk is silent along with all the earth. In his silence, he might be internalizing all that God has said. He might be deeply considering what it means for the righteous to live by his faith and the true ramifications of the statement that one day all the earth will be filled with the knowledge of the glory of God, as the waters cover the sea. What else could be done at this point but be silent before the One who can pronounce these things *and* carry them out! "In calling for all the earth to be hushed in the presence of the LORD, Habakkuk was acknowledging the need for him also to stop searching and striving for an explanation to all his dilemmas" (Prior, p. 260). From now on, Habakkuk can focus on God and God alone.

Habakkuk's prayer and song

Chapter three presents itself in a markedly different tone than the two previous chapters. The entire chapter is free from depression, despair and bewilderment. Habakkuk boldly prays for God to revive His work, praises the Lord with a deep expectation for His appearing and declares how much he himself has found in God. This chapter is a picture of new Habakkuk, who has gone through the depths with God and has emerged from that journey a changed person. "The introduction, content, mood and style of chapter 3 all indicate an immense sea-change in Habakkuk's approach to God and to the situation in which he finds himself" (Prior, p. 262). Habakkuk's response is full of joyful, buoyant prayer and praise. It is a fitting response to the wonderful words Habakkuk heard in earlier chapters. "The prophet expresses the feelings which the divine revelation of judgment described in Hab. 1 and 2 had excited in his mind, and ought to excite in the congregation of believers" (Keil, p. 414).

Habakkuk begins the chapter by testifying that he has indeed heard a report concerning God and that the report deeply affected him. "O Lord, I have heard the report of you, and your work, O Lord, do I fear" (Habakkuk 3:1). Clearly the report of God *and* His work is shocking to the prophet. It is awe inspiring. The only thing he can say after hearing about such a mighty work and Worker is, "I do fear." This shows how deeply the news affected him, as if the prophet were in the presence of a person who is the mightiest power and has truly seen that awesome power in action. I agree with Keil, in understanding that Habakkuk was struck by a greater scope of God's work than merely the judgment of Chaldeans. "The word…(I am alarmed) does not compel us to take what is heard as referring merely to the judgment to be inflicted upon Judah by the Chaldaeans. Even in the overthrow of the mighty Chaldaean, or of the empire of the world, the omnipotence of Jehovah is displayed in so terrible a manner, that this judgment not only inspires with joy at the destruction of the foe, but fills with alarm at the omnipotence of the Judge of the world" (Keil, p. 415). Now Habakkuk sees God and God alone! The marvelous report he heard was a window into the secret realms of God as He unfolds how He will work out His purpose—how the righteous would live by faith, how the entire earth will be filled with the knowledge of God and how all authority opposed to God will be swept away.

With that deep impression wrought into his heart, Habakkuk prays concerning God's work, "In the midst of the years revive it; in the midst of the years make it known; in wrath remember mercy" (Habakkuk 3:2). He pleads with God that God would revive His work, that God would make His work known, and that God would remember mercy as He is carrying out the judgment of His wrath. It is as if Habakkuk sees something so profound, so real, and now he boldly asks God, "Yes, Lord! Do it!" The word "revive" is a command for God to make His work alive. The word "does not merely mean to restore to life and keep alive, but also to give life and call to life. In Job 33:4,…the reference is not to the impartation of life to an inorganic object, but to the giving of life in the sense of creating; and so also in Gen. 7:3 and 19:32,…means to call seed to life, or raise it up, i.e., to call a non-existent thing to life" (Keil, p. 415). Habakkuk has just heard the report about God's work. Now he is yearning from his whole being that God would call His work to life, would impart life to it and would characterize His work by life. He yearns that God's work would not merely be a lifeless destruction of the ungodly. Rather, He pleads that God's work would result in life. He asks that God's work would produce a new creation, full of the divine, eternal, uncreated life of God.

He also boldly prays for God to make His work known. He is praying that God's work would not simply be recognized by a select few who have eyes to see it. It would not be accomplished hidden in a corner. Rather, it would be seen by eyes across the entire earth and would thus affect the entire world and beyond. Habakkuk himself is filled with awe, fear, respect and hope for God and God's work. He yearns that all men, all creatures, all angels and every authority could also know that same awesome work. Keil understands this prayer to be Habakkuk's prayer for God to complete His eternal administration. "Nevertheless the view which lies at the foundation of this application of our passage, viz., that the work of God, for the manifestation of which the prophet is praying, falls in the centre of the years of the world, has this deep truth, that it exhibits the overthrow not only of the imperial power of Chaldaea, but that of the world-power generally, and the deliverance of the nation from its power, and forms the turning-point, with which the old aeon closes and the new epoch of the world commences, with the completion of which the whole of the earthly development of the universe will reach its close" (Keil, p. 4:16).

Habakkuk also prays that in the midst of all this wrath, God would remember mercy. The words he uses here are interesting. ""Wrath" and "mercy" are picturesque words. "Wrath" comes from a root word which means "to tremble" or "to shake." "Mercy" comes from a word associated with the womb, indicating the compassion and tenderness which Habakkuk requested from the Lord" (Barker, p. 356). Habakkuk realizes that God's great wrath will come and shake the heavens and the earth. This will be the most momentous, awesome event. He is praying that as this great destruction happens, God would also remember creation. He is praying for mercy, for a womb to bring forth life in the midst of the wrath. As

God carries out His universal judgment upon unrighteousness in the Gentiles and Jews, He should remember to also create, give birth and bring forth new life. Habakkuk is praying here that God would save some who love Him and would bring them forth into newness, blessing, and grace.

A psalm of praise

In the next seventeen verses, Habakkuk proclaims a Psalm of praise. It is one of the most amazing and beautiful passages of the Bible, because it portrays God's future appearing for the salvation of His people and the judgment of the wicked in terms of historical moves God has made with His people. It is reproduced here in its entirety.

> 3 God came from Teman, and the Holy One from Mount Paran. Selah His splendor covered the heavens, and the earth was full of his praise.
> 4 His brightness was like the light; rays flashed from his hand; and there he veiled his power.
> 5 Before him went pestilence, and plague followed at his heels.
> 6 He stood and measured the earth; he looked and shook the nations; then the eternal mountains were scattered; the everlasting hills sank low. His were the everlasting ways.
> 7 I saw the tents of Cushan in affliction; the curtains of the land of Midian did tremble.
> 8 Was your wrath against the rivers, O Lord? Was your anger against the rivers, or your indignation against the sea, when you rode on your horses, on your chariot of salvation?
> 9 You stripped the sheath from your bow, calling for many arrows. Selah You split the earth with rivers.
> 10 The mountains saw you and writhed; the raging waters swept on; the deep gave forth its voice; it lifted its hands on high.

> 11 The sun and moon stood still in their place at the light of your arrows as they sped, at the flash of your glittering spear.
> 12 You marched through the earth in fury; you threshed the nations in anger.
> 13 You went out for the salvation of your people, for the salvation of your anointed. You crushed the head of the house of the wicked, laying him bare from thigh to neck. Selah
> 14 You pierced with his own arrows the heads of his warriors, who came like a whirlwind to scatter me, rejoicing as if to devour the poor in secret.
> 15 You trampled the sea with your horses, the surging of mighty waters
> — Habakkuk 3:3-15

Because Habakkuk uses so many metaphors and allusions, it may help the reader if I restate the central features of Habakkuk's praise in the next three paragraphs. His rich poetry surely portrays a glorious vision of the coming of the Lord.

Verses three through six describe the appearing of the Lord in glory. He comes from Teman, the capital city of Edom and Mount Paran, a mountain in the land of Ammon. The Lord led Israel from these same mountains as the nation set out to cross the River Jordan and enter the Good Land. God's glorious appearance in His move affects the heaven and earth. The heaven is filled with His splendor and the earth with His praise. His appearance is brilliant and shining, just like a bright star might shine. In His hands are bright lights, like lightning or like brilliant, strong rays emanating from His hands. The brightness is so great that it veils His true and awesome power. The brightness of the burning star is clothing something even greater, more powerful, and more intense—the very presence of God Himself. His appearance is not only bright; it is also terrible. In front of Him goes a terrible pestilence, which no man or beast can withstand. Behind him are burning sparks that seem like a plague. In such glory and terror, God stands still and surveys the earth, measuring it and demonstrating that He intends to possess it. His gaze is so powerful that it shakes the nations, scatters mountains that seem to have been there forever and causes hills to bow prostrate before Him. The nations, the mountains and the hills are forced to bend to the overpowering presence of God. In spite of all their staying power, glory, and might, they must yield to Him whose ways are everlasting. Thus, Habakkuk portrays the appearing of his great, glorious terrifying God.

In verses seven through eleven Habakkuk describes how the earth reacts to God's awesome appearing. Habakkuk switches to the first person in verse seven and declares how he is observing the two nations of Cushan and Midian trembling in affliction due to the coming of the Lord. Cushan may refer to the king of Mesopotamia (Judges 3:8). Some think this is another word for the kingdom of Cush, the nation south of Egypt. The nation of Midian tried to frustrate Israel as they entered the land of Canaan (Numbers 25:1). God's appearance strikes fear in both of these nations. Habakkuk rhetorically asks if the Lord's wrath is against the rivers or sea when He comes in His terrible array, riding on His chariot of salvation. The answer to this question is obvious—of course, the Lord is not angry at rivers and seas. He disturbs these waters, because He is coming for the purpose of salvation. His chariot is even named "salvation." The Lord in glory readies Himself for war—He strips the sheath off His bow, so that it is ready for firing. "Calling for many arrows" is actually three nouns—staves, oath and word—which Darby translates well, "The rods *of discipline* sworn according to *thy* word." This phrase indicates that the arrows God is about to shoot are for discipline, just as God promised in the past and made firm in His word. God judges with waters by splitting the earth with rivers. The mountains witness this and travail as if they are in labor. The waters continue to rage and rush onwards. Even the great deeps, where boundless waters reside, open and rush forth. Those watery depths sound out their voice and lift up their hands. Even the sun and moon are affected. They stand still in their place as the arrows from the bow of the Lord flash forth and His spear glistens with brilliance.

Verses twelve through fifteen focus on the true reason the Lord is coming. He is coming not because He is angry at the rivers. Rather, He marches through the earth for the salvation of His people and His Anointed. God is mighty to save! Salvation is compelling Him to appear in glorious array, as a Terror to anything that would threaten His people or His Anointed. He severely judges all those who are against Him. He crushes the head of the house of the wicked and flays him, laying him bare from thigh (even from his very foundation) to his neck. He confronts the warriors who came like a whirlwind to scatter His people and pierces their heads with their own arrows. Thus, the Lord tramples and travels through the sea with His horses as the mighty waters surge.

Habakkuk's Psalm paints a glorious picture of the coming of the Lord for the salvation of His people and the destruction of the wicked. Its powerful, picturesque poetry sets the coming of the Lord in vivid relief. The careful, considerate reader will feel the glory of the Lord's appearance. He will realize how His glory will reach the heavens and every corner of the earth. The inquisitive, contemplative reader will see the terror that the nations will feel at the Lord's appearing. He will be impressed with how the word of God will bring discipline, just like mighty, rushing waters overpower barriers. No earthly fortress or heavenly body will provide refuge. The perceptive, insightful reader will taste how precious God's people are to

Him and how valuable His Anointed is to Him. He will realize that God in His glory comes for their salvation. God will be a refuge for His people and an absolute terror for His enemies, who will be beaten down, pierced and even flayed. Anyone who has imbibed this vision will surely be comforted by the Lord. That person will be at rest, realizing that salvation and strength belong to God. All that we are to do is praise.

Habakkuk's Psalm is also picture of how the word of God and especially the history of God's work with His people can come alive in a servant of the Lord. Almost every image Habakkuk uses here is connected with multiple past events related to God and His people. If a person were to write down verses related to each line, the page would be full of references. Habakkuk draws images from the exodus, from Joshua's conquest of the land, from the struggles of the judges and from David's experiences fighting his enemies. Surely, Habakkuk had known these stories for a long time. However, when he was questioning God, wondering why God seemingly did not hear his prayers, he knew of the Exodus story, but it did not bring him out of despair. That was the old Habakkuk of chapters one and two. In this Psalm, however, the new Habakkuk of chapter three is encouraged because there is a new vitality to the old stories he knew for so long. Many different passages from the Hebrew Scriptures come alive. Based on them, he expressed his hope and expectation for God's great, future salvation. Consider these four different stories that might have inspired Habakkuk's Psalm.

Habakkuk's Psalm may have been mainly referencing the Exodus. Moses describes God coming from Sinai, Teman, and Mount Paran, in brilliant array with flashing lightening in His hand (Deuteronomy 33:2-3), just as Habakkuk describes God's brilliance as coming from Mount Paran and Teman. Moses saw God in brilliance on Sinai (Exodus 24:17), so Habakkuk sees His brightness. Moses describes how pestilence went before God and how plague followed him, (Exodus 9:3, Deuteronomy 32:24), just as Habakkuk relates these to God's move. When God left Sinai, the mountains were scattered before Him as He went along His everlasting ways (Psalm 68:7-8), just as Habakkuk speaks about the mountains quaking. God took out His wrath upon Midian before they went into the good land (Numbers 31:1-12), just as Habakkuk sees that nation in terror. It is evident from the Psalms that God's wrath was not against the rivers or sea (Psalm 114:5), although he passed through the Red Sea and crossed the Jordan River. Habakkuk states this. Moses and the Psalms describe God riding as He went through the wilderness (Psalm 68:4, 33 Deuteronomy 33:26), just as Habakkuk sees him riding on His horse, the chariot of His salvation. Just as God split the earth with the river of water that came out of the rock (Exodus 17:6), Habakkuk declares God split the earth with rivers. Just as God's march was associated with the pouring forth of abundant rain, waters coming from the deep, and his arrows of lightening flashing here and there (Psalm 77:17), Habakkuk describes the raging waters, open depths, and flashing arrows of God. Just as God crushed the heads of His opponents as He marches from Sinai (Psalm 68:7,21), Habakkuk sees God crushing the head of the house of the wicked into order to bring salvation to His people. Just as the Exodus showed that God's way was in the sea and His paths were in the mighty waters (Psalm 77:19), Habakkuk declares that God treads on the sea and the raging waters.

On the other hand, Habakkuk's Psalm may have been mainly referencing the glorious works that Joshua experienced. For example, the ark was considered God's chariot (1 Chronicles 28:18), and as the priests carried the ark across the river Jordan (Joshua 3:11-17), God was riding upon His chariot of salvation, just as Habakkuk declares. Just as Joshua saw the Captain of the Lord's armies hold his unsheathed sword in preparation for the coming fight (Joshua 5:13-15), Habakkuk saw God unsheathe His bow, ready for the conflict. Just as Joshua commanded the sun and moon to stand still as he consumed the enemy (Joshua 10:13), Habakkuk declares that the sun and moon stand still. Just as God sent the hailstones, His arrows, from above upon the enemy armies (Joshua 10:11), Habakkuk sees God's arrow going forth. Just as Joshua commanded the Israelites to stand on the neck of the kings (Joshua 10:24), so here Habakkuk sees the enemies laid bare from thigh (or foundation) to the neck.

On the other hand, Habakkuk's Psalm may have been referencing the song of Deborah and the recent battles in the time of the judges. Deborah opens her song with God marching from the field of Edom (Judges 5:4), just as Habakkuk opens with God coming from Teman, the capital city of Edom. Deborah sings about the earth quaking, the mountains shaking, and the clouds dripping with water (Judges 4:5-6), just as Habakkuk declares the mountains were scattered as God marched through the earth. The book of judges speaks about the defeat of Cushan-rishathaim and Midian, just as Habakkuk writes about the tents and curtains of Cushan and Midian trembling. Just as Deborah sings about the stars from heaven fighting against Sisera and the torrent of Kishon sweeping him away (Judges 5:19-20), Habbakkuk speaks about the arrows speeding away from God and raging torrents of water. Just as Sisera was pierced in the head by Jael (Judges 5:26), Habakkuk writes about how God will pierce the heads of the attacking warriors using their own arrows.

On the other hand, Habakkuk's Psalm may have been mainly referencing David's experience of God giving him victory over his enemies. David saw God appearing and marching in brightness (Psalm 18:12), just like Habakkuk saw Him in brightness. Just as David prayed that God would send forth His arrows (Psalm 144:5), Habakkuk sees rays emanating from God's hands. Just as David saw God covering Himself with a cloak of light (Psalm 104:2), so does Habakkuk see God veiled in brightness. Just as David saw God's pestilence going before Him when the Philistines mishandled the ark (1 Samuel 5:9), Habakkuk wrote about pestilence going before Him. David saw the foundations of the mountains trembling (Psalm 18:7), just like Habakkuk. He saw God ride on His cherub (Psalm 18:10), just as Habakkuk saw him ride and travel on His chariot. David saw God wield His arrows, open channels of water upon the earth and lay bare the foundations of the earth (Psalm 18:14-15), just as Habakkuk wrote about God's arrows, the raging waters, and the deep giving forth its voice. Just as David saw God as His saving defense to His anointed (Psalm 28:8), Habakkuk realized God was going forth for the salvation of His anointed.

A survey like this shows that Habakkuk's words are not his own invention. When he saw God appearing, affecting the earth, bringing salvation and judging His enemies, He saw God's future move in the context of so many moves that God had already made. Habakkuk did not come up with any original thought. Instead, the word of God that he knew and that was dear to him, took on new relevance and new meaning. Suddenly, the stories of Moses, Joshua, Deborah and David are no longer simply stories of long ago. The move of God in those times became the hope for what Habakkuk sees as God's future move. The word became living, active, sharp and operative in Habakkuk. This might be a wonderful example of how the word was mingled with Habakkuk's faith. As his faith grew and the word became alive, Habakkuk also became alive, encouraged and free from despair. Habakkuk is a wonderful example of the righteous living by faith. Living by faith is not simply being happy that one is not judged by God. Living by faith is an active, true, solid enjoyment of God's promises. It is an enjoyment and a partaking of God Himself.

Habakkuk's glorious praise

The remainder of Habakkuk's Psalm is a testimony of the new Habakkuk, who is buoyant, full of trust in God and empowered by his fresh vision of God. "Verses 16–19 form the second part of the psalm, in which the prophet describes the feelings that are produced within himself by the coming of the Lord to judge the nations, and to rescue His own people; viz., first of all, fear and trembling at the tribulation (vv. 16, 17); then exulting joy, in his confident trust in the God of salvation (vv. 18, 19)" (Keil, p. 426). God changes people. Encountering God makes an impact on a person's life. Habakkuk came face to face with God through his questions, prayers and, most recently, through the vision he saw. "He now describes the impact of this prayer encounter with the living God. He has been profoundly challenged and, indeed, changed by this time in the place of prayer. The Habakkuk who speaks in these four verses is a very different person from the Habakkuk to whom we were introduced at the beginning of the book" (Prior, p. 270).

> 16 I hear, and my body trembles; my lips quiver at the sound; rottenness enters into my bones; my legs tremble beneath me. Yet I will quietly wait for the day of trouble to come upon people who invade us.
> 17 Though the fig tree should not blossom, nor fruit be on the vines, the produce of the olive fail and the fields yield no food, the flock be cut off from the old and there be no herd in the stalls,

> 18 yet I will rejoice in the Lord; I will take joy in the God of my salvation.
> 19 God, the Lord, is my strength; he makes my feet like the deer's; he makes me tread on my high places. To the choirmaster: with stringed instruments.
> — Habakkuk 3:16-19

These verses give us a clear picture of the new Habakkuk's passion, resolution and joy in the Lord. We can learn a lot from each aspect. First, we realize how passionate he is. When he recognizes the grandness of the move of God, the hope of His salvation and the terror that will come upon the unrighteous, his whole person, even his physical body is affected. He proclaims, "I hear, and my body trembles; my lips quiver at the sound; rottenness enters into my bones; my legs tremble beneath me" (Habakkuk 3:16). This verse indicates how deeply Habakkuk feels the things of God. Habakkuk is like Jeremiah in this sense, because Jeremiah deeply felt the message he spoke. The word "body" is literally "belly." Habakkuk's belly trembled. "Into the bones there penetrates *râqâbh*, rottenness, inward consumption of the bones, as an effect of alarm or pain, which paralyzes all the powers, and takes away all firmness from the body (cf. Prov. 12:4; 14:30)" (Keil, p. 427). Prior describes how this is an effect of God's living word, "God's word has struck deep into Habakkuk's inner being. That is why he is so shaken. 'He was not exempted from the turmoil that pervades and characterizes the chapter.' God had not spoken merely into his mind, but into his inner parts'. He cannot stand outside this experience and rationalize its content. He cannot be purely cerebral and communicate God's words to him and to his people in a dispassionate manner. What he describes here is a vivid, personal example of what we read elsewhere in Scripture; for instance: 'the word of God is living and active, sharper than any two-edged sword, piercing to the division of soul and spirit, of joints and marrow, and discerning the thoughts and intentions of the heart' (Heb. 4:12)" (p. 272).

Even though Habakkuk is trembling in awe of God's future terror, he is also quietly trusting. In that restful trust, he will patiently wait for God's work, saying, "Yet I will quietly wait for the day of trouble to come upon people who invade us" (Habakkuk 3:16). This quiet waiting is a sharp contrast from the argumentative person we saw at the beginning of the book. Habakkuk has grown in the Lord. "What an amazing transformation! Because the prophet had been honest with God and took his genuine questions to a caring God, Habakkuk began to look at the world from a different perspective. Habakkuk had moved from "how long?" (Hab 1:2) to "I will wait patiently" (Barker, p. 374). Waiting for God is possibly the hardest thing any believer can do. It is so easy to want something to happen now or to try to do it alone. Habakkuk is now mature, able to trust, waiting patiently for the move of the Lord.

Verses seventeen and eighteen describe the prophet's resolution. Even though his earthly situation will become bleaker, he has set himself to rejoice in the Lord. He will not merely wait patiently in a stoic sort of way. No, as he is waiting, he will rejoice. He boldly declares, "yet I will rejoice in the LORD; I will take joy in the God of my salvation" (Habakkuk 3:18). Morgan explains the sense of this verse. "To translate literally from the Hebrew would almost startle us. To do that is to find that he said: "I will jump for joy in the Lord; I will spin round, so filled with gladness that he speaks so hilarious, so filled with gladness that he speaks of dancing and spinning round." His joy was so exuberant, and could only find expression in such language. Notice, however, that is was in "Jehovah," in the "God of salvation," that he had such an experience. It was not the result of circumstances but of triumph over them" (Morgan, p. 97). For Habakkuk to rejoice in this situation means that he has found something richer in God Himself. Prior speculates that Habakkuk discovered "that true blessedness consists, not in receiving good things from his hand, but in a personal relationship of trust between individual and his or her God: I will joy in the God of my salvation. He is my Saviour" (p. 276). Barker echoes this, describing Habakkuk at this juncture,

> His circumstances have not changed. The outer world with its evil conduct and rapacious warfare remains the same. God's people remain in time of lamentation. The prophet, however, turns to praise. Why? He has heard God's voice and seen God's vision. He knows the ultimate outcome of history. Thus vv. 17 and 18 serve as fitting climaxes to the psalm of Habakkuk and to the book as a whole. Here the prophet accepts God's program, thus resolving his contention with God expressed so strongly in chaps. 1–2. "Even with all the punishment imagery …, the fact that the book concludes with the prophet rejoicing in the saving power and strength of God indicates that Habakkuk felt Yahweh's impulse to judge in no way dismisses the Lord's loving nature"
> —Barker, p. 374

Habakkuk goes farther still. Not only is he rejoicing, but he is also empowered in the Lord. "GOD, the Lord, is my strength; he makes my feet like the deer's; he makes me tread on my high places" (Habakkuk 3:19). Here Habakkuk quotes a precious declaration from David. It has become truly alive to Habakkuk.

> The next two clauses are from Ps. 18:34, "He maketh my feet like hinds," according to the contracted simile common in Hebrew for "hinds' feet;" and the reference is to the swiftness of foot, which was one of the qualifications of a thorough man of war (2 Sam. 1:23; 1 Chron. 12:8), so as to enable him to make a sudden attack upon the enemy, and pursue him vigorously. Here it is a figurative expression for the fresh and joyous strength acquired in God, which Isaiah calls rising up with eagles' wings (Isa. 40:29–31). Causing to walk upon the high places of the land, was originally a figure denoting the victorious possession and government of a land. It is so in Deut. 32:13 and 33:29, from which David has taken the figure in Ps. 18, though he has altered the high places of the earth into "my high places" (*bâmōthai*). They were the high places upon which the Lord had placed him, by giving him the victory over his enemies.
> —Keil, p. 428

Prior sees this as an example of how Habakkuk read the account of David's experience and allowed that word to become living, relevant and true in his own time and in his own condition.

> In echoing David, Habakkuk seems to be taking the shepherd king's words and giving them deeper meaning. David had composed the psalm at a time of deliverance and victory. Habakkuk uses the words to express a faith which trusts God and rejoices in him while it is still very dark. Moreover, whereas David testified to God as the One who 'girded' him with strength, like and outer layer of protection, Habakkuk declares that God, the Lord, is my strength, an inner reservoir of boundless resources. Both Habakkuk and David bear witness to the ability to move nimbly like a deer on dangerous terrain. They are given the strength, not just to stand firm and to cope in the face

> of immense adversity, but to rise up above it and to make swift progress—to climb, not simply coast. Habakkuk has discovered the secret of turning the hills and mountains into opportunities to discover more of God's strength in his inner being.
> —Prior, p. 278

The hind's feet which God had given him, brought Habakkuk up to his high places. These places are not merely emotional highs. Rather they signify the heights reached when a person is joining with God for the accomplishment of His eternal purpose. Keil writes concerning this. "The figure must be taken as a whole; and according to this, it simply denotes the ultimate triumph of the people of God over all oppression on the part of the power of the world, altogether apart from the local standing which the kingdom of God will have upon the earth, either by the side of or in antagonism to the kingdom of the world" (Keil, p. 428).

We see then, how the process Habakkuk experienced with God led him from his despair to the highest places. The strength the Lord was to him and the feet the Lord gave him, allowed Habakkuk to rejoice and rise up to the high places of the fulfillment of God's eternal plan.

CHAPTER NINE

ZEPHANIAH

The book of Zephaniah can easily be divided into three simple sections. The first speaks of God's coming judgment on the earth and on Judah (Zephaniah 1:2-18). The second contains Zephaniah's command for the people to gather together, seek the Lord, and shows them how God's judgment on the nations will result in a remnant inheriting a blessing (Zephaniah 2:1-3:8). The third portrays God's future salvation and kindness towards the Gentiles and Israel (Zephaniah 3:9-20).

To grasp the arc of Zephaniah's thought, I think it is especially helpful to consider the only two exhortations found in the book. In his first exhortation, Zephaniah commands the people to "gather together" to seek the Lord (Zephaniah 2:1). In the second exhortation, God commands the people to "wait" until God's work is completed (Zephaniah 3:8). These exhortations form "hinges," called "hortatory hinges" by R.B.

Chisholm, that punctuate the book (Barker, p. 393). One could understand the entire book in context of these hinges. Section one declares the coming judgment upon the world and Judah. Under this thought of approaching judgment, the readers are ready to hear the first exhortation—gather together and seek the Lord. The gathering gives Israel a front row seat to witness the second section, which describes God's judgment of the nations and Judah that will result in a remnant of God's people inheriting their portion from the Lord. The thought of this approaching inheritance prepares the readers for the second exhortation—wait on the Lord. As the people wait, God moves to restore His people and bless the Gentiles, which is described in the third and final section. This, in short, is the message of Zephaniah.

Judgment on Judah and all creation

Zephaniah paints a grand picture of God's coming judgment in his first section (Zephaniah 1:2-18). The salient reason God will stretch out His hand "against Judah" (Zephaniah 1:4) is because of the nation's deep degradation. God will judge their "idolatrous priests" (Zephaniah 1:4), the hypocrisy of "those who bow down and swear to the Lord and yet swear by Milcom" (Zephaniah 1:5) and "those who have turned back from following the Lord" (Zephaniah 1:6).

The approaching calamity will not affect Judah alone, as evidenced by Zephaniah's opening verses. The entire earth, all created things, will feel God's judgment. "I will utterly sweep away everything from the face of the earth," declares the LORD. "I will sweep away man and beast; I will sweep away the birds of the heavens and the fish of the sea, and the rubble with the wicked. I will cut off mankind from the face of the earth," declares the LORD" (Zephaniah 1:2-3). The judgment due Judah will fall upon the entire creation—the beasts, the birds, even the fish. In Genesis chapter one, God creates the fish and birds, then beasts and finally man. He grants man to have dominion over all the animals He made. Here in Zephaniah, the judgment due man falls upon all the creation over which he has been given charge. Such judgment of the earth happened during the great flood (see Genesis 6:7). "By playing upon this threat, Zephaniah intimates that the approaching judgment will be as general over the earth, and as terrible, as the judgment of the flood" (Keil, p. 127).

Be silent before the Lord

After God's grand introduction of judgment, Zephaniah counsels the people not to defend, justify or try to explain their actions. "Be silent before the Lord God! For the day of the Lord is near" (Zephaniah 1:7). His advice is full of significance and is intended to make the hypocritical worshippers in Jerusalem quiet down and consider the magnitude of the coming consequences.

> Zephaniah interjects a word of advice to the people, advice that immediately hushes any attempt at self-defense. In so doing the prophet, not Yahweh, becomes the speaker who introduces the book's central theme: the day of the Lord. In preparation for the instruction of the Lord, the prophet counseled silence. In the Hebrew text the word for "silence" is an interjection usually translated as "hush!" or "keep silence." The placing of the word at the beginning of the sentence and the use of "Sovereign Lord" emphasizes the importance of the demand. "'Be silent before the Lord God!' is the priestly cry before the sacrifice." The sacrifice motif that follows joins this to the following section. The prophet calls for "submission,

> fear, and consecration." Since the day of the Lord was near, Zephaniah wanted all the people to think of the significance of the event and give God the awe due his holy name
> —Barker, p. 424

The "day of the Lord" referred to here by Zephaniah is that same coming "day" mentioned by Joel and Obadiah, in which all the evil in the world will be judged and all that is worthy will be brought into the good of God's glorious salvation.

The judgments associated with the day of the Lord

The remainder of this section (up to Zephaniah 1:18) consists of listing who will be affected by the day of the Lord, what it will be like and the extent of the earth that will be affected. On that day of sacrifice, God will punish "the officials and king's sons and all who array themselves in foreign attire" (Zephaniah 1:8). At Zephaniah's time, the king sought the Lord, but was surrounded by those who didn't. Some of these dressed in foreign attire. "With foreign dress came foreign manners and worship, especially idolatry" (Feinberg, p. 224). Merchants in many different quarters of Jerusalem will also be affected, "all the traders are no more; all who weigh out silver are cut off" (Zephaniah 1:11). God will punish the men in Jerusalem who question God in their hearts, saying, "The LORD will not do good, nor will he do ill" (Zephaniah 1:12).

The day will be bitter, a time when even mighty men cry aloud. "A day of wrath is that day, a day of distress and anguish, a day of ruin and devastation, a day of darkness and gloom, a day of clouds and thick darkness, a day of trumpet blast and battle cry" (Zephaniah 1:15-16). The Lord speaks in 1:17, "I will bring distress on mankind....their blood shall be poured out like dust" (Zephaniah 1:17). Zephaniah speaks himself concerning that day in 1:18, confirming God's words, "In the fire of his jealousy, all the earth shall be consumed; for a full and sudden end he will make of all the inhabitants of the earth" (Zephaniah 1:18).

Exhortation to gather together

Just like Joel commanded the Israelites to gather together in order to repent before the day of the Lord (Joel 2:16), Zephaniah also encourages the people to gather together in light of this day.

> 1 Gather together, yes, gather, O shameless nation,
> 2 before the decree takes effect —before the day passes away like chaff— before there comes upon you the burning anger of the Lord, before there comes upon you the day of the anger of the Lord.
> 3 Seek the Lord, all you humble of the land, who do his just commands;
> seek righteousness; seek humility; perhaps you may be hidden on the day of the anger of the Lord
> —Zephaniah 2:1-3

Zephaniah's plea to gather is tinged with irony due to his word choice. He doesn't use a typical word for "gathering," like what would be used for a gathering at the temple or gathering to hear God's word. Instead, he uses a word that is derived from the word "straw," implying that when he asks them to gather together, he is asking them to bunch themselves together so that they could be ready to be burned in the fire. The NET translates this verse, "Bunch yourselves together like straw, you undesirable nation". Keil describes this, "The summons in v. 1 is addressed to the whole of Judah or Israel.

The verb *qōshēsh*, possibly a *denom.* from *qash*, signifies to gather stubble (Ex. 5:7, 12), then generally to gather together or collect, e.g., branches of wood (Num. 15:32, 33; 1 Kings 17:10); in the *hithpoel*, to gather one's self together, applied to that spiritual gathering which leads to self-examination, and is the first condition of conversion" (p. 137). Barker views this summons as an intentional shock to the nation, "Zephaniah 2:1–2 attempts to shock and insult Judahites into joining the remnant" (p. 445).

It is evident that Zephaniah is pleading with all the Israelites that they would turn themselves around, seek the Lord, and, by doing so, might be hidden from the bitter, forthcoming day of judgment. Here, Zephaniah is trying to call out a remnant from the mass of people who are largely obstinate deviators from the true God. "Having diligently followed the requirements of the law of the Lord, they are encouraged to pursue righteousness further. If it please the Lord, they may be hid, preserved, in the day of the Lord's wrath (Is 26:20)" (Feinberg, p. 227). He is addressing his plea especially to the humble, those who by necessity are dependent on God. ""Humility" refers to the "moral and spiritual condition of the godly" who have "absolute dependence on God." The "humble" seek God, keep his commands, wait on God, and are guided by him. They are dependent on him in everything. "They are conscious of divine approval and are confident that in the eschaton God will save them"" (Barker, p. 449). Zephaniah is calling to this humble group so that might seek the Lord. "Zephaniah's climactic message involved the necessity of repentance and the importance of looking to God in righteousness. Zephaniah used the verb "seek" three times in this verse, each time as an imperative. Judah must realize that "the only adequate refuge from the consuming wrath of Yahweh may be found in Yahweh himself"" (Barker, p. 447).

The remnant will possess the nations

The remainder of the second section of Zephaniah, from 2:4 to 3:5, could be viewed as a plea to this assembled bunch of "stubble," presenting reasons to them so that they would seek the Lord and perhaps be hid in that fearful day. The motivation Zephaniah gives in verse four is that the nations, in particular Gaza and its neighboring cities, will be judged. How this is supposed to be a reason for seeking God is a matter of interpretation. Some think that when Israel hears that the Gentiles, those living in Gaza, will be judged, Israel will realize even more vividly that God's judgment will land upon them. Thus, they will be motivated to seek the Lord. While this may be true, the entire section speaks of something even more than that.

This section reveals that God's judgment of the nations will result in the nations turning to the Lord and, furthermore, in the remnant of Israel possessing the lands of the judged Gentiles. The motivation for seeking God is that God is preparing the scene, through the judgment of the Gentile nations, for the remnant of Israel (those who turn, seek the Lord, and are hidden in His day of judgment) to inherit the land. "Accordingly, the call to repentance is not simply strengthened by the renewed threat of judgment upon the heathen and the ungodly in Judah, but is rather accounted for by the introduction of the thought, that by means of the judgment the heathen nations are to be brought to acknowledge the name of the Lord, and the rescued remnant of Israel to be prepared for the reception of the promised salvation" (Keil, p. 137).

As an example of how Zephaniah portrays the coming inheritance consider his description of God's judgment upon the land of the Philistines. "The seacoast shall become the possession of the remnant of the house of Judah, on which they shall graze, and in the houses of Ashkelon they shall lie down at evening. For the LORD their God will be mindful of them and restore their fortunes" (Zephaniah 2:7). Zephaniah describes that the remnant of Israel will graze like sheep in the restored possession and will restfully inhabit that land under the kind care of their Lord. "The metaphor "portrays the remnant of Judah lying down like sheep in the wasteland that was once Philistia. Before this pastoral image Yahweh only cares about Judah's destruction, but now is their shepherd who creates a haven for His 'sheep'"" (Barker, p. 457). God describes the judgment of Moab, adding a similar thought, "the remnant of my people shall plunder them, and the survivors of my nation shall possess them" (Zephaniah 2:9).

In this speech to the remnant, God and Zephaniah describe how God's judgment of the nations will result in the Gentiles turning to God. They highlight nations from the four directions of the compass: Philistine to the east, Moab to the west, Cush to the south and Assyria to the north. These four representative nations convey the thought that all the nations on the whole earth in every direction will fall under the judgment of God. When those nations are cut off, all the gods that were worshipped by them will be shown to be absolutely worthless. "The LORD will be awesome against them; for he will famish all the gods of the earth" (Zephaniah 2:11). Their gods being "famished" means they will be made lean and wasted away. The nations, being released from their false gods, will bow down to the one true God, "And to him shall bow down, each in its place, all the lands of the nations" (Zephaniah 2:11). "Then will men worship the one true God, each from his own place, that is, each in the place where he lives, thus making the worship of the Lord universal" (Feinberg, p. 229).

Both God and Zephaniah speak in this section. Some statements are made by Zephaniah speaking in the third person. Others are made by God speaking in the first person. Combined, the section could be considered as a symphony played by God and prophet to woo the bunch of stubble so that some might seek God. Barker notes this when he considers the transition from Zephaniah's speaking in the third person in Zephaniah 2:7 to God speaking in the first person in Zephaniah 2:8. "The voice of Yahweh returns with the unusual function of "filling out the *prophet's* message." Such interchange between the functions of the prophetic speaker and the divine speaker show they work as "interchangeable revealers" so that "the word of the two is shown as one united word." The people were to understand that these words were not the musings of an obscure prophet but the words of the Lord himself" (Barker, p. 458).

In chapter three, verses one through five, Zephaniah paints a picture of how Jerusalem "the rebellious, defiled" and "oppressing city" (Zephaniah 3:1) will be severely judged. He describes her recalcitrant, obstinate attitude, "She listens to no voice; she accepts no correction. She does not trust in the Lord; she does not draw near to her God" (Zephaniah 1:2). She rejects God's law, as evidenced by her not listening, nor accepting correction. She rejects God's grace, as evidenced by her not trusting in nor drawing near to God. Her officials, judges, prophets, and priests are worthy of punishment. They became corrupt even though the Lord had given them ample opportunity to know Him, learn from Him and draw near to Him. God had been dwelling in their midst, giving them easy access to Him. Zephaniah declares, "The LORD within her is righteous" (Zephaniah 3:5), showing forth His justice every morning. The tangible presence of the Lord in the city made Judah even more guilty because of their corruption and forsaking of their Savior who so eagerly stretched out His hands to them.

God's plea for His people to return to Him

In verse six God takes over the dialogue from Zephaniah and pleads earnestly with the group gathered in Jerusalem. He pleads with the recalcitrant Jews, summarizing how He has judged the nations in preparation for them to be at peace and to possess their inheritance. He pleads, "I have cut off nations; their battlements are in ruins; I have laid waste their streets so that no one walks in them; their cities have been made desolate, without a man, without an inhabitant" (Zephaniah 3:6). God is telling them that He has prepared absolutely everything. All His people have to do is walk there, graze in the pastures and lie down to rest under His caring, tender shepherding (cf. Zephaniah 2:7).

In verse seven, God reveals His expectations for how His people would react to all the provisions He set before them. "I said, 'surely you will fear me; you will accept correction. Then your dwelling would not be cut off according to all that I have appointed against you'" (Zephaniah 3:7). These words give us a window into God's heart and expectation. God portrays Himself just like an expectant father, who genuinely hopes that the measures he has taken to correct his son would touch his son's heart. If God sees just the slightest turn—a little fear, a little "accepting of correction"—then He would reverse all the judgments that are waiting in the wings to fall upon the city. Of course, God, who knows everything, knows what will happen with His people. "God speaks after the manner of men in condescension to man's infirmity; not as though God was ignorant of the future contingency, but in their sense, *Surely one might have expected* ye would under such circumstances repent: but no!" (Jamieson et al, Vol. 1, p. 710). These words reveal His expectations, heart, passion and earnestness to reach His people. "The divine, "I said,"" as Motyer observes, "brings us right into the divine mind and heart"" (Barker, p. 483).

God commands the remnant to wait for Him

No matter how much God did to woo His people, their response was not at all towards Him. God concludes, "But all the more they were eager to make all their deeds corrupt" (Zephaniah 3:7). God's solution to the recalcitrant behavior of the masses of His people is to counsel those who have an ear to hear Him to "wait." ""Therefore wait for me," declares the Lord" (Zephaniah 3:8). This command is especially addressed to those who have set themselves to seek Him.

Waiting for the Lord may be one of the most difficult things that a believer can do. Here God counsels those seeking Him to simply wait. Keil sees the positive side of the term used here for waiting, commenting that it "is only used for waiting in a believing attitude of the Lord and His help (Ps. 33:20; Isa. 8:17; 30:18; 64:3)." He explains, "The train of thought is this: the believers are to wait for the judgment, for it will bring them redemption" (Keil, p. 155). Barker considers the magnitude of the challenge that God is putting before His people with this small word. "Waiting for God's vindication is neither desirable nor easy. Yet, waiting on God is the only choice for those who love him and seek to live according to his commands. Patience is not natural, either for the wicked or the righteous, but God called on the people to wait on him for their deliverance—a deliverance which would come in the form of God's judgment against the nations" (Barker, p. 485).

The glorious restoration

Just what are the people to wait for? God marvelously describes it in verses eight through thirteen. God will defeat the nations of the earth, "in the fire of my jealousy all the earth shall be consumed" (Zephaniah 3:8). He will bring His salvation to the Gentiles, "For at that time I will change the speech of the peoples to a pure speech" (Zephaniah 3:9). And, He will purify Israel, "I will remove from your midst the proudly exultant ones....I will leave in your midst a people humble and lowly. They shall seek refuge in the name of the Lord" (Zephaniah 3:11-12). God is charging the remnant to wait for Him until He marvelously removes all the wicked obstacles, turns the Gentiles into believers and purifies His people. God describes His coming salvation as seizing His prey, "for the day when I rise up to seize the prey" (Zephaniah 3:8). "The prey for which Jehovah will rise up, can only consist, therefore, in the fact, that through the judgment He obtains from among the nations those who will confess His name, so that the souls from among the nations which desire salvation fall to Him as prey (compare Isa. 53:12 with 52:15 and 49:7). It is true that, in order to gain this victory, it is necessary to exterminate by means of the judgment the obstinate and hardened sinners" (Keil, p. 154).

The Gentiles saved

God describes His "prey" in verses nine and ten, which, by the way, presents a wonderful Old Testament example of how God will reach the Gentiles.

> 9 "For at that time I will change the speech of the peoples to a pure speech, that all of them may call upon the name of the Lord and serve him with one accord.
> 10 From beyond the rivers of Cush my worshipers, the daughter of my dispersed ones, shall bring my offering.
> —Zephaniah 3:9-10

God's salvation of the Gentiles begins with their lips. Previously, the names of many idols and sinful things passed through their lips. "The lips are defiled by the names of the idols whom they have invoked (cf. Hos. 2:19, Ps. 16:4)" (Keil, p. 156). The words that came out of their lips were the fruit of what was in their heart, namely, many other gods. Those gods might have been their focus as they considered their lives, hopes, safety, fortunes and expectations. When God touches what comes out of their lips, this means He has converted them and changed their whole inner being. "God turns to the nations a pure lip, by purifying their sinful lips, i.e., He converts them, that they may be able to call upon Him with pure lips. Lip does not stand for language, but is mentioned as the organ of speech, by which a man expresses the thoughts of his heart, so that purity of the lips involves or presupposes the purification of the heart" (Keil, p. 156). When the Gentile's lips are purified, they are freed to call upon the name of the Lord. This calling is no small or incidental affair. It is not simply a vain repetition of the name of the Lord. The Hebrew word used here for "to call" "always signifies to call solemnly or heartily upon the name of Jehovah" (Keil, p. 156). Calling is a picture of relationship. "Calling on the name of the Lord means reaching out in faith for his all sufficient grace" (Barker, p. 488).

Furthermore, they will serve the Lord "with one accord" (Zephaniah 3:9), which in Hebrew is literally "with one shoulder." It presents a picture of many people lending a shoulder for the carrying out of a common task. Think of a yoke of oxen, where both pull together. Here, God's people are brought into a unity of service on behalf of the one God. "To serve sh^{e}khem 'echâd, with one shoulder, is to serve together or with unanimity. The metaphor is taken from bearers who carry a burden with even shoulders; cf. Jer. 32:39" (Keil, p.

156). "The Hebrew says literally that they would serve with "one shoulder," thus with unity. Not only do the people serve in a unified whole, but it is universal—"all of them"" (Barker, p. 489).

The service that the Gentiles carry out with their shoulders involves bringing offerings to God. God declares that they shall "bring my offering" (Zephaniah 3:10). Many commentators consider these offerings to be the Israelites who are scattered among the nations. "As an example of the way in which they will serve the Lord, it is stated in v. 10 that they will offer the widely scattered members of the Israelitish church as a sacrifice to the Lord. Compare Isa. 66:20, where this thought is applied to the heathen of all quarters of the globe" (Keil, p. 458). Feinberg echoes this, "In their converted condition, the nations will show their willingness to be used by the Lord in behalf of Israel. From beyond the rivers of Ethiopia they shall bring the dispersed of Israel to their own land as and offering to the Lord (Is. 49:22-23; 60:4-9; and 66:20)" (Feinberg, p. 233). This shows that the main service of these Gentile converts involves serving people. Their service is not in temple rites or abstaining from certain foods. Rather, their service involves bringing God's people, in this case the scattered Israelites, back to God Himself. I think that there are many applications to this picture. The main service of any believer is to bring other people into the presence of God Himself.

The progression of this picture of the Gentiles' salvation experience is wonderful. God purifies their lips, signifying that they are now purified on the inside. Out of their purified hearts comes words from their purified lips. By these lips they call upon the name of the Lord, meaning that they have a close relationship with Him. Then, they serve Him with one shoulder in one accord. Such service consists in bringing offerings to God. Those offerings, just as Paul describes in Romans 15:20, are people, presented to God for His enjoyment. What are the Israelites to "wait" for, as God commands them to do in Zephaniah 3:8? They are to wait for God to enact all that He has described in these verses. God will do it and will make the whole earth a suitable place where His name is called upon, where people serve Him and where offerings for Him originate.

The purification of Israel

God doesn't stop there. He will also work with His own people, the Israelites, purifying them by the strength of His sovereign power, "The congregation, being restored to favour, will be cleansed and sanctified by the Lord from every sinful thing" (Keil, p. 158). Whereas before the Lord had to plead with Israel to turn from hypocrisy to Him, now He will actively move to purify His poeple. He declares "then I will remove from your midst your proudly exultant ones" (Zephaniah 3;11) and "I will leave in your midst a people humble and lowly" (Zephaniah 3:12). The word translated "lowly" is explained beautifully by Keil. It "signifies bowed down, oppressed with the feeling of impotence for what is good, and the knowledge that deliverance is due to the compassionate grace of God alone; it is therefore the opposite of proud, which trusts in its own strength, and boasts of its own virtue. The leading characteristic of those who are bowed down will be trust in the Lord, the spiritual stamp of genuine piety" (Keil, p. 159). The remnant of seekers in Jerusalem will fittingly respond to the Lord, "They shall seek refuge in the name of the Lord" (Zephaniah 3:12). They will not lie, nor practice unrighteousness. The Lord will protect them, just like a good shepherd will protect his sheep, "For they shall graze and lie down, and none shall make them afraid" (Zephaniah 3:13).

God's work among both the Gentiles and the Jews, as outlined in these verses, will combine into an awesome testimony of His salvation. "The confessors of His name, whom the Lord will procure for Himself among the nations through the medium of the judgment, will offer to Him His dispersed nation as a sacrifice (vv. 9, 10). And the rescued remnant of Israel, in their humility, will trust in the Lord, and under the pastoral fidelity of their God have no more foe to fear, but rejoicing in the blessed fellowship of the Lord, be highly favoured and glorified (vv. 11–20)" (Keil, p. 155).

Exhortation to rejoice

After such a grand picture of the effects of God's salvation, Zephaniah's tone, exhortations and attitude completely change. He becomes bubbling, buoyant and overflowing with praise. He exhorts the people to rejoice, tells them that all their enemies are vanquished and vividly describes how God is in their midst in the most loving, caring and rejoicing way.

> 14 Sing aloud, O daughter of Zion; shout, O Israel! Rejoice and exult with all your heart, O daughter of Jerusalem!
> 15 The Lord has taken away the judgments against you; he has cleared away your enemies. The King of Israel, the Lord, is in your midst; you shall never again fear evil.
> 16 On that day it shall be said to Jerusalem: "Fear not, O Zion; let not your hands grow weak.
> 17 The Lord your God is in your midst, a mighty one who will save; he will rejoice over you with gladness; he will quiet you by his love; he will exult over you with loud singing.
> —Zephaniah 3:14-17

Previously, Zephaniah counselled the people to be silent, wail and gather together as if they were a bunch of stubble getting ready to be burned (Zephaniah 1:7, 11; 2:1). Here, his exhortations are completely different. Now he exhorts them to "sing aloud," "shout," and "rejoice and exult with all your heart" (Zephaniah 3:14). Previously, Zephaniah warned of the coming day of judgment. Now, those judgments are gone—"The Lord has taken away the judgments against you" (Zephaniah 3:15). Previously, Zephaniah described God as full of wrath, having "the fire of his jealousy" (Zephaniah 1:18), and full of anger (Zephaniah 2:3). Now, he portrays God in a completely different light: "The King of Israel, the Lord, is in your midst" (Zephaniah 3:15). He is a "mighty one who will save" (Zephaniah 3:17). "The word translated "mighty" is *gibbôr*, an adjective usually used as a noun, often translated "hero" or "warrior" as in 1:14. It is used most frequently with military activities to describe one "who has already distinguished himself by performing heroic deeds." In this case the word speaks of God who is "a warrior who brings salvation"" (Barker, p 495).

God is also full of love, both on the inside and as evident from the outside, "He will quiet you by his love; he will rejoice over you with gladness" (Zephaniah 3:17). G. Campbell-Morgan is very inspired by this scene. He likens God here to a mother with her child. "Then follows a picture of exquisite beauty. Let me say at once it is the picture of motherhood. It suggests the mother with the child in her arms. I cannot help feeling that Zephaniah had watched such a scene. He had seen her looking at the child, and rejoicing over it. Then he had seen her so full of joy that no word escaped her. She was silent in her love. Until, finally, no longer able to remain silent, she broke forth into singing. This is the prophet's picture of God" (Morgan, p. 88). The juxtaposition of silence and love paints a powerful image. "Silence in His love is an expression used to denote love deeply felt, which is absorbed in its object with thoughtfulness and admiration, and forms the correlate to rejoicing with exultation, i.e., to the loud demonstration of one's love. The two clauses contain simply a description, drawn from man's mode of showing love, and transferred to God, to set forth the great satisfaction which the Lord has in His redeemed people, and are merely a poetical filling up of the expression, "He will rejoice over thee with joy." This joy of His love will the Lord extend to all who are troubled and pine in misery" (Keil, p. 161). Barker gives a fitting conclusion, "This amazing love of God for human beings is inexplicable. Human minds would never dream up such a God. Human actions or human character could never deserve such love. God's love comes in his quiet absorption because this is who God is" (p. 496).

Zephaniah prepares the people for God's first-person words at the end of his book, by warmly comforting the people, telling them how intimate God is with them and how available He is to them. "Verses 17 and 18 make the transition from speaking about God in the third person to God's speaking in the first person. The first word of 3:17 is the divine personal name for the Lord. The reason why the people can rejoice is that the Lord is in their midst. Here "all tension built over the threatened judgment is relieved as the foreshadowing changes to fulfilled promise. By using this method of interrelating promise and completion the book's structure is tightly bound by allusion and concrete image"" (Barker, p. 495). God, who is in their midst and comforting them in His love, seeks to reassure His remnant who is now waiting for Him. This remnant will yet have to pass through many trials, tears and hardships before the salvation that they just heard about will come to pass. "In order, therefore, to offer to the pious a firm consolation of hope in the period of suffering that awaited them, and one on which their faith could rest in the midst of tribulation, Zephaniah mentions in conclusion the gathering together of all who pine in misery at a distance from Zion, and who are scattered far and wide, to assure even these of their future participation in the promised salvation" (Keil, p. 162).

In the last three verses of Zephaniah, God speaks to His people directly, proclaiming how He will gather His people and make them a praise throughout all the earth. The gathering God describes in this section is in sharp contrast to the one that Zephaniah previously described (Zephaniah 2:1). There it referred to a gathering of sticks to be burned in judgment. Here is it a gathering for celebration, comfort and testimony. Three times God wonderfully promises to gather this group, "I will gather those of you who mourn for the festival" (Zephaniah 3:18), "I will save the lame and gather the outcasts" (Zephaniah 3:19) and "I will bring you in, at the time I will gather you together" (Zephaniah 3:20). The two Hebrew words used for "gathering" in this section are used positively in other Old Testament passages. They refer to gathering food, to assembling for the purpose of worshiping the Lord and to collecting people in order give them a sense of belonging. After God deals with all the oppressors of His people, He will save the lame and gather them all together (Zephaniah 3:19). Once He has gathered them, He will comfort them by enjoying festivals together, "so that you will no longer suffer reproach" (Zephaniah 3:19). Furthermore, God will exult His people. He will "change their shame into praise and renown in all the earth" (Zephaniah 3:19) and He will make them "renowned and praised among all the peoples of the earth" (Zephaniah 3:20). Thus, God's people's fortunes will be fully restored. In that exultant gathering, God's restored people will be a glorious testimony of God's wonderful salvation.

CHAPTER TEN

Haggai

Haggai's prophecies are refreshing in their simplicity. He uses straightforward, simple words, and has few visionary utterances. His prophecy can easily be divided into four distinct prophetic burdens. In the first (Haggai 1:1-15), Haggai encourages Zerubbabel, Joshua and the people that it is indeed time to build the temple of the Lord, even though they do not think the time has come. All who hear begin to fear the Lord, are stirred up and eventually begin the rebuilding work. In the second prophesy (Haggai 2:1-9), which he uttered one month and twenty-one days after the first, Haggai encourages the people to be strong and continue to build, even though some of the builders think that the temple they are building is nothing in comparison to Solomon's. His third prophecy, (Haggai 2:10-19), which was uttered two months and three days after the second, announces to the people that God will now greatly bless them due to their obedience and fear of Him. The final prophesy (Haggai 2:20-23) is addressed only to Zerubbabel and contains the most visionary words offered by Haggai. He tells Zerubbabel that God is about to shake the entire earth and that He has chosen Zerubbabel and will make him like a signet ring on His finger. This is a clear prophecy of the Messiah, the grand vision with which Haggai ends his message.

Each of Haggai's prophecies is addressed to a different audience. The first is to Zerubbabel and Joshua, the second to everyone—Zerubbabel and Joshua and the people, the third is a question addressed to the priests, and the fourth to Zerubbabel alone. In a way the arc of Haggai's message can be understood by simply looking at who he addresses. He begins with the leaders, helping them see that the time for action is now. He continues with all the people, encouraging them to continue, even though it may seem like their efforts are fruitless. He then turns to the priests, teaching them that true holiness comes from obedience and that results in blessing. Finally, Haggai addresses Zerubbabel alone, as if at the end, his vision is full of the leader Zerubbabel who is a type of Christ—His rule and His kingdom. Haggai grows from the addressing the leaders and the people with their problems, through holiness, and ends in a grand vision of the Messiah.

Bring wood and build the house

His first word is addressed to Joshua the priest and Zerubbabel the governor. These two represent the entirety of the leadership of the people. Haggai realized that for anything to change nationally, he first has to address the leaders, their attitude, their problem and their condition. First, he tells them what the people they are leading are thinking, "These people say the time has not yet come to rebuild the house of the

Lord" (Haggai 1:2). The problem is that the people do not think it is time to build the temple. In fact, they might never think that the time is right. The other, unspoken problem is that the leaders did nothing throughout all the years to change this perception so the people would restart the building. So, Haggai talks to the leaders, "Is it a time for you yourselves to dwell in your paneled houses, while this house lies in ruins?" (Haggai 1:4). When Haggai describes their houses as "paneled" he is pointing out the luxury of their private dwelling; paneling indicates "the inside walls covered or inlaid with costly wood-work. Such were the houses of the rich and of the more distinguished men (cf. Jer. 22:14; 1 Kings 7:7). Living in such houses was therefore a sign of luxury and comfort" (Keil, p. 475). He contrasts this with the temple, which Haggai calls God's "house" and which lies in ruins.

To this sad situation Haggai abruptly charges Zerubbabel and Joshua, "Consider your ways" (Haggai 1:5). The literal Hebrew rendering of this phrase is to "set your heart upon your roads." Haggai pleads for these people to have great exercise of heart concerning their actions and the results. "To set the heart upon one's ways, i.e., to consider one's conduct, and lay it to heart. The ways are the conduct, with its results. J. H. Michaelis has given it correctly, "To your designs and actions, and their consequences" (Keil, p. 476). Jamieson et. al. also notice this, saying the phrase is "literally, "Set your heart" on your ways. The *plural* implies, Consider both what ye have done (actively, La 3:40) and what ye have suffered (passively) [JEROME]. Ponder earnestly whether ye have gained by seeking self at the sacrifice of God" (Vol. 1, p. 476).

What they are to ponder earnestly is their great efforts and investments over the past twenty some years verses their paltry returns. Haggai describes this simply and well, "You have sown much, and harvested little. You eat, but you never have enough; you drink, but you never have your fill. You clothe yourselves, but no one is warm. And he who earns wages does so to put them into a bag with holes" (Haggai 1:6). He admonishes them exactly what to do to remedy their sorry situation, "Go up to the hills and bring wood and build the house, that I may take pleasure in it and that I may be glorified, says the Lord" (Haggai 1:8). To put it simply: the people were neglecting God's house, which was lying in ruins. The remedy was for them to go to the mountain—any mountain, get wood from there, bring it to the house and build the house of the Lord. The result would be glory. That is a very simple request and a clear-cut path for correction.

Haggai then explains a little more about the inward waywardness of the people and the problem God has with them. Inwardly the people are looking in the wrong direction, "You looked for much," (Haggai 1:9) says the Lord. They are not looking for the Lord's glory or for the temple. Rather, they are stretching themselves, expecting and straining their eyes to look for "much." Keil says, that they "fixed your eye upon much" (p. 477). Jaimeson says they, "literally "looked" so as to turn your eyes "to much." The *Hebrew* infinitive here expresses *continued* looking. Ye hoped to have your store made "much" by neglecting the temple" (Vol. 1, p. 712). The Lord's response is to blow away the "much" that they are looking for. "when you brought it home, I blew it away" (Haggai 1:9). All of this occurs because God's house lies in ruins, while each person "busies himself with his own house" (Haggai 1:9). The people are busy, literally "running" for the sake of their houses. However, God's house is in ruins. Keil remarks that the description ""busies himself with his own house" does not mean "every one runs to his house," but "runs for his house," ל denoting the object of the running, as in Isa. 59:7 and Prov. 1:16. "When the house of Jehovah was in question, they did not move from the spot; but if it concerned their own house, they ran"" (p. 478). The result of this attitude and inaction towards God's house is that God calls for a drought on the land. The heavens withhold their dew and the earth withholds its produce.

The people respond and start building

Zerubbabel, Joshua and the people all react marvelously to the preaching of Haggai. They obey the voice of the Lord and the words of Haggai. The first thing that generates in them, is a healthy, good fear of God. "And the people feared the LORD" (Haggai 1:12). What a glorious first response! Before any outward action is performed, their inward *attitude* towards God becomes fruitful: "The first fruit of the hearing was, that the people feared before Jehovah" (Keil, p. 479). Maybe at this point they realize that in the future they will not answer to a king, an earthly ruler, or a financial advisor. The only One whose answer they have to prepare to give is to the God of the universe. All other things are small.

After such healthy fear is generated with them, Haggai confirms and God stirs within them. It is like the floodgates of heaven are open. "Then Haggai, the messenger of the LORD, spoke to the people with the LORD's message, "I am with you, declares the LORD." [14] And the LORD stirred up the spirit of Zerubbabel the son of Shealtiel, governor of Judah, and the spirit of Joshua the son of Jehozadak, the high priest, and the spirit of all the remnant of the people" (Haggai 1:13-14). Obedience is the joyous result of the Lord's presence with them. When they obey, the Lord adds fuel to the fire by stirring up their spirit. So, with revived, buoyant spirits, they resume the work on the house of the Lord on the twenty fourth day of the month, twenty-three days after Haggai spoke his first words.

Haggai's speaking broke through all the self-centeredness, financial, and even theological barriers that were holding back the leaders and the people from working on the temple of the Lord. They were afraid of the people around them. Haggai put a fear in them for the Lord, which was greater than their fear of the people. They were seeking much, that is, financial and material gain. Haggai showed them their poor returns and the reason God was blowing their "much" away. They might have been thinking that the temple didn't mean that much. Afterall, the temple didn't save the Jews from Babylon. Furthermore, the foundation that they had already laid was so small. Compared with Ezekiel's visionary temple, the "temple" they were making did not seem that important. After all, it was Cyrus, a Gentile king, who came up with the idea in the first place. Haggai addressed the theological issues by clearly stating that God desired a built-up temple. God Himself, "would take pleasure in it" that He "may be glorified" (Haggai 1:8). The time was now. The importance was real. The barriers were not insurmountable. Haggai clearly said "go" and eventually the people went and built.

Darby looks at this as Haggai's way of bringing the people to see the importance of the temple in their imperfect age. "The temple was necessarily the centre of this imperfect and intermediate state of the people. It was there, if God allowed the re-establishment of their worship, that the hearts of the people should centre. That was the outward form in which their piety as a people should be expressed. It was thus that the return of their heart to God should be manifested. Whatever deficiencies there might be in the restored Levitical service, still, it was the house of God, to which was attached all that could be re-established, and was the centre of its exercise" (Darby, p. 598).

Furthermore, Darby sees that Haggai stirred the people to action by getting them right inwardly with the God they served. Then they would have a right reaction to all the outward challenges that they faced. "The prophet, without troubling himself as to the king's intentions, encourages the people by turning their thoughts to Jehovah Himself, and shewing them that, after all, Jehovah reigned, cared for them, and would have them act in view of what He was for them, and seek His glory. For, weak as they were, He would thus be in relationship with them" (Darby, p. 601).

The second word—the future glory will be more than the past

Twenty-seven days after the people began the rebuilding work on the temple, Haggai speaks his second message. He addresses this message to everyone—Zerubbabel, Joshua and all the people—because everyone is putting their shoulders into the building work, after they had responded to Haggai's first message. His specific words concern the old men, whose memories might have become a stumbling block to the builders. Haggai asks, "Who is left among you who saw this house in its former glory? How do you see it now? Is it not as nothing in your eyes?" (Haggai 2:3). The young workers might have been excited and inspired as they cleared rubble, brought wood and built on the foundation that was laid some twenty years ago. They might have been full of joy that finally they could participate in a move of God, just as they had read about their ancestors doing many generations before them. However, their joy is tempered by another prevailing feeling emanating from the old men. The ones who had seen Solomon's temple look at the house they are building and consider it to be "nothing." Keil describes their comparison with Solomon's temple resulting in them thinking what they are doing is an absolute zero, "as not existing (nothing), so is it in your eyes" (p. 481).

The builders surely face many outward things that might cause them to despair. First, the temple they are building is a sad comparison to Solomon's. There is no way a group of around 40,000 people who are just establishing themselves in Judea could compete with the nation-scale, God-blessed resources Solomon used to build the first temple. Second, the people have only been interested in the temple for about the past two months. Now they are working, but they do not have a good track record of serving the Lord. Third, Haggai delivers his address on the last day of the feast of tabernacles, when the people were supposed to bring portions from the produce of their fields in to the temple. The produce this year is meager, un-blessed and gaunt. In the old mens' eyes, the evidence is disheartening, even to the point where they think "this is nothing."

Haggai's message addresses this perception by turning the people to see many inward, intangible yet real things of God. He points out that God is with them, that His word is true and firm, that His Spirit is with them and that the future glory of the house will be even greater than the past glory. Haggai is doing everything he can to pry these old men away from looking at the past and the outward things of the present.

He begins by exhorting each of the parties he addresses to "be strong." "Yet now be strong, O Zerubbabel, declares the Lord. Be strong, O Joshua, son of Jehozadak, the high priest. Be strong, all you people of the land, declares the Lord" (Haggai 2:4). If anyone has ever received such an exhortation—"be strong"—from a respected leader, that person knows how deeply encouraging that is. In fact, before Solomon embarked on his great building work for the temple, David used these same words as exhortation to his son. "Then David said to Solomon his son, "Be strong and courageous and do it. Do not be afraid and do not be dismayed, for the LORD God, even my God, is with you. He will not leave you or forsake you, until all the work for the service of the house of the LORD is finished"" (1 Chronicles 28:20).

Similarly, just as David encouraged Solomon to work because the Lord was with him, so also does Haggai encourage the people, "Work, for I am with you, declares the LORD of hosts" (Haggai 2:4). It is so much easier to accomplish a task when a person is supported and has a close, resourceful companion at his side. The greatest encouragement for work on the temple is that the Lord Himself is right there. They don't have to wonder if they are ok, if they will be overrun by enemies, if they are doing the right thing or if they are understanding God's will correctly. All uncertainty evaporates as they put stone upon stone, timber into timber and place the furniture with the Lord right there beside them. How encouraging, how comforting and how real it is to work alongside the Lord!

Haggai also encourages them based on the solid, firm word of God, which promises God's ever-present Spirit. He says, "according to the covenant that I made with you when you came out of Egypt. My Spirit remains in your midst. Fear not" (Haggai 2:5). The Hebrew translated "covenant" here is literally, "The word I cut." God reminds them of His enduring word and describes how he "cut" the word to make it firm. The word "cut" is usually associated with a covenant God makes. Jamieson et al. remark, "The *Hebrew* for to "covenant" is literally "to cut," alluding to the sacrificial victims *cut* in ratification of a covenant" (Vol. 1, p. 713). Here God is encouraging the people to remember the solid covenant which God made and the animals that were split apart to confirm the words, making them firm and secure promises.

God's firm, outwardly cut word, as emphasized by the physical sacrifices at the covenant initiation, points to an inward, mystical fact: God's Spirit is in their midst. Taylor et al., explain the thought here. "Haggai's point is that just as the Lord covenanted to be with Israel as far back as the exodus event, and just as his presence had been evident throughout their prior history, so now the community should confidently face their difficulties in the enabling power of the Spirit and free from the paralysis of fear about the future" (p. 157). God's promise insures that they can enjoy the living, active, enlightening, empowering, revealing and life-imparting Spirit of God as they work on the temple. The temple may not look outwardly glorious, but the Spirit of glory in their midst is very real. His presence is their great encouragement.

Haggai continues his prophetic encouragement by reminding the returned exiles that God will shake the entire known universe. "For thus says the LORD of hosts: Yet once more, in a little while, I will shake the heavens and the earth and the sea and the dry land" (Haggai 2:6). With this thought, he challenges those old men who were pining for the temple of Solomon's glory. It was as if he were saying to them, "This new temple may look like nothing in your eyes. But, let me tell you, there is no firm alternative. All the nations will be shaken." This is no new message to anyone who has been listening to the voices of the prophets. Two-hundred years ago Isaiah prophesied that in the day of God's anger, He would "make the heavens tremble, and the earth will be shaken out of its place" (Isaiah 13:13). Before Isaiah, Joel prophesied great shakings and warned people that the only refuge is the Lord Himself, "The LORD roars from Zion, and utters his voice from Jerusalem, and the heavens and the earth quake. But the LORD is a refuge to his people, a stronghold to the people of Israel" (Joel 3:16). Shaking is a picture of destruction. When

Tyre's walls shook from Nebuchadnezzar's armies the end was near (Ezekiel 26:10). When Samaria's thresholds are shaken their overthrow is imminent (Amos 9:1). Shaking will erase the authority of the kingdoms. It will decapitate all opposition in heaven and earth and will leave only God's kingdom and house remaining. Haggai repeats this oft spoken fact so that the old men would get it into their head. "Don't despise what you are doing. There is no firm alternative. The heaven and the earth will be shaken. There is no firmer place to invest anywhere on the earth. Look to the right place, to the only place which will survive the shaking."

Haggai's final encouragement is his declaration that the future glory of the house they are building will be greater than any past glory. In saying this, God is making it abundantly clear, that the temple they are building is not irrelevant. God is interested in it and God will bring glory to it. Once the great shaking happens, all the glory of the kingdoms will be released from their authority. Then God's house will be filled with glory. "⁷ And I will shake all nations, so that the treasures of all nations shall come in, and I will fill this house with glory, says the LORD of hosts. ⁸ The silver is mine, and the gold is mine, declares the LORD of hosts. ⁹ The latter glory of this house shall be greater than the former, says the LORD of hosts. And in this place I will give peace, declares the LORD of hosts.'" (Haggai 2:7-9). The Hebrew phrase for "treasures of the nations" in verse seven has been interpreted differently over the ages. Keil reviews that, "most of the earlier orthodox commentators understood the Messiah, after the example of the Vulgate, ...and Luther's "consolation of the Gentiles" (p. 484). This may very well refer to the Messiah, although Keil himself understands the plural of the Hebrew word "treasures" to disallow this interpretation. He, along with many others, understands the "treasures of the nations" to be, "the valuable possessions of the heathen, or according to v. 8 their gold and silver, or their treasures and riches" (p. 485). The vision of all the nations bringing their glory to the dwelling place of God is surely an enduring theme and a clear truth of what will be. The nations even bring their glory to the New Jerusalem (Revelation 21:26). The end result is that the house of God is the recipient of all the glory such that the latter glory will be greater than even the glory of Solomon's temple. The glorified, riches-filled temple will be the site of peace for the entire earth. This view should greatly encourage the builders, because they should realize that God will elevate their work to glorious realms and make it a sign of peace for the entire earth. They are not simply placing brick upon brick in an obscure corner of the Persian Empire. They are playing a role in fulfilling God's plan for the earth.

How dare those old men think that what was going on in the rebuilding of the temple was "as nothing!" Haggai's words show that these guys were earthly to the uttermost. These sorry individuals looked at the hut-like temple that they were building, the paltry harvest and the sad group of people and concluded "this is nothing." They forgot God was with them. They forgot the words of the covenant God cut with the people. They forgot the Spirit. They forgot that God was going to shake the heavens and the earth and that all opposition from those realms was unstable and temporary. They forgot that God would bring the treasures of all nations to the house. They forgot that God was the source of glory and the conduit for communicable glory. The forgot that peace would be in Jerusalem, because it is the city of peace according to God's promise. How dare they forget! How dare they risk tempering the fervency of the youth by too much knowledge of the outward things and so called "wisdom" from their experience. I thank the Lord for Haggai. Through him, God could turn back the people to see heavenly and divine things.

The third word—blessings for obedience

Two months and three days after Haggai's word to the old men, he gives his third prophesy. This word is addressed as a question to the priests and deals with holiness and blessing. Haggai first asks the priests how far holiness can be transferred by the holy meat that is sacrificed at the altar. Concerning that offered meat, Moses says, "Whatever touches its flesh shall be holy" (Leviticus 6:27). Based on this verse, Haggai asks in essence, "how far can this holiness go?" He says, "'If someone carries holy meat in the fold of his garment and touches with his fold bread or stew or wine or oil or any kind of food, does it become holy?'" (Haggai 2:12). Because the food is touched with the fold, the holiness is not transmitted, therefore, "The priests answered and said, "No"" (Haggai 2:12). Then Haggai asks another question about the transfer of uncleanness, particularly from one who has become unclean through contact with a dead person. This is one of the strongest forms of uncleanness, requiring seven days and two washings to eradicate, concerning which Moses writes, "And whatever the unclean person touches shall be unclean, and anyone who touches it shall be unclean until evening" (Numbers 19:22). Haggai asks, "If someone who is unclean by contact with a dead body touches any of these, does it become unclean?" (Haggai 2:13). Because the unclean person touches the food, his uncleanness is transmitted to the food, which then becomes unclean. Thus, "The priests answered and said, "It does become unclean"" (Haggai 2:13).

Haggai replies to the priests in front of the people and applies these scenarios to their current condition, "So is it with this people, and with this nation before me, declares the LORD, and so with every work of their hands. And what they offer there is unclean" (Haggai 2:14). One could imagine Haggai pointing to the altar as he was saying "what they offer there."

The altar Haggai is pointing to is a very familiar sight for the returned exiles. One of the first things that the remnant did when they arrived in Jerusalem was to build the altar (Ezra 3:3). From that early time, they offered regular sacrifices, free-will offerings and celebrated the feasts according to what should be offered upon the altar (Ezra 3:5). Haggai's application to them is to tell them that the holiness of the meat sacrificed at that altar did not transmit to them. It did not permeate beyond the garment "fold" to make the priests, the people, the produce of the land, or the nation holy. Furthermore, the people were unclean in the same way that a person who touches a dead body is unclean. That uncleanness in the people corrupts their sacrifices and all their work, so as to make the whole enterprise unclean before the Lord.

Haggai proceeds to illustrate how the meat from the altar did not result in the "bread or stew or wine or oil or any kind of food" becoming "holy." He reminds them how little they had received from the land up to this point. "When one came to a heap of twenty measures, there were but ten. When one came to the wine vat to draw fifty measures, there were but twenty" (Haggai 2:16). Haggai quotes Amos, who spoke about two hundred years earlier, in order to explain what was happening in the nation. "I struck you and all the products of your toil with blight and with mildew and with hail, yet you did not turn to me, declares the Lord" (Haggai 2:17 quoting Amos 4:9). As Amos reveals, the problem with the people is that they did not turn to God. When they saw blighted harvests, they never asked God, "Why?" or, "What are You saying?" or, "How might have we erred?" Instead, they blundered on, offering holy gifts at the altar but never seeing that holiness transfer to their land. Instead, Haggai pointedly declares, "Indeed, the vine, the fig tree, the pomegranate, and the olive tree have yielded nothing" (Haggai 2:19).

However, now, Haggai is heralding a great change. He boldly declares God's turn of heart, reporting that God is now declaring, "But from this day on I will bless you" (Haggai 2:19).

It is surely wonderful that God begins blessing His people. However, upon a little consideration, it is not obvious exactly why He begins blessing them now, on the twenty-fourth day of the ninth month. Commentators differ in their opinion. Some, like Jamieson et al., understand "this day" to be "*the day* of their obedience" (Vol. 1, p. 715), that is, the day that they started to rebuild the temple. Why was the twenty-fourth day of the ninth month a special day when blessing was given, even though they started rebuilding the temple three months earlier, on the twenty-fourth day of the sixth month? Jamieson understands this period to be a testing period, where they built, but didn't see immediate blessing. It was almost as if God were teaching them persistent obedience, which was then followed by blessing. "We may trust God's promise to bless us, though we see no visible sign of its fulfilment (Hab 2:3)" (Jamieson et al, Vol. 1, p. 715). In this case, the "dead" body which made the people unclean was their disobedience to the command of God to build the temple. Once they became obedient, they were clean, and were thus able recipients of divine favor, albeit delayed for testing's sake.

Another view considers the "dead body" that made them unclean to be their contact with the unclean nations. Even though they offered sacrifices at the altar and had begun the work of rebuilding the temple, all of these were considered unclean, because the people were not yet separated to God in an absolute way. Thus, Haggai's word shows that it was not just obedience to the outward commands of God to rebuild the temple that was important. No, it was also important that their life was holy, that their contact with the nations was not defiling. This agrees with Haggai's quote from Amos. The quote tells them that the proper reaction to blighted crops was to return to God, not merely do work of rebuilding. God's demand was higher, purer and pointed toward a narrower way. God was pleased that they were building the temple and encouraged them to continue building through hardship. However, it was not enough. They also had to return to Him in their heart and fully separate from the unclean nations. Then, they would see blessings flow. In support of this view, we read that "the priests and the Levites had purified themselves together; all of them were clean" (Ezra 6:20), in preparation for the Passover feast. Furthermore, the Passover was celebrated by all the people who had, "separated himself from the uncleanness of the peoples of the land to worship the Lord, the God of Israel" (Ezra 6:21). To become clean, God's people needed a clear separation from the nations around them.

> According to Haggai the people were in a deplorably sinful condition, and everything they came in contact with was thereby defiled due to their impurity. As a result, both their work on the temple and the religious sacrifices they periodically offered were unacceptable to the Lord. Like a cancer that has invaded a human body, bringing destruction and disintegration to the cells it comes in contact with, so these people were bringing spiritual defilement to everything they touched. Until the issue of their spiritual condition was resolved, no amount of religious activity they performed would be acceptable to the Lord. Haggai had uncovered and laid embarrassingly bare a need for repentance on the part of the people if their efforts at restoration were to enjoy the blessing and acceptance from God for which they hoped." The situation was desperate, but in the unit that follows the prophet moves the matter to a resolution
> —Taylor, p. 179

Dennett sees the sinful condition as a result of the people "defiled by evil associations" (p. 15). "The point here is that the Jews cannot be made holy by unholy fellowship with their pagan neighbors; instead, they and their worship will become corrupted by such associations" (NET, Notes).

Haggai's fourth word—Zerubbabel will be like the Lord's signet ring

Later the same day on which Haggai gave his third word, the twenty-fourth day of the ninth month, a fourth word came to Haggai. This last word is unique because Haggai addresses it to Zerubbabel alone. All Haggai's attention now rests on the governor. He is not looking at the house, the people, the failed harvests, the despair, the blessing of harvests, the cleanness or uncleanness, or the holy and defiled. All are set aside for this last word. Haggai is not only occupied with the governor, but with the One—the Messiah—who will come after Zerubbabel. Haggai sees the One who will eventually occupy his position and what that future Occupant means to God. This last word is elevated, soaring, and transcendent.

Haggai's third and fourth prophesies are related, beyond the fact that they are given on the same day. "There is an intimate connection between the two a connection as evident as it is beautiful. The last words of the former were, "From this day will I bless you." Now the blessing of the remnant in the land became at once prophetic of the restoration and blessing of Israel in the kingdom; but this involves two things, as revealed everywhere in the prophetic scriptures, viz., the manifestation of the Messiah, and the judgment of the nations; and it is these two things which are found in this brief prophecy" (Dennett, p. 42). Thus, Haggai "shifts attention from the rebuilding of the temple to future prospects for a renewed Davidic rule" (Taylor, p. 82).

Haggai's fourth word begins with similar words contained in his second prophecy; he reviews how God will shake the nations and destroy all the kingdoms of earth (Haggai 2:21-22). In restating this, he reminds Zerubbabel that nothing in this world—no nation, no earthly power, no authority—will stand forever. Then, Haggai turns to the governor and sees with piercing insight, what Zerubbabel's descendent will be to God. "On that day, declares the Lord of hosts, I will take you, O Zerubbabel my servant, the son of Shealtiel, declares the Lord, and make you like a signet ring, for I have chosen you, declares the Lord of hosts" (Haggai 2:23).

The most striking phrase of this final prophesy is God's declaration that He will make Zerubbabel "like a signet ring." The vast majority of commentators consider this phrase to refer not to Zerubbabel himself, but to Messiah, his descendant (see Matthew 1:12 and Luke 3:27). God is saying that Messiah, Zerubbabel's descendent, will be like a signet ring to Him.

A signet ring is a well-known Old Testament object. It is a seal, which is pressed into wax or clay, and which is a sign of authority. When Jezebel wrote a letter in Ahab's name, she made the letter an official edict of the king when she, "sealed it with his seal" (1 Kings 21:8). When Judah asked Tamar what she wanted as a pledge for his payment to her, she asked for his signet (Genesis 38:18), a sure sign of his identity and a precious item related to all his official dealings. The seal became an intimate, ever-present part of the wearer, as is evident in the Shulamite's request to Solomon, "set me as a seal on your heart, as a seal upon your arm" (Song of Songs 8:6). God likened the kings of Judah as His signet ring, saying when he was displeased with Coniah, that even though he "were the signet ring on my right hand, yet I would tear you off" (Jeremiah 22:24). The seal is a symbol for official action on the part of the owner. The stamp made by a signet ring "refers to a seal made of engraved stone impressed in clay or wax to authenticate a document" (Harris, p. 334). The signet ring was an object of fine craftsmanship and exquisite workmanship, as evidenced by many of the priest's ornaments, like the gold plate on his forehead or the stones on his breastplate and shoulders, being likened to the work that a craftsman would do in making a signet ring (Exodus 28:11, 21, 36).

God making the Messiah like a signet ring, paints a powerful picture of the relationship between God and Christ. "On the day on which Jehovah would overthrow the kingdoms of the nations, He would make Zerubbabel like a signet-ring, which is inseparable from its possessor; that is to say, He would give him a position in which he would be and remain inseparably connected with Him (Jehovah), would therefore not cast him off, but take care of him as His valuable possession" (Keil, p. 497). The ring "portrays Zerubbabel as one who uniquely represented divine authority and who appeared as the Lord's coregent" (Taylor, p. 197). What this implies is that "the Messiah, represented by Zerubbabel, will be God's official seal and certainty of all his decrees" (Harris, p. 342). It means that "Christ is the "signet" on God's hand: always in the Father's presence, ever pleasing in his sight. The signet of an Eastern monarch was the sign of *delegated authority;* so Christ (Mt 28:18; Jn 5:22, 23)" (Jamieson et al, Vol. 1, p. 715).

Considering Christ as the Father's seal gives a lot of insight into how the Father is with the Son. If the Father is not doing anything, then one might hardly notice the seal on His finger. The seal is so close to Him and one with Him. This is a picture that there is just one God. However, if the Father moves, then one might notice the seal much more. Because Christ is the Father's seal, whenever the Father acts, then the seal of that act and the impression given is that of Christ. The Father never acts without Christ, the seal. Anytime the Father moves it looks like Christ, has the image of Christ and is sealed with Christ. When the Father imparts life, gives laws, creates, reveals, inspires, forgives or redeems then He uses the seal, Christ Himself. Christ is God's active instrument, through whom He exercises authority, creates, transforms and conforms to His image. This "Christ seal" has been meticulously, artfully, and perfectly shaped to represent the exact image worthy of God. Christ is God's sign of authority, His stamp of approval. Christ the seal is with the Father at all times. Christ the seal is ever present and ready to carry out all the wisdom of the Father.

Christ being God's seal also is seen in the New Testament. The Father has put His seal upon the Son, "For on him God the Father has set his seal" (John 6:27). Furthermore, in Christ the believers are sealed, which is the work of the Holy Spirit, "In him [Christ] you also, when you heard the word of truth, the gospel of your salvation, and believed in him [Christ], were sealed with the promised Holy Spirit" (Ephesians 1:13). Haggai has thus given us a window into the workings of the Trinity, which is expanded in the New Testament. God the Father set His seal upon Christ, who is the signet ring on the Father's hand. Thenceforth, the Father's work bears the image of Christ. The Father's special work is to make the believers share that same image, the same seal that is engraved on His signet ring. That work, according to the New Testament is done by the Spirit, who has sealed the believers (Ephesians 4:30). Thus, we see the Father as the ring wearer, the King; the Son as the seal upon His finger, the sign of His authority and work; and the Spirit who applies what God is doing and makes God's believers into the same image that the seal bears. This is the grand working of the Triune God.

The church fathers also look at the Father and Son in terms of ring wearer and seal. Ambrose looks at the Father and Son in terms of a living seal. "How then do you wish the Son of God to have made these things? Like a signet ring which does not feel the impression it makes? But the Father made all things in wisdom, that is, He made all things through the Son, who is the Virtue and Wisdom of God" (Ambrose, p. 309).

Augustine uses a seal and the likeness that a seal has to human sight, to explain the Father and Son. In his book, "On the Trinity," he looks for pictures of the Trinity in the common things of life. He introduces the topic, "Let us try, then, if we can, to discover in this outer man also, some trace, however slight, of the Trinity. …Let us use, then, principally the testimony of the eyes" (Augustine, p. 144). Augustine describes how an object that a person sees impresses itself as an image in that person's mind. He likens this process to a seal impressing itself on wax. In this everyday process, in which a person can remember the image of an object after he has seen it, he sees the Father (as the object observed) and the Son (as the image of the object in the mind). This, he sees, as a ring imprinted on wax. "For when a ring is imprinted on wax, it does not follow that no image is produced, because we cannot discern it unless when it has been separated. But since, after the wax is separated, what was made remains, so that it can be seen; we are on that account easily persuaded that there was already also in the wax a form impressed from the ring before it was separated from it" (Augustine, p. 146). Augustine's example is applied to the Trinity in this way. When the seal makes an image in the wax, it is like an object that a person sees making an image in that person's mind. This is like God the Father (the object seen) making Christ His seal (the image in the mind). In this example Augustine sees the uniqueness of Christ as being the only One who can receive the imprint of the seal and keep the image stamped upon it. "But if the ring were imprinted upon a fluid, no image at all would appear when it was withdrawn" (Augustine, p. 146). Just like a dull mind cannot remember the object seen, because an image was never made in the mind, any other substance cannot bear the image of God. Christ, however, is different. Because of His humanity and His specialness, He is able to fully bear the image of God, just like a sharp mind can recall the image of a body even after the body is removed from view. This is the wonder and marvel of Christ, who has been made a signet ring by the Father.

From this profound description we see how Haggai's vision was full of the Messiah as he gave his final prophetic word to Zerubbabel, the ancestor of the coming Messiah. Haggai delved into how the Messiah would be with God. He saw how the Father would choose the Messiah and how the Messiah would be united with the Father as a signet ring.

CHAPTER ELEVEN

Zechariah

The book of Zechariah divides itself more easily than most prophetic books into simple sections. The first is Zechariah's initial charge to the people to return to the Lord so the Lord might return to them (Zechariah 1:1-6). The second contains eight visions that Zechariah received in one night (Zechariah 1:7-6:9). In the space of one evening, Zechariah is shown the nations who have persecuted the Jews and who are now at rest, God's jealousy to restore Jerusalem, the restoration of the fallen priesthood, the rebuilt temple, the shining of God's people as a lampstand, the purification of Israel and the judgment of the sinful nations of the world. The third section contains Zechariah's speaking to the people of his generation, including his crowning of Joshua and his response to the men from Bethel who ask about fasts (Zechariah 6:10-8). In Zechariah's response, he shows that he has learned a lot from the night visions. The fourth section contains two oracles, one concerning the Gentiles nations and the other concerning Israel connected by a prophetic sign concerning God's shepherding of the nation (Zechariah 9-14). In the oracle concerning the nations Zechariah describes how God will judge the nations, save some of them as a remnant, bring in the Messiah and regather and restore Israel. The section between describes how God will try to shepherd the nation and how His shepherding will be rejected. The oracle concerning Israel shows how Jerusalem will be surrounded by armies, the Lord will protect His people, pour out His Spirit, and purify the nation. Then, the whole earth will be gloriously restored.

God's plea for the nation to return

Zechariah's opening words are a direct plea from God for His people to draw closer to Him. "Return to me, says the LORD of hosts, and I will return to you, says the LORD of hosts. Do not be like your fathers, to whom the former prophets cried out" (Zechariah 1:3-4). Zechariah speaks these words to the people after they had recently responded to the preaching Haggai by starting to rebuild the temple again. In opening with this statement, it is very clear that Zechariah sees something lacking in the returnees. Even though they have returned from Babylon, they have not fully returned to God. Even though they had responded to the preaching of Haggai and resumed the building of the temple, they have not paid adequate attention to their nearness with God. If they would fully return to God, then God would fully return to them. The goal is a mutual returning—a mutual joining where God and His people dwell together.

Just like the people had recently responded to Haggai's words and resumed the rebuilding of the temple, the people respond to Zechariah's words. Zechariah describes that the people "repented and said, 'As the LORD of hosts purposed to deal with us for our ways and deeds, so has he dealt with us'" (Zechariah 1:6). This indicates that the people demonstrated some "return" to the Lord. The word for "repented" here is the same word the Lord charged the people to do—return. Furthermore, they acknowledged that the hardships that their ancestors went through were consequences of the actions of the community at that time. This indicates that the people who listened to Zechariah had some humility, in that they saw that *they* were the problem and were not blaming past judgments on an unrighteous God. Their return and humble realization were both good signs.

However, it is hard to know if this was an adequate response on the side of the people. They did repent and understand that all the past dealings that God had with them were merited because of their wicked deeds. However, it is not clear if they really had fully returned to the Lord. Possibly, at this point, they didn't even know what it meant to fully turn to the Lord. It is also possible that Zechariah himself didn't know the full implication of the people returning to the Lord and the Lord returning to them. One way to look at the rest of the book of Zechariah is that it contains God's description of what His initial plea means; what "return to Me and I will return to you" looks like is the rest of the book of Zechariah. We will see that it involves God's intentions, the Messiah coming, the cleansing of the people, the work of the Spirit, the shining of the lampstand, truth and justice and the restoration of all the earth. Only with these elements do we fully see the extent, the intimacy, the power, the glory, and the wonder of the union of the mighty God with His people. Only here do we see the full return of man to God and God to man. It is with this in mind that we go to the next section: the visions of Zechariah.
Zechariah's night visions

On one eventful night, the eleventh month of the second year of Darius, Zechariah saw eight visions that must have surely changed his life forever. Together the visions present a concise, clear view of God's grand plan for His people, the Messiah and the nations of the earth. These visions show God's anger at the nations for their maltreatment of His people and His choice to restore Jerusalem (Vision 1—the man on the red horse). They show how God will rightly judge the nations who have assaulted Israel (Vision 2—the horns and craftsmen) and, as a result, will dwell with His people in Jerusalem along with the remnants of those same nations (Vision 3—the man with the measuring line). They show Zechariah how God will restore the current degraded priesthood of Israel and will bring in the Messiah, who He calls the "Branch" (Vision 4—Joshua). They show how God will inspire Zerubbabel to complete the building of the temple and make His people a bright shining lampstand (Vision 5—lampstand and olive trees). They conclude by showing how God will eradicate iniquity from His land (Vision 6 and 7—the flying scroll and the ephah vessel) and how the wrath of God will find rest in regards to all the nations of the earth (Vision 8—the four chariots). Together, these visions teach Zechariah about God's choice of Jerusalem, His intention to judge and restore the nations, His plan to glorify the currently degraded priesthood headed by Joshua the high priest, His intention to have Zerubbabel complete the rebuilding of the temple and make His people shine, His way of cleansing the land from iniquity and His final judgment of all the nations on earth. Not a bad lesson series for a single night's visions!

The man on a red horse

The first vision teaches Zechariah that God is about to move to restore Jerusalem and, at the same time, is angry with the nations who have previously terrorized Israel. God shows Zechariah a scene that unfolds in the midst of a grove of fragrant myrtle trees growing in a deep ravine. In that valley, he sees a group of red, sorrel and white horses standing before the Angel of the Lord, who is also standing among the myrtles. The horses are led by a man riding a red horse. The Lord had sent them to patrol the earth and now they are reporting back to the Angel of the Lord, saying, "We have patrolled the earth, and behold all the earth remains at rest" (Zechariah 1:11). At this point, the Angel of the Lord cries out, 'O LORD of hosts, how long will you have no mercy on Jerusalem and the cities of Judah, against which you have been angry these seventy years?' (Zechariah 1:12). The Lord answers with words of comfort, saying that He is indeed exceedingly jealous for Jerusalem. He has returned to Jerusalem and declares that His house will be built there—"the measuring line will be stretched out over Jerusalem" (Zechariah 1:16). At the same time, He is exceedingly angry with all the nations who are now at rest, because in the past He was only a little angry, but they furthered the disaster. Now, however, He "will again comfort Zion and again choose Jerusalem" (Zechariah 1:17).

Myrtle trees are fragrant, low lying, evergreen trees with delicate white or pink flowers. They appear in passages that describe God's restoration (Isaiah 41:19). Here they may represent the returned Israelites, who are fragrant to God, yet in a low estate—in the deep ravine. The Angel of the Lord, God Himself, is with them, among the myrtles in their low estate. The report of the patrolling horses emphasizes that God knows about the nations who have put Israel in their low condition. They are at rest and Jerusalem in decimated. Now,

God is intending to move to make things different. It is not good that the nations are at rest and that there is no movement among them. God is exceedingly angry with the nations and He intends to restore Jerusalem. He is with His people and intends to comfort them and witness His house built in the currently ruined city. When He declares He will stretch out His measuring line over Jerusalem, He is indicating that a great building will take place. This vision assures Zechariah that God knows the conditions of the nations, cares about the decimation of Jerusalem and is with His people in their low estate. Furthermore, it assures Zechariah that God is seeking to bring His people comfort and mercy through His establishing of Jerusalem.

Four horns and four craftsmen

Zechariah's second vision teaches him that the nations who scatter Israel will be cast down and terrified according to God's masterful craftsmanship. In this simple vision God shows Zechariah four horns and four craftsmen. The horns have scattered Jerusalem and the craftsman have come to terrify and cast down the horns.

The horns, a symbol of power, represent nations who have lifted up their strengths against the land of Israel to scatter it. Many commentators see in these horns the four kingdoms of Daniel chapters 4 and 7; namely, Babylon, Persia, Greece and Rome. The word translated here as "craftsmen" is a Hebrew word that is used to describe an engraver of stones, a metal worker or a carpenter. These skilled workmen terrify the horns of the nations and cast them down. Thus, they are a picture of the many ways, miraculous and otherwise, God has at His disposal to limit the destruction the horns, the nations, may inflict upon Israel. God, as a Master Craftsman, can even make something of beauty out of that destruction! Some craftsmen could be the other nations that helped overcome the horns. Possibly, the last craftsman is Christ, just as the Mountain cut out without hands crushes the last kingdom in Daniel 2:34-35. This vision assures Zechariah that God's provision is larger than the fury of the nations set against Israel. His craftsmen can terrify them and produce something of His workmanship from their destruction.

The man with the measuring line

In Zechariah's third vision, he beholds a man walking and holding a measuring line in his hand. When Zechariah asks him where he is going, he replies, "To measure Jerusalem, to see what is its width and what is its length" (Zechariah 2:2). Another angel approaches Zechariah's tour-guide angel, and declares, "Run, say to that young man, 'Jerusalem shall be inhabited as villages without walls, because of the multitude of people and livestock in it. And I will be to her a wall of fire all around, declares the LORD, and I will be the glory in her midst'" (Zechariah 1:4-5). After this vision, the Lord tells Zechariah about His intention for three different parties. First, to the Jews who are still captive in Babylon, He commands them to escape. Second, to the nations who plundered Israel, the Lord declares that they themselves will be plundered by their own slaves. Finally, to Israel, the daughter of Zion, God commands them to "sing and rejoice," for, He says, "I come and I will dwell in your midst" (Zechariah 2:10). Furthermore, He declares that there will be a day when even the nations are included in His people with whom He dwells in Jerusalem. He says "many nations shall join themselves to the LORD in that day, and shall be my people. And I will dwell in your midst, and you shall know that the LORD of hosts has sent me to you" (Zechariah 2:11).

This vision causes Zechariah to see how utterly marvelous are God's thoughts concerning the future Jerusalem. As Zechariah sees the man with the measuring line intending to measure the city, his thoughts must go to the details and characteristics of what Jerusalem will be in God's plan. Instead of hearing the results of the measurements—how many cubits are its width and length—God shows Zechariah something much more. God Himself will be a wall around Jerusalem. He will also be the glory within her. Such words surely denote more than a city of stone and brick on the earthly sight of Jerusalem. Eventually, this heavenly city will include not only the Jews, but also the Gentiles—many nations will become His people—and God will dwell with them as they dwell in the city. What Zechariah sees here is the mutual dwelling of God with man, man with God. He sees Jews and Gentiles as one people dwelling together with God Himself as wall of fire around them and the glory in their midst. In light of this marvelous vision, the glory of the nations fades, as their very own slaves plunder them. In light of this marvelous divine-human entity all those in captivity should flee from where they are in order that they also could become a part of this marvel. When God declares this marvelous vision, it makes sense that it would involve the coming of the Messiah, who was sent by the Father Himself. Thus, the Lord mysteriously declares, "I will dwell in your midst, and you shall know that the Lord of hosts has sent me to you" (Zechariah 2:11).

Joshua clothed anew

Zechariah's fourth vision teaches him that God will restore the degraded priesthood of Israel and will eventually make way for the Messiah, the Branch. God shows Zechariah a scene held at God's divine court. There, Joshua, the high priest, dressed in filthy robes and standing in front of the Angel of the Lord, is being accused by Satan who is standing beside him. God's attendants are surrounding the court, ready to do His bidding. The Angel of the Lord speaks to Satan, saying, "The LORD rebuke you, O Satan! The LORD who has chosen Jerusalem rebuke you! Is not this a brand plucked from the fire?" (Zechariah 3:2). He thus rebukes Satan and describes Joshua as a brand plucked from the fire—a survivor of the Babylonian captivity. The Lord then commands the waiting attendants to remove the filthy garments from Joshua and put festive robes upon him. The Lord tells Joshua, "Behold, I have taken your iniquity away from you, and I will clothe you with pure vestments" (Zechariah 3:4). At this point, Zechariah interjects his thought into the scene as well. In addition to giving Joshua pure vestments, Zechariah requests, "Let them put a clean turban on his head" (Zechariah 3:5), which the attendants do under the approving gaze of the Angel of the Lord. Zechariah's request shows how passionate he is in regards to the full restoration of the priesthood of Israel—new robes are great; a clean turban is even better.

After Joshua is newly clothed, the Angel of the Lord challenges him with these words, "If you will walk in my ways and keep my charge, then you shall rule my house and have charge of my courts, and I will give you the right of access among those who are standing here" (Zechariah 3:7). In saying this, the Angel is promising Joshua rule over His house and rare access to God Himself, just like His attendants at His court have access to Him. This promise is contingent on Joshua's faithfulness towards the Lord.

Additionally, the Angel of the Lord introduces the coming Messiah as a Branch and a Stone to Joshua. He tells Joshua and his "friends who sit before you"—the rest of the priests—that God "will bring in [His] servant, the Branch" (Zechariah 3:8).

Furthermore, He will set a stone before Joshua, "on the stone that I have set before Joshua, on a single stone with seven eyes, I will engrave its inscription, declares the Lord of hosts, and I will remove the iniquity of this land in a single day" (Zechariah 3:9). When the Angel introduces the Branch and the Stone, he is promising the coming of the Messiah, who, as a Branch, will build the spiritual temple of the Lord and who, as a Stone, will be the foundation for such a building. This promise results in blessing for everyone, "In that day, declares the Lord of hosts, every one of you will invite his neighbor to come under his vine and under his fig tree" (Zechariah 3:10).

The lessons of this dramatic scene are relatively straightforward. Just as Joshua received festive robes and a clean turban, God will restore the priesthood of Israel, even though they are "brands plucked from the fire," or survivors from the Babylonian captivity. Just as He claims in the vision that He will do this because He has chosen Jerusalem, God's acts of restoration will be based on His choosing of the city and His desire to restore it, not any merit that the brand has in himself.

God's words to Joshua show that the restored priesthood is not an end in itself. It actually is a step the nation must take towards a richer, more heavenly blessing—the coming of the Messiah. If Joshua is faithful, God will give him charge, authority, rule, and will give him special access to Himself. Furthermore, this will lay a foundation for the Messiah, Christ, to come. Messiah will come as a Branch, signifying a sprout that grows out of a cut-down tree, that is full of life, vigor, and freshness. That sprout will actually accomplish the building work of God (see Zechariah 6:10). This Messiah will also be a stone with seven eyes, who is good for God's building and whose eyes see all things for the interest of God and His work.

A shining lampstand

Zechariah's fifth vision teaches him that God's people will become a shining lampstand, working together under the move of the Spirit. For this vision, Zechariah's tour-guide angel wakes him up, like a person who has just woken up from sleep and asks Zechariah what he sees. The freshly awakened Zechariah replies that he sees a golden lampstand with seven lamps upon it. On top of the lampstand is a golden bowl for oil, with forty-nine pipes that allow the oil to flow to the lamps, seven pipes per lamp. Two olive trees, representing sons of oil, stand beside the lampstand, one on each side. The branches of the olive trees are connected via two pipes to the golden bowl. They empty their oil, called gold, into the bowl, which then supplies it to the lamps.

When Zechariah asks what he is seeing, his tour-guide angel replies, "This is the word of the Lord to Zerubbabel: Not by might, nor by power, but by my Spirit, says the Lord of hosts. Who are you, O great mountain? Before Zerubbabel you shall become a plain. And he shall bring forward the top stone amid shouts of 'Grace, grace to it!'" (Zechariah 4:6-7). In answering Zechariah with these words, the angel indicates that the entire scene is a working out of the Word of God, by the power of God's Spirit. The great mountain of difficulties that are before Zerubbabel will be overcome. Eventually, Zerubbabel will set the top stone—the last, uppermost stone—in order to complete the building of the temple. The setting of the top stone is a picture of God's grace.

The word of the Lord then comes to Zechariah encouraging him even more for the building of the temple. God informs him that Zerubbabel's hands have laid the foundation of the temple and that his hands will finish it. "For whoever has despised the day of small things shall rejoice, and shall see the plumb line in the hand of Zerubbabel. "These seven are the eyes of the Lord, which range through the whole earth'" (Zechariah 4:10). This word addresses a thought among some that the building of the temple has so far been like a "small thing," which seems insignificant. Those small things should not be despised. Furthermore, they will rejoice, along with the seven eyes of God, because a plumb line—a line for building—will be in Zerubbabel's hand and he will be able to fully complete the building of the Lord's house.

The lesson Zechariah sees from this vision is awe inspiring. From this vision he would understand the glorious potential that God's people have to shine to the world. Shining comes when all the people are in cooperation together under the work of the Spirit. The olive trees are "sons of oil," servants of God faithfully supplying oil—the Holy Spirit—for God's enterprise. These are most likely Joshua and Zerubbabel for the time Zechariah is prophesying. These sons of oil are connected to other faithful people, who make up the pipes to convey the oil to the bowl, the bowl containing the oil, and other channels to bring the oil to the lamps in a full and complete way (signified by seven pipes to each). This spiritual cooperation amongst God's people results in God's glorious shining.

God's description of the building efforts that will eventually result in the completion of the temple serve as concrete example of how God's people at that time will work together to produce a shining testimony. The challenge at hand is the rebuilding of the temple. Zerubbabel laid the foundation. Zerubbabel's hands laying the top stone "with shouts of grace, grace to it" paints a mystical and heavenly picture of the temple completion that is possible under the working of God's grace.

The flying scroll and the ephah vessel

Zechariah's sixth and seventh visions go together. Both visions address how iniquity will be eradicated from the land of God's people. Zechariah first sees an enormous flying scroll, ten cubits by twenty cubits. The tour guide angel says, "This is the curse that goes out over the face of the whole land. For everyone who steals shall be cleaned out according to what is on one side, and everyone who swears falsely shall be cleaned out according to what is on the other side" (Zechariah 5:3). The Lord will send out this scroll into the house of the thief and of the one who swears falsely by the Lord's name. It will lodge in their house, consuming the timbers and the stones.

The scroll addresses two odious things in God's eyes, stealing and swearing falsely in the Lord's name. It is interesting that stealing concerns the second table of the law and taking the Lord's name in vain concerns the first. This scroll shows that God will visit each person who is guilty, will enter their house and consume it completely.

Next Zechariah sees an ephah basket, which is a bushel basket for grain, with a lead cover over its mouth. When the lead cover is lifted, Zechariah sees a woman, who is called wickedness in the ephah. The woman is thrust back down into the ephah and the lead cover is thrown over the top. Then two women with wings like a stork's lift the basket and take it away to Shinar, where they will sit it on a pedestal in a house made for it.

The ephah containing the woman is a picture of the sinfulness of the people, especially in relation to commerce. The ephah being carried to Shinar signifies that all the iniquity of the land will be banished to its home in Babylon, which is in Shinar. God will take away all the sins of the land, pile them up in Babylon in anticipation of Babylon being judged and destroyed. Zechariah will surely learn from these visions that the Lord will purify His people, eradicating every sin so that they might be a people apart from sin and holy to God.

Both these visions teach Zechariah that God will eradicate iniquity from the land of Israel. It is interesting that these visions don't address sins being cleansed or washed away. Rather, they both portray sins being eradicated or taken away from the land.

The four chariots

Zechariah's eighth and last vision teaches him that God's judgment will fall on the nations. He sees four chariots coming out from between two bronze mountains. The chariots are pulled by horses of different colors: red, black, white and dappled. The angel describes that these chariots have just presented themselves before the Lord and are now going out to the four winds of heaven. The black and white horses are going toward the land of the north, most likely Babylon. The dappled are going towards the south, most likely Egypt. All of them are eager to go, so are pleased when the angel commands them, "Go, patrol the earth" (Zechariah 6:7). As they set off, the angel turns to Zechariah and says, "Behold, those who go toward the north country have set my Spirit at rest in the north country" (Zechariah 6:8).

The chariots teach Zechariah that God's judgment will fall on the nations. When they come from the presence of the Lord through the bronze mountains, Zechariah would think of judgment, the meaning of the metal bronze. When he sees the horses going to the north, he would realize that they are going there to set God's "Spirit at rest" in the north country. His previous vision showed him wickedness in the Ephah going to make home in Babylon, a city in the north country. Now, that north country will be judged. Egypt, likewise, will receive her just punishment. These two nations together—Babylon and Egypt are symbolic of all the nations, indicating that all the nations will be judged and made right in God's eyes.

Putting the lessons of the visions together gives us a good idea of how complete and encompassing Zechariah's education was. In one night he saw how God is jealous for Jerusalem, how the nations who have harmed Israel will be limited, how God will be a wall of fire around Jerusalem, how God will dwell in Jerusalem with His people—Jews and Gentiles—and will be the glory therein, how God will purify the degraded priesthood to bring in the Messiah, how God's people will be a shining lampstand, how God Himself will eradicate sin from Israel, and finally how God will judge all the nations of the world to make the whole world right. Not a bad lesson for one night!

Zechariah's words to his generation — Crowning Joshua

If the night visions brought Zechariah to see heavenly, mysterious, glorious, and divine things, the next section of Zechariah's prophesy shows us how he is brought back to earth to minister the people of his generation. Zechariah is to collect real gold and silver from some Israelites who just returned from Babylon. He is to make crowns with the metals and place them onto the actual head of Joshua. When he places the crowns, he should speak to Joshua about the coming "Branch," saying, "Behold, the man whose name is the Branch: for he shall branch out from his place, and he shall build the temple of the LORD. It is he who shall build the temple of the LORD and shall bear royal honor, and shall sit and rule on his throne. And there shall be a priest on his throne, and the counsel of peace shall be between them both"

(Zechariah 6:12-13). Then, Zechariah is to place a crown in the finished temple of the Lord, as a reminder to those who have returned from Babylon. He concludes that even more people will come from afar to build the temple of the Lord if the people listening to him will diligently obey the voice of the Lord their God.

Zechariah's act of crowning Joshua accomplishes at least two things. First, it takes Zechariah from the realm of seeing visions into the practical challenges of working with the people directly in front of him. Before he had seen Joshua in a vision. Now he sees him with his own eyes and touches his head with his hands. Before he had heard about the Branch as the Lord spoke to Joshua in the vision. Now, Zechariah himself is speaking concerning the Branch to Joshua. This sign brings Zechariah down to earth, makes his ministry concrete, and connects what he saw in the vision with the people in front of him.

Second, his words to Joshua give much more insight into the Branch. In the previous vision God simply said to Joshua that He would bring in His servant the Branch. Here Zechariah elaborates in very important ways. He describes how the Branch will grow by declaring, "He will branch out from his place." He links the Branch with the building of the temple, "He shall build the temple of the Lord." He declares how the Branch will be both king and priest—" He will be a priest on His throne" (Zechariah 6:13 NASB)—just like Joshua, the high priest (representing the priesthood) at that time, was given a crown (representing the kingship) in Zechariah's demonstration. He elaborates how the Branch will produce genuine peace, "the counsel of peace shall be between them both" (Zechariah 6:13). This signifies that "The Messiah, who unites in Himself royalty and priesthood, will counsel and promote the peace of His people" (Keil, p. 555). In Zechariah's practical words to Joshua, he elaborates on the vision of Messiah as Branch and makes His work and person much richer to the nation.

A Question about fasts

Almost two years after Zechariah's night visions (and about two years before the completion of the temple) a group of Israelites come to Jerusalem and ask the priests and prophets if they should continue holding a yearly fast in remembrance of the burning of the temple by the Babylonians (Zechariah 7:3; Jeremiah 52:12-13). The response from God that comes to Zechariah is full of realizations similar to what Zechariah saw in his night visions.

Before revealing a picture of the future, Zechariah first reviews the questioners' history of falling away from God. He tells them that while it was true that the nation did fast during the past seventy years of captivity, it was not, in fact, for God, but rather for themselves. This false fasting was just like their fathers before them, who stubbornly refused to follow God's commands from their heart. Instead, they "made their hearts diamond-hard lest they should hear the law and the words" of the prophets (Zechariah 7:12).

Zechariah proceeds to declare that the current day, however, is a new era. This era is one in which God has chosen Jerusalem and will dwell there with His people. God joyfully declares "I have returned to Zion and will dwell in the midst of Jerusalem, and Jerusalem shall be called the faithful city, and the mountain of the Lord of hosts, the holy mountain" (Zechariah 8:3). God will bring His people from east and west so that old men and women will sit in Jerusalem while boys and girls play in its streets. God declares, "They shall be my people, and I will be their God, in faithfulness and in righteousness" (Zechariah 8:8).

God applies this vision directly to the people's situation. He reminds them that before the foundation of the temple was built, this city was a desolate place. There was no wage for man or beast; there was no safety from attack. Now, that God is moving to restore Jerusalem, things will be different. "The vine shall give its fruit, and the ground shall give its produce, and the heavens shall give their dew. And I will cause the remnant of this people to possess all these things" (Zechariah 8:12). All that is required of the people is that they heed the words of the former prophets, which are the same commands God is giving them today. "These are the things that you shall do: Speak the truth to one another; render in your gates judgments that are true and make for peace; do not devise evil in your hearts against one another, and love no false oath, for all these things I hate, declares the LORD" (Zechariah 8:16-17).

God then converts the fasts that the men were inquiring about into celebrations, saying that they "shall be to the house of Judah seasons of joy and gladness and cheerful feasts. Therefore love truth and peace" (Zechariah 8:19). He concludes His response by emphasizing how Jerusalem will be a joy to both Jews and Gentiles, "Many peoples and strong nations shall come to seek the LORD of hosts in Jerusalem and to entreat the favor of the LORD" (Zechariah 8:22).

Zechariah's response to this simple question of fasts paints a very high and glorious picture of the future city God has in mind. God will dwell in the city. It will be called a faithful city, or city of truth, firmness, or trustworthiness. The mountain upon which it sits will be called a holy mountain (Zechariah 8:3). The people in this joyful city will be God's people and He will be their God in faithfulness and righteousness (Zechariah 8:8). The people themselves will speak truth, render true judgments that promote peace and devise no evil in their hearts towards one another (Zechariah 8:15-17). Their years will be punctuated with seasons of joy and cheerful feasts, and they will love truth and peace (Zechariah 8:19). They will have a glorious effect on the entire earth. Men from many different nations will seek God in Jerusalem. "Ten men of the nations will take hold of the robe of a Jew, saying, 'Let us go with you, for we heave heard that God is with you'" (Zechariah 8:23). The description of the future has so many good words: faithful, true, holiness, faithfulness, righteousness, true judgments, peace, joy and cheer. This is what happens when God is dwelling with His people and when His people truly belong to Him. This is God's dream for His city and the best He has in His mind for His people.

Zechariah has really grown in his description of what God has in store for His people. In his first word to the people, Zechariah pleads with them, telling them that God is saying "Return to Me and I will return to you" (Zechariah 1:3). Now, after the night visions, Zechariah conveys a much richer picture of what that mutual return looks like. Just like he saw the vision of the man on the red horse, now Zechariah declares how God has chosen Jerusalem. Just like he saw the vision of the man with the measuring line, Zechariah now conveys how God will dwell with His people in the city and how the nations will also be there and dwell with Him. Just like he saw in the vision of Joshua, the iniquity will be taken away so that the mountain can be called holy, the people will truly walk in God's ways and there will be true faithfulness in the city. Just like Zechariah saw the lampstand in the vision, now he declares that the people will shine to the nations to the point that all the nations will know that God is in Jerusalem. Here Zechariah's ministry is rich; his realizations profound. When some Israelites come to ask a simple question about fasts, then they receive a profound word of God's coming salvation of His people and its effect on the nations of the earth. Now, in Zechariah's experience the lessons of the night visions are incorporated into his ministry, making his ministry high, transcendent and profound.

The Oracles

The remainder of Zechariah's work is composed of two oracles, one concerning the nations with reference to Israel (Zechariah 9-10) and the other concerning Israel with reference to the nations (Zechariah 12-14). In between these two oracles Zechariah demonstrates the role that God as a rejected shepherd will play as He shepherds God's people (Zechariah 11).

The oracles section of Zechariah's work shows an even more profound aspect to his ministry than can be seen in his answer to the fast question. That answer showed how Zechariah had incorporated lessons from his night visions into his practical ministry to the people. Zechariah's speaking in this final section elevates itself into a higher, more profound realm. It shows maturity, growth, revelation, and clarity that can only come from a servant who is very much in the Lord's hands.

The richness and uniqueness of this section surely comes because of its many direct prophecies of Christ and the Holy Spirit. These divine utterances catapult this section of the prophets to sublime realms. Previously Zechariah had prophesied about Christ in a relatively oblique way. In his visions he saw that He is the Branch and the stone with seven eyes, good for God's building. Additionally, other visions contained references to Christ through the character called the "Angel of the Lord." In this oracle section, however, Zechariah's descriptions of the Messiah become richer, more precise and fuller. From the visions we knew Messiah would be a King on a throne. In the oracles we find out how the Messiah King comes, "Behold, your king is coming to you; righteous and having salvation is he, humble and mounted on a donkey, on a colt, the foal of a donkey.... he shall speak peace to the nations; his rule shall be from sea to sea, and from the River to the ends of the earth" (Zechariah 9:9-10). From the visions we saw how the Stone was engraved, which might have some reference to Messiah's suffering and death. In the oracles we see much more detail. We see the rejection that led to Messiah's death, "Then I said to them, "If it seems good to you, give me my wages; but if not, keep them." And they weighed out as my wages thirty pieces of silver. Then the LORD said to me, "Throw it to the potter"—the lordly price at which I was priced by them. So I took the thirty pieces of silver and threw them into the house of the LORD, to the potter" (Zechariah 11:12-13), and we see how He was pierced in His death, "when they look on me, on him whom they have pierced, they shall mourn for him" (Zechariah 12:10).

Furthermore, the oracles show us how Messiah was God's Shepherd, the One who stood next to Him, and how He was struck according to God's own design, ""Awake, O sword, against my shepherd, against the man who stands next to me," declares the LORD of hosts. "Strike the shepherd, and the sheep will be scattered"" (Zechariah 13:7). The oracles show us how God pours out His Spirit, "And I will pour out on the house of David and the inhabitants of Jerusalem a spirit of grace and pleas for mercy" (Zechariah 12:10). Additionally, they show us God's rich provisions for the sins of His people, "On that day there shall be a fountain opened for the house of David and the inhabitants of Jerusalem, to cleanse them from sin and uncleanness" (Zechariah 13:1). The oracles show us how Christ will return to the earth, "On that day his feet shall stand on the Mount of Olives that lies before Jerusalem on the east" (Zechariah 14:4). Finally, they show us many descriptions of the glorious kingdom established after Messiah's return. Putting all these verses together gives quite a wonderful picture of Christ's humble coming, His shepherding care, His kingship, His salvation and righteousness, His rejection by His own people, His piercing, His being struck by God, the sheep that scatter when He is struck, the pouring out of the Spirit, the coming of Christ in the clouds, the wailing and repentance of the Jews, the eradication of sin, the descent of Christ to Olivet, and the coming kingdom. Zechariah's night visions were marvelous, but his oracles most surely top them.

Before we briefly review the content of these oracles, it is interesting to note that Zechariah gives no indication of what year he speaks these oracles or performs his shepherding demonstration. This absence is unlike any other section in Zechariah, or Haggai for that matter, who both usually indicate the year, month, and even day of their prophesies. It is almost as if the messages in the oracles are timeless, not meant for a simple thought of temple reconstruction or any mere temporal concern. They don't need a time marker, because they, like Christ, are for all time.

The first oracle: the nations are to be included and Israel is to be restored

We begin by looking at chapters nine and ten, the oracle concerning the nations, which Zechariah calls "Hadrach." This oracle does not merely speak about the nations. Rather, it presents a grand overview of the restoration of the entire earth; covering the salvation of the nations, the Messiah and details of the struggle that will establish the coming kingdom.

The oracle begins by announcing God's judgment that will fall on the Gentile cities of Tyre, Sidon and Damascus. When the neighboring Philistines see the severity of the judgment on these places, they will writhe in anguish and God will stop all their pagan practices. After their judgment, this oracle shows us that an amazing thing will happen: the remaining people from these nations "shall be a remnant for our God" (Zechariah 9:7). This statement indicates that the remaining Gentiles will turn to God and become His people.

The oracle then turns to the nation of Israel. God will encamp around them and their Messiah will come, as indicated by Zechariah's encouragement, "Rejoice greatly, O daughter of Zion! Shout aloud, O daughter of Jerusalem! Behold, your king is coming to you; righteous and having salvation is he, humble and mounted on a donkey, on a colt, the foal of a donkey" (Zechariah 9:9). The salvation that Messiah brings will cause world peace under His extensive rule, which is "from sea to sea, and from the River to the ends of the earth" (Zechariah 9:10).

The peace God brings in will not happen automatically. It will only happen after God works in His nation to make things right between them and the other nations. Previously, the other nations oppressed Israel. Now, God will make Israel strong to fight against those oppressors. Thus, He declares, "I will stir up your sons, O Zion, against your sons, O Greece" (Zechariah 9:13). God Himself will fight alongside them, protect them and save them. Based on this glorious hope, Zechariah encourages the Israelites to pray for God's blessing, "Ask rain from the LORD" (Zechariah 10:1), he charges them.

Zechariah concludes his oracle by focusing on how important shepherds are to the people. Their lack of a good shepherd is evident in their drifting away to idolatry. Zechariah emphasizes this by contrasting the fact that God will truly answer their prayers, unlike all their household gods, who do not answer prayers. He describes that the people had been seeking help from these false gods, because they did not have a shepherd to help them. In fact, they had bad shepherds who led them astray (Zechariah 10:2-3). The remainder of the oracle describes how God will be a real shepherd to them. Under His care they will become great, "like a majestic steed in battle" (Zechariah 10:3). He will bring out strong men from among them and will make them like mighty warriors. Finally, God will gather His people who have been scattered among the nations and bring them back to His land. He "will make them strong in the Lord, and they shall walk in his name" (Zechariah 10:12).

Zechariah demonstrates how Christ is a shepherd

Chapter eleven describes how shepherds are related to Israel, expanding on what Zechariah mentioned in 10:2-3. Zechariah highlights Israel's rejection of the Messiah and lays a foundation to speak about the effect of that rejection in chapters twelve through fourteen. It begins with the desolation of the leaders (the cedars, the oaks, the cypresses), which most likely will happen by means of an occupation by a foreign power (Zechariah 11:1-3). The flock, God's people, is then in bitter straits; the people are being ruthlessly bought and sold by merchants looking for gain (Zechariah 11:5). Additionally, God Himself declares, "I will no longer have pity on the inhabitants of this land" (Zechariah 11:6). God reveals that he will judge the flock and then demonstrates how that will happen in terms of the flock's rejection of their Shepherd—the Messiah Himself.

To demonstrate this, God sends Zechariah as a shepherd in the vision who represents God Himself coming as shepherd in the person of Christ. He rightly comes to shepherd the poor of the flock with two staves, "beauty" and "union"

(Zechariah 11:7). Three of the current shepherds of Israel are bad, so he displaces the three. However, the flock is still unreceiving. Thus, Zechariah breaks the staff "beauty," which causes the afflicted of the land to see that this is the word of the Lord (Zechariah 11:10-11). It is evident that these afflicted, while they recognize the word of the Lord, do not advance beyond to the point of repenting or receiving the shepherd's care. When Zechariah asks them to pay him his wages they give him only thirty pieces of silver, the price of a dead slave. The Lord tells Zechariah to throw that "lordly price" they gave him to the potter (signifying a low-priced vessel) in the Lord's house (Zechariah 11:12-13). Zechariah then breaks his other staff "Union" to sever the union between Judah and Joseph (Zechariah 11:14). After the rejection, God asks Zechariah again to shepherd the people, but this time for ill, not for good. Zechariah then comes in the person of a foolish shepherd, who represents Antichrist who shepherds the people in an evil way (Zechariah 11:15-17).

In this chapter Zechariah has masterfully portrayed a large portion of the history of Israel in terms related to shepherding. He introduces the nation as a wandering flock, who is beset by God's judgments. The shepherds they have are all bad. God sends His Messiah as Shepherd who seeks to gather the flock into unity, symbolized by the staff "bonds," and give grace to the flock, symbolized by the staff "beauty." However, the flock rejects the Shepherd Messiah and is thereby rejected fully by God. In the end, God allows another, evil shepherd to arise. This shepherd will be antichrist, who will lead God's people away and will prepare the setting for the great events at the end time.

The second Oracle: Israel purified under the Jerusalem siege and the final restoration

Chapters twelve through fourteen, the oracle concerning Israel, outline events that focus mainly around Jerusalem, which becomes a center after the reign of antichrist begins. It is fitting that this oracle appears after the foolish shepherd, representing Antichrist, is introduced in chapter eleven.

Chapter twelve sets the scene—many nations are surrounding Jerusalem, besieging it. Even though the Israelites had by this time forsaken God and sought an alliance with the evil kingdoms of the world, all their efforts did not prevent the nations from attacking them. In spite of all this, we see that God intervenes by His own sovereign grace to deliver His wayward people. "On that day I will make Jerusalem a heavy stone for all the peoples. All who lift it will surely hurt themselves. And all the nations of the earth will gather against it" (Zechariah 12:3). God strikes the besiegers' horses with blindness and their riders with madness. He makes the people of Judah and Jerusalem strong to fight against the enemy. Additionally, He Himself will fight, declaring, "I will seek to destroy all the nations that come against Jerusalem" (Zechariah 12:9).

In the midst of this intense conflict, God does something wonderful for His people. He pours out His Spirit upon them. "And I will pour out on the house of David and the inhabitants of Jerusalem a spirit of grace and pleas for mercy, so that, when they look on me, on him whom they have pierced, they shall mourn for him, as one mourns for an only child, and weep bitterly over him, as one weeps over a firstborn" (Zechariah 12:10). God's pouring out of the Spirit of grace coincides with an appearance of the pierced Messiah in the clouds. The Spirit filled people look on the Messiah and have a visceral, powerful reaction—they mourn. They mourn like they lost their only son and they mourn alone—wives and husbands separate.

The Spirit of pleas of mercy and the prayers that the Israelites prayed when they received that Spirit results in the events outlined in chapters 13—Israel's cleansing and refining. For this a fountain is opened for sin and uncleanness. All the idols will be cut off and all the prophets and spirits of uncleanness will be removed. If anyone does prophesy, his father and mother will pierce him through. Any prophet who has ceased prophesying will want to hide the fact that he has any history of prophesying, especially if he had been pierced in the past for prophesying. If anyone asks him what his wounds are, he would say that he is simply a worker of the soil, he was sold in his youth, and was wounded in the house of his friends (Zechariah 13:3-6).

At this point, there is an interruption of the flow of thought of the oracle. It could be called a "Messianic interruption." It is almost as if the "wounds" that this prophet claimed he suffered in the house of his friends triggers a great exclamation from the Lord. The Lord goes deeper, indicating the underlying motivation for the wounds. In the light of the wounded prophets, God suddenly blurts out about *one* wound of *the One* Shepherd, that would affect all the nation. He says, "'Awake, O sword, against my shepherd, against the man who stands next to me,' declares the LORD of hosts. "Strike the shepherd, and the sheep will be scattered; I will turn my hand against the little ones'" (Zechariah 13:7). Here God describes who is wounded—"my shepherd…the man who stands next to me." This indicates that Messiah is God's sent Shepherd, who is standing next to God Himself. Messiah is working with God and is shepherding as God shepherds. It should also be noted that God Himself beckons the sword to awake and strike His Messiah-shepherd. Thus, God declares that it is according to His own will that His Shepherd would be struck.

When the Shepherd is struck the sheep will be scattered. This was fulfilled in part when Christ was wounded on the cross. At that time, the Apostles scattered. In the final siege of Jerusalem, which is the final refinement of God's people, there will be an even greater scattering than that. This scattering will result in the nation truly becoming the people of God. In the intense heat of this final Jerusalem siege, God will refine His people. He "will put this third into the fire, and refine them as one refines silver, and test them as gold is tested. They will call upon my name, and I will answer them. I will say, 'They are my people'; and they will say, 'The LORD is my God'" (Zechariah 13:9).

Chapter fourteen describes in more detail how Israel emerges from the refining. God will bring all the plunder that the nations took from Israel back to Israel. He will descend to earth on the Mount of Olives. The mountain will split, and the refined nation will escape through the valley. Finally, the Lord will return to the earth with all His saints, "Then the LORD my God will come, and all the holy ones with him" (Zechariah 14:5).

This glorious return changes everything on earth. Due to the brightness of the Lord's presence the day appears different, "On that day there shall be no light, cold, or frost" (Zechariah 14:6). Previously the land was dry, but now Jerusalem will be the source of water, "On that day living waters shall flow out from Jerusalem" (Zechariah 14:8). The entire land will be a fertile plain and Jerusalem will dwell securely. The nations that set themselves against the Lord's people will be defeated and their wealth will be brought to God's people. All the earth will worship the Lord. "Then everyone who survives of all the nations that have come against Jerusalem shall go up year after year to worship the King, the LORD of hosts, and to keep the Feast of Booths" (Zechariah 14:16). Any family that does not go to celebrate the Feast of Booths will have no rain on them. Finally, in that day Jerusalem will be completely holy; all the bells of horses shall be inscribed with the inscription "Holy to the Lord." Also, the entire land will become holy like the temple is holy. Just as every pot is holy in the temple, in this new land, "every pot in Jerusalem and Judah shall be holy to the Lord of hosts" (Zechariah 14:21). All will be holy to the Lord!

Thus ends Zechariah's grand prophesy. A deeper study of this is well worthwhile, since this section not only outlines crucial events transpiring in association with the Lord's second coming, but, it also describes crucial aspects of the Messiah. These are a product of a mature, learned, and experienced prophet who has gone through the trenches of serving the Lord in visions, in ministering to the people of his generation and in shepherding the people according to God's thoughts.

CHAPTER TWELVE

Malachi

Malachi's writing lends itself to a simple division into four basic sections. The first covers God's love for the nation of Israel as demonstrated in His love for Jacob (Malachi 1:2-6). The second contains a series of complaints that God has against the people (Malachi 2:7-3:15). This section covers major topics such as polluted sacrifices, marriage to foreign wives and tithing, as well as minor topics, such as bad attitudes that lead people to believe serving God is vain. The third section describes a wonderful result of Malachi's speaking—the people who fear the Lord gather together, something that God distinctly notices and values (Malachi 3:16-18). The fourth section covers encouragements and promises God gives to those who fear Him to ready them for the coming day of the Lord (Malachi 4:1-6).

As the book progresses, Malachi includes two specific references to Christ. In the third section, he likens Christ to a refiner's fire and to a man who refines gold and silver (Malachi 3:2-3). In the fourth section he describes Christ as "the Sun of righteousness, with healing in its wings" (Malachi 4:2). These marvelous depictions portray Christ coming in His glory, separating the metal from the dross, and healing His servants, just as the sun's rays bring health and goodness to people.

Section one: "I have loved you"

Malachi opens his speaking with words of comfort from God, "I have loved you" (Malachi 1:2), says God tenderly, thus laying the foundational thought for the entire book. After the people respond, "How have you loved us?" the Lord replies in a most interesting way: He asks them to think about Isaac's sons—Esau and Jacob. "Is not Esau Jacob's brother?' declares the LORD. 'Yet I have loved Jacob but Esau I have hated'" (Malachi 1:2-3). God then paints the picture what His hate for Esau means for Esau. He describes how He has laid waste to Esau's country and "left his heritage to jackals" (Malachi 1:3). Then, He declares how Esau's ruin will be permanent, no matter how hard Esau may try to reverse the fall, "'They may build,' declares the Lord, 'but I will tear down'" (Malachi 1:4). Such a permanent ruin—the fruit of the Lord's anger towards Esau—will provide a testimony of God's greatness to the children of Jacob, "you shall say, 'Great is the LORD beyond the border of Israel!'" (Malachi 1:5).

God's choice of using Jacob and Esau as examples for asserting His love to Israel speaks volumes. At Malachi's time both nations descended from these men were experiencing ruin and destruction. Esau, which occupied the mountain region south east of the land of Canaan had been destroyed by the Babylonians, just like the Israelites had. It was at this juncture in time, after the destruction of both, that God's love could shine. Even though Edom would build itself up again, God would tear them down. However, with Jacob it is different. God loves Jacob, and this means that they will not be in ruins forever.

This statement shows us a profound picture of God's love. His love doesn't prevent us from going through trials, but it does promise us future restoration. Here, God's love didn't prevent Israel from being carried off to Babylon. God's love didn't cause them to return from Babylon and immediately set up a glorious kingdom in Judea. However, what God's love did assure them of, is that they will not be in ruins forever.

The patriarch Jacob is the perfect example of God's unchanging love, because in many ways his life is similar to Israel's national life. Jacob didn't do anything to deserve God's love; he was chosen and loved by God at his birth. Because of this unwavering love, Jacob could never do anything in his life to lose that love. His lies, his lack of prayer, his bargaining with God did not cause God to withdraw His love. Instead, *eventually* his descendants would be glorified. Likewise, the nation of Israel was chosen and loved by God, period. Even their current errant behavior could not disqualify them from God's love, because they never did anything to deserve it in the first place. Additionally, Jacob spent time away from the land of Canaan, while Esau became rich in his father's house in Canaan. However, this temporary difference did not change their final outcomes. In the end Jacob was still glorified and Esau was still decimated. Jacob's example provides strong comfort to the nation before Malachi lists their deficiencies. Additionally, as they consider Edom, they will see that Edom will never rise again, no matter how hard they may try. This will be added proof to them of how great their God is in His influence throughout the entire earth.

Section two: God's complaints against Israel

Malachi's next section shows that God's unwavering love toward Jacob does not mean that God approves of everything that Jacob does. This becomes more than evident as Malachi details the many deficiencies of the nation.

Polluted sacrifices

He begins with the priest's profane practice of offering polluted sacrifices at the altar. God reasons with them about how He is their Father and therefore should receive the honor due a father. God declares, "A son honors his father, and a servant his master. If then I am a father, where is my honor? And if I am a master, where is my fear?" (Malachi 1:6). In the matter of sacrifices, the priests and people are not honoring their Father or fearing their Master.

The priests are despising the Lord's name by saying that the table of the Lord, which is the altar at the temple, may be despised. They allow the people to despise the altar by offering polluted sacrifices—blind, lame, and sick animals, even animals taken by violence—instead of healthy ones. God reasons with them, saying, "Present that to your governor; will he accept you or show you favor? (Malachi 1:8). God would rather that the entire temple would be closed, "Oh that there would be one among you who would shut the doors" (Malachi 1:10), rather than these evil offerings. On top of this, their attitude toward offering something to the Lord is terrible. They consider sacrificing to be tiresome, exclaiming "What weariness this is," as they "snort" (exhale in frustration) begrudgingly at the task (Malachi 1:13). The Lord contrasts the priests' treatment of Him with the treatment that He will eventually get from the nations of the earth. God declares that, one day, "from the rising of the sun to its setting my name will be great among the nations, and in every place incense will be offered to my name, and a pure offering" (Malachi 1:11). He concludes with "I am a great King" and that "my name will be feared among the nations" (Malachi 1:14).

If the priests do not take this to heart, adjust their ways and honor the Lord's name, the Lord will allow His judgment to fall upon them. He will "send the curse" upon them, "curse" their "blessings," and will even spread the dung of their offerings upon their faces, so that when the dung is carried out of the temple, as required as part of the sacrifice, they also will be carried out with it (Malachi 2:1-2).

The priest's offence is deepened because they are corrupting the covenant, the agreement, that God made with Levi. Throughout its history, the tribe of the tribe of Levi has been a picture of special obedience and special relationship with God. When Moses saw the golden calf and the people reveling in idolatry, he called out "Who is on the Lord's side?" (Exodus 32:25). The tribe of Levi responded and followed Moses' instructions to slay their brothers. For this Moses declared to them, "Today you have been ordained for the service of the Lord" (Exodus 32:29). This special relationship was called a "covenant of peace" after Phineas, another member of the tribe of Levi, turned back God's wrath by killing Zimri and Cozbi in his zeal to purify the sons of Israel (Numbers 25:10-14).

God intended that the Levites would be a genuine help to Israel as they followed the Lord. His covenant with them was full of life and peace. Levi was to fear the Lord. He was to stand in awe of the Lord's name. He was to be a beacon of right teaching and peace in the midst of the nation. "True instruction was in his mouth, and no wrong was found on his lips. He walked with me in peace and uprightness, and he turned many from iniquity. For the lips of a priest should guard knowledge, and people should seek instruction from his mouth, for he is the messenger of the Lord of hosts" (Malachi 2:6-7).

However, instead of building people up, the priests became a corrupting influence. They themselves have turned aside from the way. They caused many to stumble by their instructions. God finally warns them, that He will abase them in the eyes of all the people if they indeed continue in their despised ways of offering.

Foreign wives

The next major complaint God has against the people concerns the matter of marrying foreign wives and divorcing the wives of their youth. Before Malachi addresses this issue, he reminds the people how God is their Father and about the covenant of their fathers. "Have we not all one Father? Has not one God created us? Why then are we faithless to one another, profaning the covenant of our fathers?" (Malachi 2:10). In saying this Malachi joins himself to the people, claiming that God is his Father also and that he also, along with them, is profaning the covenant of their fathers.

The problem here is that they married foreign wives, "daughters," Malachi describes them "of a foreign god" (Malachi 2:11). That, Malachi points out, is a sin against the sanctuary of the Lord (Malachi 2:11). In marrying their new wife, they have divorced the wife they married many years ago. Thus, the Lord's altar is now covered with tears of the wives they divorced. When the priests or the people make offerings after having done this, the Lord no longer accepts their offering.

In divorcing their wives, the priests violated something very fundamental in God's intention for His people. God gave their wives to them, and even sealed that union with His Spirit. In this way, God was seeking godly offspring, a continuation of the race who would love and serve Him. When the Israelites broke their marriage, they demonstrated that they had no regard for their wife by covenant, no regard for the Lord's arrangement, and no regard for the spirit. Malachi argues, "Did he not make them one, with a portion of the Spirit in their union? And what was the one God seeking? Godly offspring" (Malachi 2:15). He charges the people to guard themselves, "So guard yourselves in your spirit, and let none of you be faithless to the wife of your youth" (Malachi 2:15). Malachi pleads strongly with his people, "guard yourselves in your spirit, and do not be faithless" (Malachi 2:16).

These two sins, offering polluted sacrifices at the altar and divorcing to marry the daughter of a foreign god, are two heinous sins that corrupted the nation. One cheapens what is offered to God; the other corrupts the closest relationship God intends for a person. One is Godward; the other involves a human relationship that is under the eyes of God. It is interesting that Malachi specifies what is profaned by the people in each case. When they despise the food of the altar, God declares that they have profaned His name (Malachi 1:12). When they are faithless to their wives, Malachi declares that they have profaned the sanctuary (Malachi 2:11). Profaning the name can be an individual act, between the Levite and God Himself. However, taking a foreign wife affects more than the individual's relationship with God. God intends that Judah would be a holy people, even a sanctuary to God Himself (Psalm 114:2). The faithless treatment of a wife of one's youth, results in this sanctuary being profaned and made common. It has an effect on the corporate aspect of the Israelite's life. He causes his wife to shed tears on the altar, profanes the covenant of his fathers, and makes what was supposed to be holy—a corporate sanctuary for God—common.

Crooked justice

The next complaint that Malachi raises against the people involves their deep misunderstanding of God in His justice. They say, "Everyone who does evil is good in the sight of the LORD, and he delights in them," and they ask, "Where is the God of justice?'" (Malachi 2:17). They have become upside down in their understanding of morality, justice and rightness. They look at the wicked who are prospering and declare that God is delighting in them. Furthermore, they see the wicked thrive without retribution and they ask if God is even there. They wonder, "Where is the God of justice?"

God's comfort to the nation

Malachi 3:1-5 contains God's clear answer to their question, "Where is God?" The short answer is, "God is coming. A messenger will come before Him. When God comes, He will surely judge, purify, refine and clean house." God says this in a much more beautiful way. It is so beautiful, that it is worth reproducing here and adding a few comments. "Behold, I send my messenger, and he will prepare the way before me" (Malachi 3:1). This indicates that Elijah, as shown in spirit by John the Baptist, will appear before the Lord comes. He is called God's messenger and will prepare the way for the Lord Himself to come. "And the Lord whom you seek will suddenly come to his temple; and the messenger of the covenant in whom you delight, behold, he is coming, says the LORD of hosts" (Malachi 3:1). God announces that He will come to His temple. This prophecy has been partially fulfilled in Christ's first coming, when Jesus entered the temple. It will be fulfilled in full at His second coming. Messiah is called "the Messenger of the Covenant," indicating that the Lord Himself will seal the covenant God made with His people Israel. Such a promise would be welcome news to anyone at Malachi's time who had witnessed God's people breaking covenants in many different forms. The Lord coming as the Messenger of the Covenant means that He, the Messiah Himself, will seal the covenant, be the guarantee, and the faithful executor of God's covenant with His people. This is a great hope.

God further comforts His people by describing how He will remove unrighteousness from them. He will judge all unrighteousness, like a refiner's fire, like fuller's soap, and like a refiner of gold and silver. "But who can endure the day of his coming, and who can stand when he appears? For he is like a refiner's fire and like fullers' soap. He will sit as a refiner and purifier of silver, and he will purify the sons of Levi and refine them like gold and silver, and they will bring offerings in righteousness to the Lord" (Malachi 3:2-3). The Lord being likened to refiner's fire and fuller's soap speaks to how the Lord will restore both the inside and outside of His people. As a refiner's fire He will burn away the mixture, alloy and foreign substances that corrupts the Levites from within. As fuller's soap he will cleanse the outside, whiten what is stained and purify the appearance. These two images are wonderful pictures of the coming New Testament salvation. In the New Testament God will sanctify, that is, make His people holy on the inside. He will also conform them to His image, which is to brighten their appearance on the outside. Together, sanctification and conformation form a complete picture of God's salvation. Malachi colorfully illustrates these two by describing how the Messiah is a refiner's fire and fuller's soap. The Lord will refine and cleanse the sons of Levi, so that all their unrighteousness will be removed. Then, they will be able to bring offerings of righteousness to the Lord with their bodies and with their hearts.

Finally, the Lord will eradicate all the unrighteous on earth. "Then I will draw near to you for judgment. I will be a swift witness against the sorcerers, against the adulterers, against those who swear falsely, against those who oppress the hired worker in his wages, the widow and the fatherless, against those who thrust aside the sojourner, and do not fear me, says the LORD of hosts" (Malachi 3:5).

God pleads for them to return

After warning them of the judgments that will fall when He comes, God changes His tone by reassuring Israel that He will not abandon them. He reassures them by saying that He has not changed His choice for them. "For I the LORD do not change; therefore you, O children of Jacob, are not consumed" (Malachi 3:6). God is firm in His choice. He chose Israel; therefore, He will not eradicate the nation, even though they might have a history of continually forsaking Him. "From the days of your fathers you have turned aside from my statutes and have not kept them" (Malachi 3:7). In spite of their history of forsaking Him, God still is seeking to restore His relationship with His people. Thus, He pleads and promises, "Return to me, and I will return to you, says the LORD of hosts" (Malachi 3:7).

It would seem that now, at this very moment, would be exactly the right time for the Israelites to return. God has shown them how they have profaned His name through polluted offerings, how they have profaned the sanctuary through divorcing their wives, how they have despised serving Him. He has shown how He will come in judgment. Now, in spite of all this, it is as if He is giving them one final opportunity, saying, "I don't change. I still desire you. If you would only return to Me, I will return to you." However, in an extremely disappointing response, Israel shows just how pitiful they are. Instead of trying to return, they just say, "How shall we return?" (Malachi 3:7).

Withholding tithes

God then proceeds to level another charge against the people—they are robbing God through withholding their tithes and contributions. The parallel section of Nehemiah notes how the Levites had to return to their fields instead of working in the temple, because their needs were not being met by the people's contributions (Nehemiah 13:10). The end result is that the people "are cursed with a curse" (Malachi 3:9). Malachi commands them to change so that they, "Bring the full tithe into the storehouse" (Malachi 3:10). In charging them such, God is prodding them to go out on a limb, prove Him and test Him so that He will show them how richly He could bless them, if they only give Him His due. "Put me to the test, says the Lord of hosts, if I will not open the windows of heaven for you and pour down for you a blessing until there is no more need" (Malachi 3:10). If they bring in the full tithes so that there is food in God's house, then God will bless them, will rebuke all the pests from destroying their crops and will make the land of Israel "a land of delight," which all nations will call "blessed" (Malachi 3:12).

Claiming it is vain to serve God

God paints a wonderful picture of what life could be like for the people if they would bring in the full tithe. God will respond richly to their giving. He will open heaven and pour out blessings. He will protect them from all destroyers. He will make them a sign to the nations because of the delight in the land. God's promise stands in stark contrast to the people's speaking against the Lord. They have said, "It is vain to serve God. What is the profit of our keeping his charge or of walking as in mourning before the LORD of hosts?" (Malachi 3:14). God had just finished speaking about the profit and blessing resulting from giving the full tithe. However, the people's response is to say that serving God is vain and that there is no profit in keeping His charge. Furthermore, they feel that the evildoers and arrogant people of the world are actually the ones who prosper. "Now we call the arrogant blessed. Evildoers not only prosper but they put God to the test and they escape" (Malachi 3:15).

God gives no response to these words spoken against Him. He gives no promise of coming judgment, nor does He seek a way to refute them. After this accusation is leveled, there is nothing but silence, as if God allows their own words to sink in while they ring in the people's ears. Now the people can judge for themselves. They know God's love. They know their failings. They know the coming judgment. They know the unchangeable choice God has made. They know His plea for them to return. They know the open heaven that might result from their full giving. They also know their own words, "It is vain to serve God." And now there is silence. Maybe they consider. Maybe they make a resolution in their heart. Maybe some people wake up, as if they had been in a stupor. Maybe others consider their true state late at night, when the silence of the darkness allow them to think deeply.

Section three: a gathering of God-seekers

Among all the children of Jacob who were loved by the unchanging God, a few gather together for one of the most momentous meetings of the entire Old Testament. "Then those who feared the LORD spoke with one another" (Malachi 4:16). This seemingly small action is *the* turning point of Malachi's book. What happened? It isn't some great army gathering together to fight for God. It isn't a great revival that sweeps through the nation. It isn't a resolution to reform the priesthood or to fix all the marriages or to start a campaign to change the attitudes of the people. It isn't even a massive outpouring of the Holy Spirit and a great move towards being a rich testimony of God. It isn't a vision that transports them to another realm, such as Ezekiel sees in his first chapter. It isn't any of these things. Instead it is merely a gathering, most likely a small one, of those people who fear the Lord. It is as if the few who feared the Lord in the past were "in the closet," largely silent, and not communicating with one another. Now, it is different. They speak to one another. Maybe they say things to each other about how much they really love God. Maybe they relate how they have been honoring Him, although secretly. Maybe they speak about their families and how they wish their children would indeed be godly offspring. At Moses' time, God commanded the people to speak His words, saying, "⁶ And these words that I command you today shall be on your heart. ⁷ You shall teach them diligently to your children, and shall talk of them when you sit in your house, and when you walk by the way, and when you lie down, and when you rise" (Deuteronomy 6:6-7). Maybe this group of God fearers speaks to one another about the wonderful works of God, just like God commanded in Deuteronomy. This gathering, where they could speak to others who fear the Lord, is finally a safe spot for them to open their hearts and speak about what is in their innermost being concerning their Love for God, their hope in God and their desire that their lives would be for God.

It seems small, but we know that this gathering is big because we see that God has a big reaction to it. God pays attention, takes notice, and hears them. While this small gathering is taking place, it is probable that many other larger "spiritual" activities were going on. Many offerings are being sacrificed at the temple. Maybe there is a great commotion in the temple as the animals are brought, slaughtered and offered. However, God pays no attention to that commotion. In fact, He prefers it if someone would just shut the doors of the temple and stop the whole thing. Instead of paying attention to the din of offering at the altar, God pays attention to this little gathering, where there are just a few who love the Lord and speak to each other. Malachi declares, "The LORD paid attention and heard them" (Malachi 3:16). God is arrested by this. His neck is straining to watch them and hear every word. Oh, what blessed words! The Lord's attention is so much more valuable than 10,000 offerings, all the tithes and all the reformed attitudes. The Lord is saying, "Well done, good and faithful servant" (Matthew 25:21), to this small group of God-fearers.

The people then do the most interesting thing. They bring out a book and write their names and their deeds before the Lord. "And a book of remembrance was written before him of those who feared the LORD and esteemed his name" (Malachi 3:16). The Lord surely treasured all whose names were in that book. These are the people who fear Him, who esteem His name. They are like jewels in the midst of coal. They are like gold, when everything else is dross and corruption. The Lord declares, "They shall be mine, says the LORD of hosts, in the day when I make up my treasured possession, and I will spare them as a man spares his son who serves him" (Malachi 3:17). God had intended that all His nation would be His treasured possession (Exodus 19). However, as we have seen with Malachi and with Israel throughout their history, many deviated from the Lord, profaned His name, and became odious to Him. However, God never ceased dreaming His dream of a nation that would be His treasured possession. Here, He finds a small group who is just what He desires. They fear Him, esteem His name, and serve Him.

It may seem insignificant. However, Theodore Austin-Sparks sees this little band as a seed of people who will eventually welcome the Messiah after His lowly birth in Bethlehem.

> And so the value that the Lord has here, as you see quite clearly, is in just a very few, comparatively. It is a "day of small things"; it is a comparatively small company about which the Lord says, 'My peculiar treasure'. The value is intrinsic. It is there that the Lord finds what His heart desires, and that which, I believe, leads us to the far greater thing. It is not that the Lord's thought ends there in smallness because the Old Testament ends with this day of small things, this little company fearing the Lord: but that is the link between the end of the old dispensation and the beginning of the new - the coming of the Lord Jesus and all that followed. For, in the four hundred years between the Testaments, there was still that little company holding to the Lord's full thought. When you open the New Testament, and begin the record as given by Luke, there you find that link - the little representative handful. Here is Anna, here is Simeon - here in Jerusalem is a company who wait for the promise, for the Messiah, looking for that day. They are linked with those who "feared the Lord". Ah, but this is something that, though outwardly small, has become so intrinsically great, making a way for the Lord to come.
> —Austin-Sparks, chapter 8

God rescues these people, just as a loving father rescues his son who is serving him. Previously, Malachi relates how even though God is a father to the nation, yet, His relationship with them is not a healthy father and son relationship; His sons do not render Him honor (Malachi 1:6) and God does not return to them. This group of people, those who are speaking to one another, is different. They esteem, fear, and serve God. God looks at them like a proud father would look at his son who took over the family business and made it prosper and thrive. These people are markedly different from the rest of the nation. God wants this difference to be displayed. "Then once more you shall see the distinction between the righteous and the wicked, between one who serves God and one who does not serve him" (Malachi 3:18).

Section four: the Sun of Righteousness

This distinction between the righteous and wicked will be most evident in the coming day of the Lord. In that day there will be a great shining of Christ. To some, that shining will be an incineration; to others, it will be healing and restoration. "For behold, the day is coming, burning like an oven, when all the arrogant and all evildoers will be stubble. The day that is coming shall set them ablaze, says the LORD of hosts, so that it will leave them neither root nor branch. ² But for you who fear my name, the sun of righteousness shall rise with healing in its wings. You shall go out leaping like calves from the stall. ³ And you shall tread down the wicked, for they will be ashes under the soles of your feet, on the day when I act, says the LORD of hosts" (Malachi 4:1-3).

The promise to the arrogant and evildoers is complete destruction, a fact Malachi poetically describes as leaving them with "neither root nor branch." This means they will no longer have any means of sprouting again—all their roots will be gone—and that they will never have any way of flourishing—every branch will be gone.

Those who fear the Lord, however, will have a much more

marvelous experience. Christ, instead of being a burning oven, will be a life-imparting, healing Sun. The Sun of Righteousness will rise! Praise the Lord! The wings of the Sun are His rays, which will fall upon the God fearers like the warm summer sun falls upon a green plant after a rainfall. In those rays there will be healing. The fact that those who fear the Lord need healing shows that they are not perfect or even necessarily healthy at the time the sun rises. However, even though they might not have health, they do have fear for the Lord, and they do serve Him. The result is that the rays of the Sun will fall on them, bringing in healing and wellness. "As the rays of the sun spread light and warmth over the earth for the growth and maturity of the plants and living creatures, so will the sun of righteousness bring the healing of all hurts and wounds which the power of darkness has inflicted upon the righteous" (Keil, p. 662).

The result is absolutely joyful. They will go forth leaping and rejoicing, just like a young calf who is set free from the stall. They will tread upon the wicked, who will be like ashes under their feet.

Remember the law and look for Elijah

Malachi concludes his prophesy with an exhortation and an announcement. He exhorts the readers to "Remember the law of my servant Moses" (Malachi 4:4), then announces, "Behold, I will send you Elijah the prophet" (Malachi 4:5), thereby directing people to watch for Elijah. Malachi was so inspired by the joyful picture of the leaping calf that he must leave his readers with essential instructions that will get them there. Malachi is saying, "How will you all get that warm, nourishing, healing Sun to shine upon you so that you will become like a jumping calf? Here are two keys. First, remember the law. Second, look for Elijah."

"Remember the law" for Malachi may hold a very different sense than the common thought of the law in most people's minds. In understanding this, one should think more of Anna and Simeon (Luke 2:22-38) than of the Pharisees or high priests of the New Testament. The Law in its true function is a tutor that educates people and prepares them to receive Christ (Galatians 3:24). The law, taken properly by those who fear the Lord, is very different from the harsh demands perceived by those who do not seek God. To God seekers the law is sweeter than honey to their mouths and are to be more treasured than fine gold (Psalm 19:10). The law, received in this way, will surely make people ready for that day. When Jesus was born, Simeon and Anna were in the temple waiting for the Messiah. They did this because they remembered the Law of Moses, which prepared them to receive the Messiah.

Looking for Elijah is a blessed endeavor. Malachi announces here that Elijah will come "before the great and awesome day of the LORD (Malachi 4:5). This was partially fulfilled with the coming of John the Baptist, who came in the spirit of Elijah (Luke 1:17). It will be fully fulfilled when Elijah comes as one of the two witnesses (Revelation 11:1-13) before the Messiah's second coming.

Malachi describes Elijah's function—to "turn the hearts of fathers to their children and the hearts of children to their fathers" (Malachi 4:6). Turning the hearts of the children to their fathers does not mean that Elijah will solve family problems. Rather, it means that the children who are presently alive will have their hearts turned to the patriarchs, like Abraham, Isaac, and Jacob, who followed God and enjoyed a covenant with Him. Consider Abraham, who sought for the city whose Architect and Maker is God. When the heart of a child is turned to him, that child will seek the same thing Abraham sought. Likewise, when the children turn their hearts by being faithful to the covenant of their fathers, the hearts of the fathers will be turned to them. Right now, the fathers are part of the great cloud of witnesses that surround the people of faith (Hebrews 12:1). When these fathers see their children becoming faithful to the covenants and to each other, their hearts will be turned to their children.

With these last two encouragements Malachi ends his words. He has succeeded in conveying God's unchanging love for His people as demonstrated in God's love for Jacob. He has succeeded in listing the many failings of God's people. He has also succeeded in causing a small group who love the Lord to come together and speak to one another. He describes how God notices this group and considers them to be His treasured possession, which He will protect as a father would protect his son. Malachi makes a clear distinction between those who serve God and those who don't. He prophesies that the arrogant will be judged, but the God fearing will be healed and restored. He ends His prophetic words with exhortations to be attentive to the Law and to Elijah, both of whom can prepare God fearers for that day.

Bibliography

<u>On the whole Bible</u>

Barnes, Albert (1996). *Barnes' Notes*. Grand Rapids, MI: Baker Books.

Biblical Studies Press. (2005). <u>*The NET Bible First Edition; Bible. English. NET Bible.; The NET Bible*</u>. Biblical Studies Press.

Chisholm, R. B., Jr. (1985). Hosea. In J. F. Walvoord & R. B. Zuck (Eds.), *The Bible Knowledge Commentary: An Exposition of the Scriptures* (Vol. 1, p. 1385). Wheaton, IL: Victor Books.

Gill, John (1810). *Exposition of the Old & New Testaments*. London: Matthews and Leigh.

Jamieson, R., Fausset, A. R., & Brown, D. (1997). *Commentary Critical and Explanatory on the Whole Bible*. Oak Harbor, WA: Logos Research Systems, Inc

Reese, Edward, (1977). *The Reese Chronological Bible*. Minneapolis, MN: Bethany House.

Ryrie, Charles Caldwell, (1994) *Ryrie Study Bible*, Chicago, Moody Press.

<u>Dictionaries</u>

Easton, M. G. (1893). *Easton's Bible dictionary*. New York: Harper & Brothers.

<u>On the Old Testament</u>

Keil, C. F., & Delitzsch, F. (1986). *Commentary on the Old Testament* (Vol. 8). Grand Rapids, MI: Eerdmans Publishing Company.

On Hebrew Words

Harris R. L., Archer Jr. G. L., & Waltke B. K. (Eds.), *Theological Wordbook of the Old Testament* (electronic ed.). Chicago: Moody Press.

Waltke, B. K., O'Connor, M. (1990). *An Introduction to Biblical Hebrew Syntax.* Winona Lake, IN: Eisenbauns.

On the Minor Prophets

Allen, Leslie C. (1976), *The New International Commentary on the Old Testament: The books of Joel, Obadiah, Jonah, and Micah*, Grand Rapids, MI.: Eerdmans Publishing Company.

Austin-Sparks T. (1953), *The Recovery of the Lord's Testimony in Fullness,* London, Witness and Testimony Press.

Barker, K. L. (1999). *Micah, Nahum, Habakkuk, Zephaniah* (Vol. 20). Nashville: Broadman & Holman Publishers.

Boda, Mark J. (2016). *The New International Commentary on the Old Testament: The Book of Zechariah.* Grand Rapids, MI: Eerdmans Publishing Company

Calvin, John (MDCCCXLVI) (1846) *A Commentary on the Twelve Minor Prophets* Translated by John Owen, Volume 1-5, Edinburgh, The Calvin Translation Society

Campbell Morgan, G., (1975), *Voices of Twelve Hebrew Prophets,* Grand Rapids, MI: Baker Books.

Coates, C. A., (1986), *An Outline of Some of the Minor Prophets.* Sussex, England: Kingston Bible Trust.

Dearman, Andrew, (2010). *The New International Commentary on the Old Testament, The book of Hosea.* Grand Rapids, MI: Eerdmans Publishing Company

Dennet, Edward (1884) *The Christian's Friend and Instructor,* vol. 11.

Didymus the Blind, (2006) *The Fathers of the Church, Commentary on Zechariah.* Washington D.C.: The Catholic University of America Press.

Feinberg, Charles L., (1990). *The Minor Prophets,* Chicago, IL: Moody Publishers.

Garrett, D. A. (1997). *Hosea, Joel* (Vol. 19A, p. 41). Nashville: Broadman & Holman Publishers.

Ironside, H. A., (2004), *The Minor Prophets: An Ironside Expository Commentary.* Grand Rapids: Kregel.

Kelly, W. (1874). *Lectures Introductory to the Study of the Minor Prophets.* London: H. W. Bloom.

Lee Witness, (1993). *Life-Study: Hosea, Joel, Amos, Obadiah, Jonah, Micah, Nahum, Habakkuk, Zephaniah, Haggai, and Malachi.* Anaheim, CA: Living Stream Ministry

Motyer, J. A. (1974). *The Bible Speaks Today, The Message of Amos.* Downers Grove, IL: Intervarsity Press.

Prior, David (1998). *The Bible Speaks Today: The Message of Joel, Micah and Habakkuk.* Downers Grove, IL: Intervarsity Press.

Pusey, E. B. (1983), The Minor Prophets, A Commentary. Grand Rapids, MI: Baker Books

Smith, B. K., & Page, F. S. (1995). *Amos, Obadiah, Jonah* (Vol. 19B). Nashville: Broadman & Holman Publishers.

Smith, George Adam (1902) *The Book of the Twelve Prophets.* New York, A. C. Armstrong and Son.

Spence-Jones, H. D. M. (Ed.). (1909). *Hosea* (p. 50). London; New York: Funk & Wagnalls Company.

Taylor, R. A., & Clendenen, E. R. (2004). *Haggai, Malachi* (Vol. 21A). Nashville: Broadman & Holman Publishers.

<u>On special topics</u>

Ambrose of Milan. (1896). <u>Exposition of the Christian Faith</u>. In P. Schaff & H. Wace (Eds.), H. de Romestin, E. de Romestin, & H. T. F. Duckworth (Trans.), *St. Ambrose: Select Works and Letters* (Vol. 10, p. 309). New York: Christian Literature Company.

Augustine of Hippo. (1887). <u>On the Trinity</u>. In P. Schaff (Ed.), A. W. Haddan (Trans.), *St. Augustin: On the Holy Trinity, Doctrinal Treatises, Moral Treatises* (Vol. 3, pp. 144–145). Buffalo, NY: Christian Literature Company.

History

Broadbent, E. H. (1931). *The Pilgrim Church*. Grand Rapids, MI.: Gospel Folio Press

Printed in Great Britain
by Amazon